Other titles by Don Levin you may enjoy

The Code

Knight's Code

Broken Code

The Gazebo
The Life Story of Alexander Lebenstein

Eight Points of the Compass

Don't Feed the Bears

Another Last Day

The Advocate
sequel to Another Last Day

Blast of Trumpets

Clarion Blast

Wisdom of the Diamond
(with Tom Bartosic)

The Leader Coach
(with Terry Edwards)

The Right Combination
(with Todd Bothwell)

Visit our website at <u>donlevin.com</u>

THE PATH

A Memoir of Discovered Faith

DON LEVIN

Author of *Clarion Blast*

authorHOUSE

AuthorHouse™
1663 Liberty Drive
Bloomington, IN 47403
www.authorhouse.com
Phone: 833-262-8899

Published by AuthorHouse 12/17/2020

ISBN: 978-1-6655-0847-6 (sc)
ISBN: 978-1-6655-0846-9 (e)

Library of Congress Control Number: 2020923343

TABLE OF CONTENTS

Preface ix

Introduction xv

1. Alpha and Omega 1
2. What is a Testimony 7
3. What is Conversion..11
4. What is Faith 15
5. What is a Jew? 17
6. Roots..25
7. Blame Mark Clark...35
8. Donnie's Home 39
9. Chick 43
10. Motherhood 47
11. Earliest Recollections...49
12. Hebrew School 53
13. The Boy Wonder Begins 57
14. Battle of Angels 61
15. Guardian Angel...67
16. Drag Race 69
17. Bar Mitzvah Season...73
18. Hand in the Glove 77

19. A New Birth Certificate 81

20. First Fight 87

21. Seder 93

22. Dating 97

23. Graduation 103

24. Suicide is not Painless 105

25. Higher Learning 115

26. Crossroads 119

27. Fort Lewis 123

28. The Bunker 127

29. We Don't Do That Here 133

30. The Disappearing Cokes 137

31. Gas Chambers 141

32. Sacred Grove 143

33. Cleanliness 145

34. Interregnum 151

35. It's a Wonderful Life 153

36. Law School 155

37. Tithing 159

38. The Miracle of Life 165

39. Taking the Plunge 167

40. The Hosanna Shout 171

41. Ordination 173

42. You Are Special 175

43. Sealing 179

44. Patriarchal Blessing 181

45. Priesthood Miracle 185

46. The Bar Exam 191

47. The Temple 197

48. And Baby Makes Seven 199

49. Black and White 201

50. Heritage 203

51. Hey Meatball 207

52. The Clothes Make the Man 215

53. Our First Missionary...217

54. Apostle's Blessing..219

55. Indestructibility...223

56. Into the Crucible Again...229

57. The Kirtland Temple...237

58. The Hand Leaves the Glove again 241

59. Sayonara..247

60. Broken Code 249

61. The Gazebo 253

62. Miracle of Forgiveness 261

63. Chippenham 265

64. Sometimes the Answer is No..269

65. Stay the Course..275

66. Transitions 279

67. Isle of Tears 287

68. The Emerald City 291

69. Million Dollar Baby 297

70. Platinum 309

71. End of the Road and a New Beginning 317

72. CUBS W1N..323

73. Family History...329

74. Tender Mercy...335

75. A Punch in the Nose 337

76. Connecting the Generations..341

77. The Plan 343

78. What's in a Name? 345

79. Pandemic 347

80. Third Act...353

81. Why I Believe...357

PREFACE

"Wherefore teach it unto your children, that all men,
everywhere, must repent, or they can in nowise inherit
the kingdom of God, for no unclean thing can dwell
there, or dwell in his presence; for, in the language of
Adam, Man of Holiness is his name, and the name of his
Only Begotten is the Son of Man, even Jesus Christ, a
righteous Judge, who shall come in the meridian of time."
Moses 6:57, Pearl of Great Price

Over the years since we joined the Church of Jesus Christ of Latter
Day Saints, I have heard people stand and bear testimony that the
Gospel of Jesus Christ, their baptism, and that their adherence to
Gospel standards has "saved" them. I have heard others proclaim that
temple ordinances have saved them spiritually. This story is about how
my reading the Book of Mormon literally saved my physical life.

One of the first lessons that really resonated with me as taught by the
missionaries was the importance of being clean because the Spirit will
not dwell where it is not clean. While this denotes spiritual and moral
cleanliness as opposed to simply physical cleanliness, I was enough of
a literalist that I always insured that I had washed my hands and was
physically clean as well before I picked up my scriptures. I have always

treated all books, but particularly my scriptures, with respect – some of my kids would even say that I border on the maniacal about avoiding cracking the spine of the book, or shudder, bending and folding pages back around while reading a paperback book.

As part of a "front-line" unit with an active mission of patrolling the West German/East German/Czechoslovakian border, service with the Second Armored Cavalry Regiment also presented me with a lot of "field" time in general. Regular rotations to the major training centers in Germany, most notably Grafenwoehr [famous for Rommel's training the Afrika Korps on these very same tank trails] kept me away from home over 80% of the time. It was nearly like being deployed overseas with an occasional opportunity to check in with my family that just happened to be in country with me.

I was on one such training rotation at Grafenwoehr, supporting Level I gunnery for the Cavalry troops, essentially living out on Firing Point 621, tucked away on the Northwest corner of the reservation. As either the Fire Direction Officer or the Officer in Charge of the firing point I was pretty much stuck out there living in the muck of February, for the better part of the entire exercise.

After ten days of living out on the range, it was finally my turn to rotate to our Tent City located near main post, and again, I began to think about the significance of being clean if I was serious about reading and studying the Book of Mormon in anticipation of my next meeting with the young missionaries who had been challenging me with assignments to read and to then pray about what I had read.

This thought was absolutely reverberating in my mind as my driver steered our jeep in from the range where I had just spent those ten days without seeing the insides of a shower or a mess Hall. Ten days of bathing and shaving out of my helmet and having hot chow brought out to the firing point in giant metal containers had definitely altered my priorities as we drove on the muddy tank trail heading for what in my mind had taken on the epic proportions of Nirvana. I could already feel the sting of the hot water on my skin, and was breathing in the steam that was going to envelope my body as I treated myself to a much needed extended stay under the shower as well as some real food, albeit from the greasy burger bar.

At the same time, I realized that in addition to these creature comforts, I was going to be afforded the opportunity to crawl into my sleeping bag on my cot and read select portions of the Book of Mormon and ponder them as I had been challenged to do by the missionaries with whom I had been meeting. While I had endeavored to read my scriptures several times while out on the range, the constant interruptions had made it pretty much an exercise in futility.

Therefore, my quandary was whether I should read or shower first. On one hand, I was afraid that by not showering and becoming [physically] clean that the Spirit might not touch my heart as I hoped it would, and on the other, I knew that the only thing keeping me upright after ten hard days in the field with long days and very short nights was the dried sweat and grime of the range; I was afraid that by showering it off that I would be too tired and too relaxed to read and that I would miss out only my opportunity to study.

I wrestled with this choice the entire way back to Camp Normandy. Upon arrival there I was still undecided and determined to say a prayer to resolve the question. I had no sooner sat down on my footlocker and cleared my mind, when I received a very distinct and powerful impression, almost a whisper that ran through my heart and mind, that it was important that I shower first, so as to strip away the dirt of the world before I began my study of the Book of Mormon. I quickly gathered up my toiletries and a clean uniform and headed for the concrete shower house about one hundred twenty five yards from my tent.

As expected, the hot water of the shower was absolutely delightful, and I literally felt the cares of the world being washed away. Ironically, I had the shower to myself, as most of the camp was attending a movie, and I stood there under the water for a long while. I had literally just turned the water off when I heard and felt a large explosive thump that seemed unnaturally close in both severity and volume. Mind you, we would often hear artillery and tank firing going on around the clock, so this was not unusual. Over time, I actually learned how to sleep through it!

However, the severity of the impact of this round made it feel different, and definitely up close and personal. Sensing that something might be amiss, I quickly dried and dressed myself, and headed back outside.

Imagine my surprise when I discovered that the source of the explosion had been an errant 8" artillery round from an adjacent training area that had completely missed the range impact area and had actually landed in our camp, with my tent near the center of the blast radius! Having already experienced the bunker blast and hand grenade debacles, it was somewhat surreal to walk over to the remains of my tent and to view the damage that the shrapnel from this 240 pound shell containing about 21 pounds of TNT had done to cots, sleeping bags, foot lockers, and the concrete pad on which it all rested.

Personnel from Range Control, the post medical detachment, as well as military police all converged on the area because this incident was a big deal, and probably meant that more than one or two heads were going to roll before all was said and done. While we jokingly refer to such incidents as an "oops" the potential for loss of life is great. Over the years I was party to several such incidents in various training areas in the US, fortunately always with the same result and no loss of life. In fact, I have shrapnel sitting on my desk from such an oops....

Miraculously, no one was injured, but there was a lot of personal gear and equipment destroyed by the exploding round, to include my footlocker and everything in it. I literally was left with the clean clothes on my back and the few personal items that I had taken with me to the shower house until I was sent to Quartermaster Sales the next day to have my personal uniforms and equipment replaced courtesy of Uncle Sam. It is the only time in my military career that I did not pay for my personal equipment as is required of commissioned officers.

Later that night after all the brass had left the area and my tent mates and I had found ourselves a new tent in which to spend the night, I settled into my sleeping bag on my cot, and began to say my nightly prayers. It was not until that moment that I had the stark realization that had I not heeded *and acted upon* the impression to take a shower *before* performing my study and reading, I could very well have been in my tent at the time that it was destroyed.

That revelation was enough to release a large dose of adrenaline into my system, and had I not already been lying down, I probably would have had to sit down. All four of my limbs instantly felt as solid as Jell-O and I could feel myself beginning to perspire and my respiration to quicken. It was probably a good 15 to 20 minutes that this condition persisted, and I was able to regain control of my body.

As the years have passed and I have shared that story on a limited basis, the reaction to it has largely been the same. Those with faith have been quick to point out that I was *blessed* because of my desire to be clean before I read from the scriptures. Others have said that I was *lucky* and that this experience is proof that "timing is everything." With the passage of forty years, the benefit of 20/20 hindsight, and the acquisition of knowledge during this period, I know that *luck* had nothing to do with my survival, and that it was my desire to be *obedient* as well as my heeding the prompting of the Holy Ghost that was the true basis of my avoiding harm.

Candidly, the impact of this lesson has become more and more significant to me as the years have passed. Back at the time of it happening, but for the realization in my sleeping bag of just how close I had come to potentially being killed, the spiritual lesson was somewhat lost on me, for it was another four years before I entered the waters of baptism. Maybe I am a slow learner after all.

INTRODUCTION

"The attributes by which we shall be judged one day
are all spiritual. These include love, virtue, integrity,
compassion, and service to others. Your spirit, coupled
with and housed in your body, is able to develop and
manifest these attributes in ways that are vital to your
eternal progression. Spiritual progress is attained through
the steps of faith, repentance, baptism, the gift of the
Holy Ghost, and enduring to the end, including the
endowment and sealing ordinances of the holy temple."
President Russell M. Nelson

I was sitting at a funeral talking to a friend about Jewish and LDS
funerals and the fact that they are as different as night and day. Whereas
a Jewish funeral is full of mourning and wailing, heartfelt grief, and a
tremendous sense of loss and finality, an LDS funeral is a church service
that is a celebrations of life; the marking of a momentous passage or
transition, and is filled with hope for a brighter and better future for
the deceased as well as promises of renewal and resurrection and the
opportunity to be together again eternally.

We speak of passing through the veil, while for Jews, dead is
certainly dead. Because they do not believe in an afterlife, it is only

natural that most Jews largely fear death. The Passover mark on the door was intended to ward off the angel of death and to spare the first born child. To this day there are no "Juniors" anywhere else in the family tree. For as it was explained to me countless times while growing up, the Angel of Death could come down and snatch the "wrong" Don if there was a Senior, a Junior, and *oi vey*, may he live and be well, a Don III. This is how it was explained to me before I had children of my own, so imagine the consternation when we had a son and named him Donald Jr.

As I recounted to my friends other parts of my conversion story, their interest grew and grew. When I mentioned that I have in the past given firesides in which I spoke of my experiences, they were quite enthusiastic about attending the next one and then suggested that inasmuch as I am an author, I should capture all of these experiences in a book not only for my own family but for others who may be seeking the truth in the same manner that I sought it for so many years. I chewed on that thought for several weeks, until one Sunday after church I sat down at my computer and in the matter of about ninety minutes had a substantial outline for what eventually became this book.

I have always believed that there are distinct seasons to our lives during which we utilize our God-given talents to further the mission of the church of Proclaim the Gospel, Perfect the Saints, and Redeem the Dead. When I look back over the last thirty-five years, I can see the seasons in which I engaged in each of these works based on the callings in which I was engaged. Now, I feel that I am most assuredly in the Redeem season, as I am attempting to capture and assemble our family history; in the last two years I have successfully grown a family tree with only thirty leaves on it to one with thousands. I am attempting to engage my grandchildren in this work, and I am keenly aware that as the connecting link between my grandparents and my grandchildren, that it is my responsibility to forge strong and lasting chains between these generations, connecting the past with the present as well as the future.

Without being overly morbid or allowing my [melodramatic] Jewish roots to show [which according to my wife and children happens fairly regularly], I am keenly aware of my legacy in general and the urgency that has often accompanied the writing of many of my books, and that I am now feeling associated with this one. When I wrote *Don't Feed the Bears* and *Eight Points of the Compass,* I was concerned with who would teach my children the very things they would need to survive in this mortal state. Writing *Another Last Day* and then its sequel *The Advocate* brought me squarely face to face with my own mortality and ministry. *Blast of Trumpets* and *Clarion Blast* were a focus and retrospective on my words & thoughts.

Broken Code, The Code, and *Wisdom of the Diamond* are largely autobiographical chronicles of my professional life even if not intended to be at the time that I wrote them.

Which now brings us to this book which will be part life story, part conversion story, as well as part family history. One of my sons has also suggested that I should video record large portions of these stories so that in years to come that the words will come alive and that they will be more than just words on a page and that future generations will *know* who I was, and why the heck I wrote so many books.

It is not ego or narcissism driving me to capture this story but rather a deeply seated spiritually received *impression* that it is the proper thing to do. In the event a story or recollection helps just one person seek and find the clarity that the Gospel has brought to my life, then I know it will have been worth the effort. We are a "record keeping people" encouraged to construct and maintain daily journals in which we are to capture significant events, spiritual experiences, and our very *history.* As more and more of my friends and acquaintances face their own trials of morbidity and mortality, I feel an equal necessity to complete this work and to capture these thoughts for posterity, especially as the Covid-19 pandemic presented me with "extra" time. I hope it will be read with an eye to that objective.

Don

CHAPTER 1

ALPHA AND OMEGA

"Knowing that the gospel is true is
the essence of a testimony.
Consistently being true to the gospel
is the essence of conversion."
Elder David A. Bednar,

For those who like to read the end of the story before reading the entire book, you are in luck. I say this because I am going to share the ending of the story right now.

We live in a very turbulent, fast-paced, ever-changing, and darn right scary world. I used to say that I did not worry so much about myself but for my children; now, I am absolutely terrified by the world that our grandchildren are going to inherit. Spiraling national debts, a politically polarized populace the likes of which we have never seen before, and this sense of entitlement from our children's generation compounded by a lack of discipline in their children's generation. It is for all these reasons that I am grateful for the Gospel of the Church of Jesus Christ of Latter Day Saints. The foundational beliefs that I have come to embrace during my time on the Path have come to mean a great deal to me as I approach the next Act in my finite stage life. The Gospel — do not be confused between the Gospel and the Church, for they are distinctly different things — provides me with the infinite Truth, eternal Justice and Integrity, and the everlasting Covenant of eternal life. Eternal life is a whole lot different than simple immortality. With each passing year and bit of insight that I acquire, the Gospel becomes all the more significant an anchor in my mortal life, and one that I want all of my progeny to embrace because of the safety it affords us against the dangers of Man and Satan.

I believe with certainty the following:

- I believe In God, Jesus Christ, and the Holy Ghost. They are three separate beings with whom I have separate and distinct relationships.
- Contrary to a lot of converts to, or investigators of, the Church, I had no problem embracing the concept that Joseph Smith was a prophet and was visited by angels. Further, that like Joseph, I often prayed with true intent to discover which church on the earth today is true.
- Russell M. Nelson is a prophet today, and someone worth emulating in so many ways. While I have admired all the sixteen prophets who have proceeded him for their spirituality and example to the world, there is something truly special about President Nelson. He is such an accomplished man, that he almost appears to possess supernatural powers. Whether it was his groundbreaking work as a world renowned cardiac thoracic surgeon, or his ability to learn languages such as Mandarin with seemingly little effort, he appears larger than life, and is a wonderful man, husband, father, grandfather, and great-grandfather. I am proud and humbled to listen to him speak as God's chosen mouthpiece on the earth today.
- I believe that the fifteen men who are ordained as apostles, prophets, seers, and revelatory at any given time in this dispensation are in fact those very things; that they have been

called of God as special witnesses. I have felt of their energy when I have met them in person and received apostolic blessings. Each apostle who we have met in person emits a special aura of the Spirit with which he is imbued. While they may be as mortal a man as I am, there is something special about these special witnesses of God.

- I believe in latter day prophets the same way that I believe that Moses was a prophet in olden times. If God spoke to us in early scripture, why is it hard to believe that he would continue this practice today?

- Trite as it may sound, but I am a Son of God and He knows me individually, the righteous desires of my heart, and that I am never alone.

- That repentance is a wonderful gift that allows each of to take advantage of the sacrifice associated with the Atonement. I thought I understood this for the first quarter century of my church membership and then I became a bishop and seemingly had my eyes and my heart opened to terms such as repentance, charity, and mercy.

- As a priesthood holder I have the power to act in His name on the earth.

- That my oath and covenant of the Priesthood means more to me than my Oath and Commission as an Army officer.

- That I am the patriarch of my family — smack dab in the middle of five generations — the common link to all of them.

- That we need to influence future generations by the example we live and not by the words we utter.

- That we need to make full use of the finite time that we have been allocated. We need to have our affairs in order so that if we are called home at a moment's notice, that we are not placed in a position to "defend" our life on earth, and that we are as worthy as we said we are when participating in our Temple Recommend interview and answered the questions of the Temple's sentinels.

- That Honor and Integrity are intertwined and represent the most important character trait with which we leave the Earth. That my true North is in fact Integrity.
- The power of prayer is an amazing thing and is often the precursor to miracles that we witness on the earth.
- The power of the priesthood in terms of healing is very very real. I have seen people that I know and care about healed by virtue of the laying on of hands.
- The temple is the place on Earth where we can be closest to our Heavenly Father. I have communed with him, seeking answers or confirmations to prayers, and received them, even if on occasion it was with answers that I did not want to hear.
- Choosing the right is something we must be prepared to do every day. That making decisions ahead of time — once — saves us countless heartache as we reconsider them time and time again.
- Satan is everywhere, doing all that he can do to seduce us to his side. He is subtle, probably looks like a movie star, and uses temptation and subtlety to undermine the foundations of good. He is not going to pick up a building and put it down across the street, but rather will use inch-by-inch subtlety and temptation to draw us close to, and then over, the line. He will use questions and doubts to undermine truth, but I am also of the mind that these same questions and doubts can be used to grow our depth and breadth of knowledge and strengthen our testimonies.
- We are all entitled to revelation — personal for ourselves, as well as for those over whom we may have stewardship. It requires us to have our radios in receive mode and not in transmit. That it is the small still voice that will often speak like a blast of trumpets *if* we are listening.
- Moderation in all things is a good way to live, not just eat.
- That there are no small acts of kindness, and that a kind word or act can often mean the world to someone who has that specific need.
- We are surrounded by angels, both mortal and immortal.

- I have *witnessed* and/or *been part of* miracles that cannot be explained either as coincidence or in terms of science.
- Faith is believing in things unseen but remain real.
- That the Holy Ghost is real, and that the promptings that we receive like *whispers into our soul* are real too, and that we will never go wrong by heeding and acting upon these promptings.
- There is financial security associated with honestly embracing the tenets of tithing and doing so with a willing heart.
- The work of salvation that we are in engaged in does extend to both sides of the veil. I love doing family history work and linking the generations of my family together. A picture attached to a name makes that person very real to me, and if they are a fallen soldier or sailor even more sacred. Visiting the grave of a fallen cousin in the Punchbowl National Cemetery in Hawaii takes on greater significance, as does learning of the death of a fellow 19-year old second lieutenant in the trenches of France during World War One. They *are* my family.
- That the Book of Mormon is as true as the Old and New Testaments contained in the Bible, and that the Doctrine and Covenants and Pearl of Great Price are also latter day scripture that I have come to embrace as truth and something written for me in these latter days.
- That it is the Gospel of which we need to have a testimony, and not the Church. The church is a vehicle that the Lord uses to further His work on the Earth.

Some other non-Gospel truths that I hold near and dear include:

- Hearing about the death of people that we taught when they were youth seems counter-intuitive and makes me even more committed to spend my time in righteous pursuits, such as capturing these thoughts and words.
- It almost feels like I am writing the last chapter of the story and that I am doing so with a tsunami of danger sitting offshore waiting to hit us with a great and devastating fury.

- Our grandchildren of all ages, (we have over a quarter century age span in that generation thus far) have grown up in the church, not knowing any different. When we talk about our "past life" with them, they are enthralled, and ask many questions about what life was life prior to our joining the Church. I would like to think that their questions answer any doubts or concerns that they may be experiencing in their own lives, and also allow them to garner an appreciation for the presence of the Gospel in their lives, and the very modest sacrifices we endured while bringing the Gospel into the family as we modeled the way as "pioneers."
- Likewise, I see these questions and doubts as seeds of Satan taking root in this generation of my family and it terrifies me that we will lose them.
- That we are spiritual beings having a human or mortal experience, and not humans seeking spiritual experiences. Far more than just perspective, this is a core belief for me with each passing year of mortality.
- That as sure as there is a Law of Gravity and other Laws of Nature, there are equally powerful laws that cover things like Tithing, Charity, and the Word of Wisdom.
- That Thomas Edison was correct when he said that there is really nothing that comes from within us, and that everything we are, want, or aspire to, is out in the Universe waiting for us to harness it.
- That I do *know* and possess a 100% certainty of these things, and don't have to "hedge my bets" by believing 99% and reserving final judgment until I am translated to the next world on my path and shown these truths with total certainty.

So now, the story behind these truths that I now hold as self-evident or as Paul Harvey used to say, "and now for the rest of the story," and *the Path* upon which I embarked so many years ago.

CHAPTER 2

WHAT IS A TESTIMONY

""Believing things on authority only means believing them because you have been told them by someone you think is trustworthy. 99% of the things you believe are believed on authority. I believe there is such a place as New York. I have not seen it myself. I cannot prove by abstract reasoning that there is such a place. I believe it because reliable people have told me so. The ordinary man believes in the Solar System, atoms, evolution, and the coalition of blood on authority."
C. S. Lewis

As a child I had it impressed upon me that telling the truth was the most important part of character. When I acted as an attorney representing clients, it was always important to me that the truth prevailed while seeking *testimony* in a court of law. For these reasons I always believed that testimony was a tangible part of speech or evidence that could readily be shared with a group or jury. It was only in the context of my seeking light and knowledge that the word *testimony* took on a new meaning.

From a gospel perspective, a *testimony* is the sure knowledge, received by revelation from the Holy Ghost, of the divinity of the work being completed in these the latter-days. Fortunately for me, and my family, there were many people along the path who were willing to take the time to help us find our way. These missionaries came in various shapes and sizes, and from all walks of life. Some were dedicated full-time missionaries serving away from home, others were locally "called" missionaries, while others were simply good friends who wanted to share with us the same knowledge that provided them joy, security, and peace of mind in their own lives.

In the spirit of full disclosure, while I did "church hop" in the course of my investigations for approximately ten years, it was the latter half of these ten years during which I limited my investigation to the Church of Jesus Christ of Latter Day Saints. In hindsight and with thirty five plus years of membership and growth under my belt, I will admit that there were certainly phases to my gaining a testimony of my own. I suspect that my testimony began with discussions based on reason and logic, and maybe even persuasive argument. This is not a testimony. It was not until I completely humbled myself with fervent prayer, study, and *action* based on faith, that I began to receive the knowledge that comes only through revelation. It was an intellectually intriguing exercise for me. As this journey progressed, I learned that the logic and reasoning that I first utilized in my pursuit of Truth were merely tools to help me along the path.

I have learned that any valid testimony must contain three great truths to be a true testimony. First, that Jesus Christ is the Son of God and the Savior of the world. Second, that Joseph Smith is a prophet of God and through whom the Lord restored the gospel to the earth in these the latter days. Finally, that the Church of Jesus Christ of Latter Day Saints is "the only true and living church upon the face of the whole earth." Doctrine and Covenants 1:30.

I was grateful to learn that anyone – to include a 'heathen' like me -- can gain a testimony of the gospel. If I were trying to reduce the process by which one can gain a testimony or create a Six Sigma quality flow chart it would look something like this:

- First, we must *desire* to know the truthfulness of the Gospel.
- Second, we must *study* the doctrines and learn the tenets of the Gospel.
- Third, we must *live* the principles in every aspect of our life; not picking and choosing those things that we wish to honor while ignoring other tenets.
- Fourth, we must *pray* for confirmation of this knowledge by the Holy Ghost.

Part of acquiring and later benefitting from this testimony requires action on our part. It is all about paying it forward through the sharing of our own testimony, living and personifying the Gospel to those around us by our examples, and truly enduring to the end.

I have also learned that men are not saved by virtue of their simply having a testimony. I have attended church with many people over the years who profess to have a great testimony but fall short on truly living the faith. Some will cut corners, equivocate, or rationalize why some "rules" are meant to be broken, and why they are correct in being "selective" in exercising their God-given agency.

By the same token, I have met an equal number of people who radiate their testimony of the Gospel and are beacons of light to those around them. I admire these people because they personify the tenets of faith and testimony. I want to be like them.

It is also noteworthy to distinguish between a testimony of the Church and of the Gospel. The Church is an organization created by the Lord to facilitate the gathering of His children here upon the earth; a place for us to learn the doctrine, and to live our mortal probationary period. The Gospel on the other hand is the Light of Christ, and the very path that was created for us so that we can once again live in the presence of our Heavenly Father. It is so easy to get caught up in the activities and functions of the Church that we can lose sight of the Gospel; but with a testimony of the Gospel, everything is possible, and we are truly in a position to have peace of mind, guidance, and direction, as well as the assurance that we will one day return to the presence of the Father.

A testimony is like a muscle; when exercised often and regularly, it grows stronger in size and endurance. When it is not exercised, it will often atrophy and wither. It is my hope that all those who read this, most notably my children, grandchildren, and those that follow, will know with certainty that I have a testimony, and am eternally grateful to those whom the Lord placed along my path through life for helping me discover answers to the three great questions: where did I come from, why am I here, and where am I going. More on that later.....

CHAPTER 3

WHAT IS CONVERSION

"Our needed conversions are often achieved more readily by suffering and adversity than by comfort and tranquility. ... Father Lehi promised his son Jacob that God would 'consecrate [his] afflictions for [his] gain' (2 Nephi 2:2). The Prophet Joseph was promised that 'thine adversity and thine afflictions shall be but a small moment; and then, if thou endure it well, God shall exalt thee on high' (D&C 121:7–8). Most of us experience some measure of what the scriptures call 'the furnace of affliction' (Isaiah 48:10; 1 Nephi 20:10). Some are submerged in service to a disadvantaged family member. Others suffer the death of a loved one or the loss or postponement of a righteous goal like marriage or childbearing. Still others struggle with personal impairments or with feelings of rejection, inadequacy, or depression. Through the justice and mercy of a loving Father in Heaven, the refinement and sanctification possible through such experiences can help us achieve what God desires us to become."
Dallin H. Oaks

The process of acquiring a testimony to the Gospel is called *conversion*. More than simply embracing a new set of tenets or beliefs, conversion is about making a *change* in the way we choose to live our life during this mortal probationary period here on earth.

Many years ago, I heard something that truly resonated with me and forever changed me and hopefully completed my personal conversion. It was in a form of a question and asked whether we are humans seeking the occasional spiritual experience or spiritual beings living a mortal existence. Wow. That changed me, and how I determined to live the balance of my life. It was so empowering and liberating at the same time. I resolved to be that spiritual being living a series of mortal experiences and almost instantly my perspective about the life I was living changed. Without sounding melodramatic, I felt as if another brick had fallen into place and that my understanding of our purpose here on the Earth was another step forward on the Path.

While I do not pretend to be transformed or any closer to perfection, I know that all the Lord is asking of me is to *strive* to be a better person today than I was yesterday, and to live a life centered on Obedience. That is pretty easy for a guy who has an extraordinarily strong sense of right and wrong. As I will address later, I had another one of those moments where another major brick was placed in the path when my feelings were validated and I learned that there is no such thing as gray – either it is black, or it is white. It is like being pregnant, either you are, or you are not.

I find comfort and security in Obedience and in conforming to the Laws of God, of Nature, and of the country to which I have sworn allegiance as a soldier for life. I should also note that there is *joy* to be found in being obedient as well. It is a concept that I have attempted to teach those around me and consider it a large part of my personal ministry.

The greatest joy, security, and comfort that accompanies conversion to the Gospel of Jesus Christ is the companionship of the Holy Ghost. I will talk a lot about that, because even before my conversion and baptism, I *knew* through personal experience that the Holy Ghost was a real personage of spirit and that it was merely a matter of *learning* how to identify it and how it could be a part of my life.

Conversion, obedience, and consciously choosing to live life by a higher set of ideals has meant far more to me than I ever imagined. A lot of people view our lifestyle choices as a series of limitations, prohibitions and don'ts, e.g. no alcohol, or tobacco, but for me I prefer to focus on all things that conversion has permitted me to embrace and the joy that it has brought into my life and that of my family.

Truthfully, I do not see the guidelines that have been prophetically shared with us as limitations. *"Moderation in all things"* has taken on gargantuan proportions in my own life for it relates to everything we do. It applies to our diet, to exercising, to the activities we choose, and the constant *balance* we seek to achieve in our lives.

While I am not a Rhodes Scholar, I am also not a total *schlepp*. It may have taken me a little while to perfect the context of how submissiveness, meekness humility, and charity all fit into my daily life, but I like to think that I am getting a handle on it. Being submissive and meek and humble are not attributes of weakness, but rather the very qualities that our Heavenly Father desires for all of us. For it is in these very qualities that we are the most teachable and able to embrace the full measure of the love that our Heavenly Father possesses for each and every one of us, no matter what kind of knucklehead we might be on any given occasion.

It is this very love that allows us to navigate the Path, with one eye fixed firmly on the horizon towards Heavenly Father, and the other on the path directly in front of our feet as we navigate the temporal world. Satan would have us forget these things and to not be converted to these Truths.

CHAPTER 4

WHAT IS FAITH

"Some say that they have not faith, that they cannot
believe. What is faith? It is confidence. What is confidence?
It is faith. Some people are striving and striving to get faith,
when saving faith is simply confidence in God, flowing
from walking in obedience to His commandments. When
you have confidence in yourself, in any man, woman, or
child, you have faith; and when you have not confidence,
you have not faith. I believe they are co-partners, and the
principle of faith and confidence is synonymous to me.
Journal of Discourses, 4:249

A conversation regarding Testimony and Conversion would be
incomplete without the inclusion of Faith. Faith. Another one of those
"touchy feely" topics that can go on forever and ever. I love it whenever
I am having a gospel discussion with anyone of another religion and
the ultimate question of "but how do you *know* what you are saying is
true?" comes up and that re-directs the conversation to the topic of faith.

How does one define a word without using the word in the
definition? Keep in mind that early on in my conversion process I was

drawn to the First Vision and the way Joseph Smith prayed for answers as to which church was the most correct. Therefore, it was quite natural for me to look to his teachings on a wide range of subjects. In teaching the laws and principles surrounding the subject of faith, the Prophet Joseph Smith outlined his presentation under three headings:

- "Faith itself – what it is"
- "The object on which it rests"
- "The effects which flow from it."

Faith, therefore, "is the first principle in revealed religion, and the foundation of all righteousness." From Hebrews 11:1: "Now faith is the substance of things hoped for, the evidence of things not seen."

Faith is based on truth and is preceded by knowledge. Until a person gains knowledge of the truth he can have no faith. As Alma said, "faith is not to have a perfect knowledge of things; therefore, if ye have faith ye hope for things which are not seen which are true." Alma 32:21.

While I recognize that this sounds like neither a logical nor legal argument, I read that, pondered it, and realized it that there was *truth* to it. As the C.S. Lewis quote at the head of chapter two indicates, while I have never been to St. Petersburg, the birthplace of my paternal grandmother, I can believe that it does exist because reliable people have told me so, and therefore I can hold a belief that there is such a place.

Because of my faith, I can also have a belief in miracles. As Joseph Smith taught, "Miracles are the fruit of faith. Faith comes by hearing the word of God." So how do I answer the question of "how do I know what I know?" Simple. I have seen miracles that defy logic or the laws of science. I have seen people with afflictions healed by the power of the priesthood. In my own family I have seen illnesses and serious conditions resolved under conditions that left medical doctors in disbelief. For this reason, I believe that faith is a gift from God that is bestowed as a reward for personal righteousness. I am grateful for my faith, and wish everyone could have it, like the companionship of the Holy Ghost, in more than just times of trials and tribulations when it is most often sought, for without faith there is only darkness.

CHAPTER 5

WHAT IS A JEW?

"Being born again is a gradual thing, except in a few
isolated instances that are so miraculous they get
written up in the scriptures. As far as the generality
of the members of the Church are concerned, we
are born again by degrees, and we are born again to
added light and added knowledge and added desires
for righteousness as we keep the commandments."
Brice R. McConkie

Over the years I have often pondered this singular question: What beliefs, choices, and lifestyle manifestations makes a Jew? It has even been suggested to me that I am not really a Jew by religion but only one through ethnicity or merely heritage. When I first heard that, I was more than a little defensive, wanted to refute it, but instead elected to ponder it as another intellectual challenge. Had I been a Jew or was my conversion less than advertised? Was I in fact perpetuating a fraud?

Attendance at most synagogues in the United States generally hover at about 20% of their congregation membership. To this end, if one does show up for services on Saturday, a greeting will often be followed by a query of what is so wrong in your life as to warrant attendance at the synagogue. While that may be shocking, it is becoming quite prevalent today. By the same token, much the same can be said for Christian faiths across Europe as organized religion becomes less important to a larger segment of Society.

So, where does that leave me? Was I ever a Jew? I can say that back in the day, I believed that Jesus Christ was a teacher, a wise man, a rabbi. He was no more a son of God than I was, though of course today I would say something completely to the contrary on both counts. I could not even begin to fathom why there was such a fixation on the crucifix by so many Christian faiths. No doubt Jesus Christ had been betrayed by his own people, and why that occurred was even more of a mystery for me.

What I did believe:

- I remember my brothers and family friends all being circumcised as a ritual that was symbolic of the binding of the new child to his faith. While today it is a readily accepted medical procedure done for a myriad of preventive health reasons, back in the day it was still an important religious ritual. In some instances I would even attend the *bris* (the actual ceremony at which it was performed) that was done at home under the supervision of a *mohel* who is not a rabbi but is licensed under strict requirements to perform this rite. While today this procedure is routinely done in the hospital after birth, and before a boy is sent home, it was still something of importance when I was growing up in the 1960s and into the 1970s.
- I remember being taught to be proud of my Jewish heritage. As the son of a first generation American (my father), I was always hearing about life in the old country from his mother, the perils of traveling to America, and of course Ellis Island. Growing up in Skokie, Illinois (at the time the highest concentration of Holocaust survivors in the United States), I was keenly aware of my roots. But more on that later.

- When it was [financially] possible I attended Hebrew School in an effort to learn the language so that I could read from the Torah in anticipation of my own Bar Mitzvah and the rite of passage of becoming a man in the eyes of God at the age of 13.
- Whenever I attended any form of worship service at the synagogue, I would cover my head with a *yarmulke* as a sign of respect that the Messiah has not yet arrived back here on the Earth.
- I believed that there was no Afterlife and that if we lived a good life, that we would somehow be taken care of by a benevolent God.
- We celebrated *Hannukah*, or the Festival of Lights, which commemorated the oil lamp that inexplicably kept burning for eight days.
- God is God. He is one. Man was made in God's image, but we were certainly not his spirit children. Therefore, there is no trinity of God, Jesus Christ, and the Holy Ghost.
- God was the Creator of all things, and that was a statement of fact. There was no need to "prove" that God existed. It was a given.
- I later learned that it was because the faith places such an emphasis on education that my paternal grandmother was adamant that all of her grandsons would achieve a college education, and that it was the most important thing we could do at that stage of our lives. To this end, we were rewarded with $500 upon graduation – not an insignificant amount of money to her or to us. If we were to continue and earn an exalted master's degree in any discipline, then we would receive an additional $1,000. I learned from her that education and a sincere love of learning was an element of our faith that had been embedded in her by her father back in the old country.
- I was taught that service to my God should come from my heart without condition or the seeking of personal riches.
- I was taught that I should strive to live a life of charity and desire to share my own good fortune with my fellow man. I

remember hearing about how important to my own life this would be, and that I should always strive to be able to render such acts of kindness.

- The Rabbi is a wise man, and while viewed as a member of the clergy, he is the teacher of the congregation. He did not possess any special privileges nor God-like qualities. I also learned that if the rabbi was not popular, the congregation could literally fire him, and replace him by advertising for someone who "fit in" better. That has not changed to this day.

- I wore a *mezuzah* around my neck, and all my family members who owned homes had one on their front door. It was a reminder of God's presence in our lives. I remember one time when I was around ten years old, opening a mezuzah to see what was inside. True enough, there was an exceedingly small parchment inside, and while I could not see it distinctly enough, I later learned that there are allegedly fifteen verses of the Book of Deuteronomy printed on the scroll.

- At one point I wore a *chai* around my neck which is the Hebrew word for life. The word, consisting of two Hebrew letters —chet (ח) and yud (י)— is a Jewish symbol, frequently appearing on pendants and other jewelry. Chai also refers to the number 18. That is because each Hebrew letter has a numerical equivalent, and the sum of *chet* (numerical value of 8) and *yud* (numerical value of 10) is 18. As a result of its connection to the word for life, the number 18 is considered a special number in Jewish tradition. For this reason, Jews frequently make gifts or charitable contributions in multiples of $18.

In Hebrew, chai is often referred to in the plural form, *chaim* (חים), hence the boy's name Chaim and the toast *l'chaim* (לחים), which, as anyone who has seen *Fiddler on the Roof* knows, means "to life."

- The Star of David, or more accurately the Shield of David, or Mogen David (not the wine), is a six-pointed star made up of two triangles pointing in opposite directions. I never knew what, if any religious significance it had – none as it turned out, but it somehow was adopted as a popular symbol in Jewish life back in the 1600s and was thereafter associated with Jews. I believe everyone knows that Hitler and the Nazis forced Jews before and during World War II to wear it on their clothing and to mark their stores with it. Now of course it is associated with the State of Israel.

- That there were certain dietary restrictions and that meats had to be slaughtered according to certain rituals to maintain certain health standards. The practice of keeping a *kosher* house was something my grandmother did until the death of my uncle. More on that later.

- The Sabbath is the seventh day of the week, from sundown on Friday until sundown on Saturday. It is intended as a day of rest on which no work is permitted. Again, depending on the degree of attentiveness, this could range from not turning on light switches, to serving as a family day for memories, as well as synagogue worship.

- Passover. The Feast of Freedom, that commemorates Israel's deliverance from Egyptian bondage. The "highlight" of this season is of course the *Seder*. I used to attend a Seder at my aunt and uncle's house every year. Imagine the horror when my cousin and I proposed that we only enjoy the meal of bitters, herbs, unleavened bread, hard boiled eggs, nuts, and apples, on leap year. Not a good move on our part.

- *Rosh Hashanah* – the New Year, I was born on it! This was more than just the New Year as we celebrate it in Times Square and the changing of the calendar because it also ushered in the Ten Days of Penitence. This was the period when mankind passes before God's judgment bar. God would look inside a man's heart and examine not only their deeds but their intentions. This was heavy stuff and I did not understand it until I was a teenager. In some ways it was quite intimidating. It is during these ten days that the *Shofar* or ram's horn is sounded. It was a call for all to repent of their misdeeds. Doing so would provide for a more fruitful year ahead with greater dedication to the service of God.

- *Yom Kippur*, the day of Atonement. The last day of the ten day period, it is usually spent in prayer and fasting asking for forgiveness of collective rather than individual sins. Ironically, I can remember when I was a practicing attorney, we had an attorney we dealt with on a fairly regular basis who would spend that day visiting all the law offices (ours included) with whom he did business throughout the year apologizing for any of his personal offenses or trespasses. He was right back at it the next day.

What I knew about the faith even if I did not quite understand it.

- I remember a rabbi saying that we should be more focused on "human potentialities" (whatever that was) and that I was responsible for loving my fellow Jew.
- The Bible was a book of God, and that I could believe parts of it, but not all of it. That was confusing. To this end, the *Torah*, or the Five Books of Moses, consists of the first five books of the Bible from Genesis to Deuteronomy. Orthodox and Conservative Jews believe that the Torah is to be the word of God as He revealed it. A Reformed Jew believes that the Torah can be used as a measurement of truth relating to the soundness of a principle as it applies to life today. I never quite grasped this concept, as it sounded like a "watering down" of the Torah itself. Either it was from God or it was not.
- On the other hand, the *Talmud* was a compendium of legal writings by rabbis going back nearly two thousand years that strived to illustrate how Jews should live their day to day lives. It is of great import to the Conservative Jew, and less so to the Reformed Jew.
- There was not a Heaven and Hell, per se, and therefore no Satan to be contended with by us here on Earth.

- It was all about the Family and our Home; that the Home was more important than the synagogue, and that we could even survive without the existence of synagogues so long as we had our families.

It was against this backdrop that I began my ten year sojourn looking for truth, answers to the questions that literally weighed on me, and most of all, peace of mind. I just felt that in the absence of these things that there was something decidedly missing from my life.

Amazingly enough, I don't *feel* any less Jewish today, as I still cling to my heritage and as I engage in family history revel in discovering how many of my ancestors in the old country going back some ten generations were rabbis and devoted and faithful men and women.

So, was I Jew? Yeah, I think I was. I may not have had a bar mitzvah or raised my own children in the faith, but yes, I was, and remain, a Jew.

CHAPTER 6

ROOTS

"Family. Like branches on a tree, we all grow in
different directions yet our roots remain as one."
Unknown

    Alex Haley changed the world with his book entitled *Roots: The Saga of an American Family*. While he maintained that it was fiction, it was sold in the non-fiction portion of bookstores, and largely captured the story of six generations of his family from the capture and transport of his fourth-great-grandfather Kunta Kinte from Africa to Virginia to his discovering his roots in the 1960's. I remember the excitement that the television mini-series stirred, and genealogy received a shot in the arm in terms of its growing popularity. I was in college at the time and can still vividly remember that it stirred something in me as well. I wanted to know my roots. After hearing some stories from my grandparents, I resolved that some day I would be the one in the family that united all the generations of our family; that I would be the lynchpin between generations past and generations future; what I didn't count on is that it would take me forty years to really get started in earnest.

I started my family tree in 1984 shortly after joining the Church of Jesus Christ of Latter Day Saints. We are encouraged to build a four generation sheet that includes ourselves, so that meant parents, grandparents, and great-grandparents. That was not too difficult for me, but that is where three of my four branches ended abruptly for many years to come.

Sol Levin, my paternal grandfather, was born in Riga, Latvia on July 20, 1898. The oldest of seven children, he supported the family from the time he was 16 and his father David, a fish peddler on the Southside of Chicago, died at age 41, leaving his wife Ida a widow with seven hungry mouths to feed. I know that my grandfather came through Ellis Island but he never talked about that experience or the responsibilities of being the sole support of the family except to mention that his next younger brother "disappeared" for a number of years, which caused a great deal of heartburn, but reconciliation did occur later in life.

In his prime, Sol was 5'6 and topped out at 150 lbs. He was a bare-knuckle boxer of some repute, drove a taxicab for many years, and when I met him, he was still one tough bird even though he had lost two-thirds of his stomach to cancer. I remember vividly my grandmother cooking him fried eggs for breakfast and he then lathering on the Tabasco hot sauce, much to my grandmother's dismay and concern for his reduced stomach capacity.

Despite living in a residential area on the Northside of Chicago, and having only a modest yard, my grandfather had one of the greenest thumbs of anyone I have known and instilled a love of growing things in me. For years I nurtured the plants that I brought to my wife upon the birth of our children at my office and had them for many years until it was time to move from the Chicagoland area. Nearly every portion of his yard was consumed with garden beds in which we would grow tomatoes, a variety of peppers, green beans, peas, cantaloupe, watermelon, lettuce, carrots, onions, and anything else that came out of the ground. In the winter months, the basement, interior back porch and kitchen would be littered with flowerpots full of seedlings waiting for the next Spring planting season. He taught me to work hard and instilled a degree of both patience and discipline as we tended the gardens together. I can still hear his voice in my head as he would often sing to us, and if I ever forget, I am blessed to have recordings of his voice that my father made throughout the 1960s as he captured us interacting with our grandparents.

Probably the best story about my grandfather occurred when my father was a young boy and came running into the house crying. Apparently, a neighbor man had taken exception to my father playing near his yard and had the temerity to give my father a cuff to the side of the head. That was all my grandfather had to hear, and he was out the door like a shot. While I am certain the story grew into mythical proportions over the years, it was reported to me that the ensuing fisticuffs turned into a neighborhood brawl between the two men as they literally duked it out, crashing through wooden fences, knocking over trash cans, disrupting laundry drying on the line, and creating enough of a ruckus that it took four to six police officers to separate them. When asked by the ranking police officer what sparked the battle, my grandfather let it be known that nobody would ever lay a hand on either his wife or one of his sons so long as he had breath in his lungs. Having heard at least three accounts of the incident, I am confident that this is the way it went down.

On a more humorous note, because my grandfather was a taxi driver, his driver's license was his livelihood, and so protecting it was of paramount importance. After completing a fare, he was pulled over for speeding. The officer making the stop approached my grandfather's vehicle and with a very thick Irish brogue (common among police officers in New York City, Boston, Philadelphia and Chicago in the early 20th Century) asked my grandfather for his name and driver's license. When he responded, "Oh, Sol Levin", his words were slurred and said quickly enough to appease the Irish police officer who obviously heard "O'Sullivan" to his satisfaction. The result, a warning, and no costly ticket. This is another one of those stories that lived on for many years. I have the same problem on the phone when people will erroneously hear me identify myself as "Donovan," as opposed to Don Levin.

When we were not laboring in the garden together, my grandfather did his best to teach me the rudiments of boxing. We would dance around the yard, sparring with one another, working on footwork as well as bobbing and weaving. Whenever he wanted to assert his superiority, he would lightly tap me on one of my cheeks with his fingertips or an open hand. He never hurt me but impressed upon me that boxing is more about finesse and technique rather than brute strength and the ability to take a punch. Little did I know that I would put these skills into action many years later.

It has always amused me that America and its top metropolitan cities are referred to as melting pots. Nothing could be further than truth. Even today, the local *botega* will cater to Hispanic members of the neighborhood, just as will shops in the Asian Market, Little Italy, Chinatown, Little India, the French Quarter, etc. We are not a melting pot but rather an amalgam of ethnic neighborhoods or ghettos; it is the case today and has been that way for as long as we have had immigrants flowing into our country. It was no different in the 1930s when the West side of Chicago was where the Jewish community lived to include the family of Sol and Mary Levin.

As times changed, so did the neighborhoods and little by little the neighborhoods would often leapfrog over one another. Such was the case when Sol and Mary moved to the North side of Chicago, and bought the bungalow in which most of my most formative childhood memories were created. The building on the west side that they had purchased with the proceeds of the Serviceman's Group Life Insurance that they received upon the death of my uncle was retained, and they became landlords in what eventually became a black neighborhood. I can remember going with them to collect rents and to inspect the building. I was no more than four or five at the time, and I remember my grandmother making it clear that we are all God's children, regardless of the color of our skin. "People are people, and we should treat everyone as we want them to treat us." It was as close to a religious discussion that we ever had; but more on that later as well.

We would drive from the Northside to the West side of Chicago in my grandfather's pride and joy, a brand new 1963 Chevy II – the precursor to the Chevy Nova. No air conditioning, only an AM radio, no power brakes or power steering, cloth interior, this was as basic a form of transportation as one could find. When my grandfather died in November, 1972, my grandmother who did not drive, gave the car to my father so that we could have a second car in our family – my mother had just learned to drive at age 33 that same year. It was intended to be the car in which my father would commute from our suburban home to the train station for his ride to downtown Chicago. Two years later, my father *sold* me this car, which I then dubbed Julius in honor of Groucho Marx, and helped me repaint it in an effort to camouflage all the bonding material with which we had repaired the rust holes that had accumulated due to the region's use of road salt in the winter. It was a beast to drive, but it was mine, and when I drove it, I could sometimes feel my grandfather's presence in the car with me.

My paternal grandmother, Mary Lisch Levin, was a saint. I attribute most of the good in me to her influence on me as I grew up largely at her knee. When it came time for my brother and I to have the chicken pox, it was Grandma Mary who nursed us 24/7 at her house, ensuring that we ate very well. In fact, most of our life at her house revolved around food. Regardless of the meal, if you cleared your plate, you received a shiny new dime acquired at the Devon Bank located on Western Avenue, a short walk across the alley from the house, and for each additional helping, one could pocket an additional nickel. It was not uncommon for my brother and I to add ten pounds to our slight frames during a two week visit at the old homestead.

Mary Lisch was a "greenhorn" who came through Ellis Island, New York on August 1, 1913 at the ripe old age of ten years old. Having been born in St. Petersburg, Russia, she was the youngest of six children born to Ira Lisch and his wife Fenya (Fanny) Wasserman. When Ira's wife died in 1908, Mary was only five years old, and as was the tradition of the time, Ira was quick to remarry in order that he would have a wife and his children a new mother. Unfortunately, Ira's choice of a step-mother was not a good one, and when opportunity presented itself, Mary was sent to America with a traveling companion, her older brother Max, who had emigrated a couple of years earlier and was already residing in Chicago, serving as her sponsor. It is still hard to imagine the adventure of traveling from St. Petersburg, Russia at that age, with no command of the language. On many occasions we heard about how Grandma spoke no less than *eight* languages, but sadly, English was not one of them. At age ten, she found herself in kindergarten attempting to learn the language.

As we grew older, she would share more of her immigration story. Imagine our surprise when she shared how she narrowly escaped being raped by running through corn fields to escape from horse riding Cossacks.

Her brothers Yankel and Schlomo served as young members of the Czar's army, and I have a photograph of the two of them in uniform hanging on my wall.

She always spoke in reverent tones of Lady Liberty and how seeing the Statue of Liberty for the first time caused stirrings of pride in her new country. I have recordings of her vivid descriptions of this experience and cannot help but get emotional as I listen to them.

When the movie *Yentl* starring Barbra Streisand was released and showed the domed buildings of the "Old Country" my grandmother emphatically said that it was exactly as she remembered it from the time she was a little girl.

My grandmother was an *interesting* cook. I suspect that one of the reasons I to this day enjoy having a "cast iron stomach" is that she introduced so many antibodies into my digestive system. Whether it was chicken soup with homemade *kreplach* or *matzo balls* proceeded by chopped liver, or roasted chicken, or egg salad with Catalina dressing as added flavoring, or even an occasional steak dinner that she would direct my grandfather to grill at 8 o'clock in the morning, the one ingredient that you could always taste was the pure love that she used in heaping portions. Her family was her world, and her six grandsons and two [remaining] sons was her purpose for living. I never heard an unkind word from her, and when I think of Christ-like love and service, and the personification of *Charity Never Faileth*, I think of Mary.

Mary was a simple woman who endured the worst that Life can throw at a person – the death of a child. Whether she dealt with it better or worse than the next person is a moot point. I will write of this in greater detail in the next chapter, because it had the most profound of impacts on me and my family for generations to come, and contributed significantly to my dissatisfaction with what I perceived as the limitations of my Jewish faith, and instilled in me a desire for something much more. I realize now that my grandmother was indirectly responsible for sowing these seeds of discontent as I was truly seeking the true meaning of life. Ultimately, I found the doctrines associated with the Church of Jesus Christ of Latter Day Saints to be both intellectually and emotionally compelling and resonating with truth. I have often thought that these very doctrines would have brought her great solace had she embraced them into her own life while on this side of mortality. Fortunately, she has had the opportunity to do this on the other side of the veil.

She called me Handsome from the time I was old enough to remember until the day she died. She has been gone for over twenty seven years as I sit writing this, gazing at her picture and remembering the overwhelming sense of love and security that she provided to me not only as a child but also as an adult. I look to her example to more fully understand what Elder Jeffrey R. Holland of the Quorum of Twelve Apostles meant when he said: "No love in mortality comes closer to approximating the pure love of Jesus Christ than the selfless love a devoted mother (grandmother in my case) has for her child."

Sol and Mary were married in June 1921, and had three sons, Donald Aaron born in 1922, Edward born in 1925, and my father Erwin born, oops, in 1936. I have their wedding picture on my wall in our ancestor gallery, and the cut crystal water pitcher that they received as a wedding present is displayed prominently in our china cabinet. It is a prized possession because of its lineage. They were married fifty years before my grandfather died in November 1972. More on that later as well.

My maternal grandfather, Joseph Hefter was born in Chicago on December 18, 1912. He was the youngest of four children born to Don Jacob Hefter and his wife Molly Mendelovich. I knew all three of his siblings, spending time with them and their spouses on many occasions. His sister Mary was married to Ben Terkel, who was the brother of best-selling author Studs Terkel. My grandfather was a first generation

American, whose life could best be summed up as "coulda, woulda, shoulda." As a result of his example of missed opportunities, I have not been afraid of making a decision and moving forward. I believe he had a good life and enjoyed his career selling children's shoes. He *coulda* been a podiatrist, because back when he was young, the qualifications were so much less than by the time I had come along. He sold the only home they owned just before the prices in the area skyrocketed and he *coulda* nearly tripled the sales price had he waited all of two more years. They rented an apartment thereafter for the balance of his life. He did have some prowess in the stock market because I know that he and my grandmother accumulated quite a portfolio over the course of their life together. My grandfather always wore the most stylish clothes and fancied himself a bit of the ladies man, and would hug and kiss all the mothers of the children who came into his shoe store. He was also generous in terms of sharing "hand me down" clothes with my father, as well as occasionally providing my brothers and I with a pair of shoes from the store as a means by which to help out my parents. Note: never a pair of Beatles shoes or penny loafers (they are too wide and not good for your feet) either of which I would have killed for, but quality leather shoes. He did teach me never to buy cheap, non-leather shoes as they are bad for the health of your feet; also, always polish new shoes before you wear them for the first time because you protect against unwanted scuffs and cuts in the leather. I follow that advice to this day even if my children cannot fathom the logic behind it.

Joe's brothers were seven and five years older than he, and I do not recollect a lot of interaction with them except around the Jewish holidays, but even then, there was not a lot of ceremony associated with these events. It was largely an excuse to get together and to share a meal.

My maternal grandmother, Eunice Ruth Meyer, was born April 9, 1913, in Chicago, Illinois the middle child of Manuel Goldsmith and Tillie Nathanson. She is the only grandparent that provided me with any real "roots" here in the United States when I began my family history research, with ancestry going back several generations to New Orleans, LA and then back to France and Germany.

Joe and Eunice were married in 1936 and were married just shy of fifty years when my grandfather died of cancer in 1985. Their union produced two daughters, my mother Toby born in 1938 and my aunt Renee born in 1946. I remember my aunt more as a big sister when I was a child. I remember watching the Beatles with her on The Ed Sullivan Show, and to this day think of her when I hear several of the early Beatles songs.

We spent a lot of Sunday dinners with my maternal grandparents, and my grandmother was an excellent cook. Chopped liver, noodle kugel, brisket, chicken matzo ball soup, and roast beef were her specialties. She always maintained a well-stocked candy drawer in the living room, most notably with Doublemint gum, licorice twists, and Necco wafers.

There was protracted estrangement with her older brother and younger sister, and I really don't understand why, though I do know that the example it set permeated the relationship between my aunt and mother who did not speak for the last twenty five years of my mother's life which is so contrary to the emphasis that we place on family.

Both sets of grandparents maintained that they were Jewish, but I do not recall either set ever attending the synagogue unless it was for a special event, e.g. a bar mitzvah, wedding, or funeral. I do recall lighting the Chanukah menorah at my maternal grandparents' home and playing with a *dreidel* or spinning top that they provided to my brother and me.

My maternal grandparents did display a fair amount of symbolic art and accoutrements such as a regular Menorah, that reflected their Jewish heritage, and in hindsight can say that I was reminded fairly often of the fact that I was in fact a Jew.

The shoe store at which my grandfather worked was on Oakton Street in downtown Skokie, Illinois, which in the 1960s could claim the highest number of concentration camp survivors in the country. It was one of the reasons that the Skinheads marched there in the early 1980s in a show of force. I can remember walking with my grandfather and seeing people with numbers tattooed on their forearms. On one occasion when I pointed at one of them and asked the significance of the numbers, my grandfather rather brusquely told me not to point and later explained to me what it meant to be a Jew and a survivor of one of Hitler's Concentration Camps. As a seven year old, I was horrified, and thereafter had a greater appreciation for what it meant to be a Jew.

My grandfather gave me my first mezuzah to wear around my neck when I was around ten years old, and I still have it to this day. Again, while we did not ever engage in deep meaningful faith promoting discussions, I was taught from a very early age that I was a Jew, and that I should be proud of my heritage, and that I should be prepared to defend it if ever called upon to do so. Despite this "identity" I wanted more knowledge relating to God, and my purpose in life. By the time I was ten years old I had reconciled Darwin's Theory of Evolution with Genesis by determining in at least my own mind that we could have "evolved" on one of the six creative periods, because nobody could speak definitively just how long those days were. As I remember the Sunday dinner at which I proudly shared what I considered to be a rather profound and deep thought on the subject, the family was less than impressed and just attributed the theory to the fact that I was a voracious reader and was always "thinking about something." Yes, I was a bookworm and nerd.

With the gift of hindsight, I must admit that I sorely missed the spiritual guidance that I would love to have received from my grandparents [and parents]. My cousins and my friends all apparently were receiving it, especially as they prepared themselves for their individual bar mitzvahs and the rite of passage into manhood. More on that later as well. For this reason alone I remain committed to being the grandpa who talks about the priesthood, priesthood blessings, family history work, service in the temple and as a bishop, and the spiritual experiences that I have experienced both before, during, and after my conversion to the Church of Jesus Christ of Latter Day Saints.

CHAPTER 7

BLAME MARK CLARK

"The strength and peace that come from knowing
God and having the comforting companionship of His
Spirit will make your efforts eternally worthwhile."
Robert D. Hales

People often ask me what some of the most impactful events were
that led to my conversion and membership in the Church of Jesus Christ
of Latter Day Saints. In retrospect, I would say one such event occurred
nearly fourteen years before I was born, with the World War II combat-
related death of my paternal uncle, Donald Aaron Levin.

My dad's oldest brother, and the man that I am named for –
remember I mentioned earlier that it is traditional for Jews to name
for the dead as a sign of honoring their memory – was a bona fide hero
complete with Bronze Star and *five* Purple Hearts awarded for wounds
received in combat. A bayonet through the knee at Anzio Beach, a
bullet that entered his forehead and exited the rear of his head that
went *around* his skull and prompted him to walk three miles back to
the aid station; two lesser wounds, and the final posthumous award for

the wound that officially occurred when he was killed in a foxhole as a result of incoming mortar fire.

I have several postcards and letters that he wrote home from North Africa or various parts of Italy as part of the 88th Division Blue Devils. I am proud to say that many years later in the latter stages of my own military career that I was a second generation Blue Devil, and have in my curio table, the Blue Devil membership card issued posthumously to my grandparents on behalf of my uncle.

From the time I was old enough to understand, I heard many times that Donnie felt compelled to volunteer for every mission that came up in order to prove that as one of the few Jews in the unit, Jews were brave and not cowardly. This attitude and willingness to assume higher risks contributed to the number of wounds that he received. Grandma felt that Donnie's death could most notably be blamed on General Mark Clark, the Army Theatre Commander, for failing to take the boys off the line after an extended period of combat.

At the time of Donnie's death, my grandmother's faithfulness was exhibited by the fact that she did keep a kosher house, and rigorously observed all the practices associated with these dietary laws. This stopped immediately when my grandmother, and presumably my grandfather as well, embraced the belief that Donnie's death was a byproduct of God having "turned His back on her and the family." On the few occasions that we did address this topic as I entered adulthood and began my own search for God and the spiritual path that I wanted to pursue, commentary from both of my grandparents led me to the conclusion that but for Donnie's death, life in the Levin family would have been dramatically different.

My father Erwin was 8 years old when news of his brother's death arrived in the form of a Western Union telegram, copies of which I also have in my files. Life as he knew it ceased to exist. His world was turned inside out, upside down, and will be addressed in more detail in the next chapter.

My Grandfather Sol took the news of his son's death stoically, but the inner turmoil soon proved to be too much, and he suffered an emotional breakdown that landed him in Cook County Hospital. We never spoke of this episode except in passing.

My Grandmother Mary literally cried her eyes out. My brothers and I repeatedly heard that the reason she had to start wearing glasses is because she cried so much as to "hurt" her eyes. In hindsight I suspect that some of the cause may have been natural progression but that was the story from which she never deviated. As I met people later in life, we also learned that my grandmother's personality changed from that of an extrovert to the introvert that I always knew as I was growing up.

I was also viewed as her "replacement" for Donnie, and as such, I freely admit that I was doted on. While my grandparents treated all six grandsons equally, there was no doubt that as a child I was afforded more of her attention.

My Uncle Eddie, who was about three years younger than Donnie and still some eleven years older than my father, served in the South Pacific for thirty two months as part of the 4th Marine Division, seeing combat in nearly every major campaign. Despite all the horror that he saw and experienced, he came home with a great sense of humor still intact, with a sore back and lingering effects of malaria, but otherwise very well adjusted. Like many other veterans of the Greatest Generation, he never spoke about his war experiences until after 1998 when the movie *Saving Private Ryan* was released, and he felt both empowered *and allowed* to share some of his experiences. Eddie went on to marry a lovely Jewish girl, have two sons – my cousins – both of whom attended Hebrew school and had a bar mitzvah, and became a wonderful example to all of us.

Donnie's death traumatized my family. It shattered my grandparents and prompted them to question their faith, and to largely abandon the daily practices associated with it. For my father, it left a huge vacuum that was filled in other ways, which naturally later filtered down to me and my brothers.

CHAPTER 8

DONNIE'S HOME

"Our ability to endure to the end in righteousness
will be in direct proportion to the strength of our
testimony and the depth of our conversion."
Richard J. Maynes

I had long believed that we encounter angels every day. Not necessarily those from Heaven, but every day mortal angels who are intent on making a difference in the world. I am confident that you have encountered these very same angels even if you have dismissed them as merely being more kind-hearted than yourself, or someone who was inspired to do something nice for those around them. Now I can honestly say that with the *knowledge* that I hold near and dear, that I do believe that the veil separating this world from the next one can be very thin at times, and that interaction with the other side not only is permissible, but that it readily happens all of the time, and that we do interact with angels and of course the Holy Ghost as our constant companion. I will share some specific examples in subsequent chapters.

In the fall of 1948, my father was 12 years old. Like any twelve year old at that time, Saturday afternoon meant being in front of the radio for any of a myriad of popular radio programs. This was long before television became the popular medium that it is today. It was about noon and my father was laying on the floor in front of the big radio that dominated the living room, when he had an experience that left him shaken and still somewhat "spooked" by it until the day he died.

When my two uncles (his brothers) entered the military service in 1942-3, my grandmother placed a framed photo of each of them in their respective military uniforms on top of this radio. These pictures sat there undisturbed for all the intervening years. It was shortly after noon when the frame containing Donnie's photo literally came apart at the corners, prompting the glass to fall forward on the top of the radio, freeing the photograph, which then proceeded to waft to the floor. When my father shrieked and called my grandmother into the room, she looked down at the photo laying on the floor, and calmly announced, "Donnie's home." My uncle had originally been buried at a US military cemetery in Italy, and in 1948 my grandparents were given the option of having his remains brought back to the United States. They accepted the government's offer, and my Uncle is now buried in what has become the family plot in a Jewish cemetery on the North side of Chicago. My father did not question the pronouncement, and remembers the phone ringing at 5 o'clock that day, and the caller, a supervisor down at the Union Station train terminal, announcing that my uncle's remains had arrived. When my father asked when, the station master off handedly said, "the noon train." In years past, I would have referred to this sort of experience as "spooky stuff" but now realize that my grandmother had received a testimony or spiritual prompting of comfort from the Holy Ghost letting her know that the remains of her son had in fact completed his journey home.

I have discussed this phenomenon many times with my father, my brothers, as well as many of my friends within the Church. The consensus is that coincidence is not a satisfactory explanation for the occurrence. For the frame to have sat there undisturbed for six years and to come apart at exactly the moment that the train bearing my uncle's earthly remains arrived back in Chicago is just too difficult to chalk up to coincidence. As recently as this week when I started to capture the thoughts for this chapter, I had a conversation with my brother who remembers the *story* in great detail, and was still willing to identify it as such: a story that has been passed down within the family and generally accepted as having occurred as depicted.

When I pressed him, and reminded him that this was not a *story* that we read about in a magazine, or heard on television, but rather from the lips of our very father as adults, he acknowledged that there are forces out there beyond our comprehension or explanation. In any event, I remain confident that the events as depicted did occur, and that my grandmother's calm utterance was the result of what she had described to me as a "feeling of peace inside her heart."

Over the years, while we all were still living in Chicago, I took my grandmother to the family plot on many occasions and heard her recount that story time and time again. She never faltered in her words or the feelings she conveyed while relating the details of that story. I heard it again when she gave to me the metal tag that had been attached to the military casket containing his name, rank, and serial number that now rests on display in our memorabilia table.

Because I firmly believe that a parent burying a child is the most unnatural act we can perform in life, I would like to think that my grandmother did receive an inspired feeling of comfort at that time from a loving Heavenly Father.

CHAPTER 9

CHICK

"An honest heart will lead to a change of heart.
Spiritually speaking, a change of heart is not
only desirable, but essential for eternal life."
Marvin J. Ashton

My father Erwin was born in Chicago, on August 2, 1936. A first generation American, the third son of Sol and Mary Levin. Donnie, age 14, and Eddie age 11, were his idols. Donnie nicknamed him 'Chick' and the name stuck all through high school when my father played trumpet in a local band. Being the [unexpected] caboose, and with such a large gap between he and Eddie, my grandmother was embarrassed to have given birth to him at the old age of 33. For all intents and purposes, he was raised as an only child, doted on by his parents, and afforded many opportunities that his brothers did not enjoy.

Aside from being poor, his memories of his early childhood were happy ones, especially whenever his brothers were present. To this end, I heard from my grandmother how one day when he was five or six years old, he went outside with half a bagel smeared with butter, and promptly dropped it in the dirt. When he returned to the house, my grandmother informed him that there was nothing else left to eat in the house. All of that changed with the advent of World War Two. Both of his brothers left to fight America's enemies, my grandmother went to work in a factory while my grandfather continued to drive his taxi, and my father was largely left to his own devices and the influences of his friends.

Life as he knew it came to a screeching halt in October 1944 when my grandparents received that fateful Western Union telegram that notified them of the combat death of my Uncle Donnie. As previously noted, the impact of his death truly shattered the family. Gone were the vestiges of Jewish faith, the kosher house, and the love and devotion of two parents who went into deep states of mourning.

The war ended and the country returned to a new normal as the Greatest Generation returned from overseas, began college on the G.I. Bill, and started producing the Baby Boomer generation. My father was what he described as "rudderless." He had many Catholic friends with whom he would build model airplanes, attend movies, and listen to the radio. One of his friends was so talented that he has model airplanes on display at the Smithsonian Museum in Washington, D.C. It was with this circle of friends that my father's rabbi took exception, essentially giving my father the choice of the synagogue or his friends. With no direction forthcoming from his grieving parents, my father chose his friends and that was the end of his formal affiliation with religion.

My father graduated high school, attended a local junior college for a short while and then went to work. He married my mother, and they began their family which consisted of me and my three younger brothers.

My father was a voracious reader, and I can still remember the large Time-Life coffee table book *Religions of the World*. I remember opening it as a child and being encouraged to read it by my father. I also have in my possession the paperback copy of the Book of Mormon that was presented to my father by someone when I was seven years old. I remember him reading it and making some comment along the lines of "this is a very interesting book." I do not know why he kept it all the years that he did, but he did.

My father was one of the most logical people I have ever known and had a great capacity for "compartmentalizing" his emotions. He was also a great optimist. When he had a tumor removed from his back and was told that 90% of the time that it would grow back cancerous, he calmly said that he would be in the 10%, and in fact that was the end result.

The years passed, my parents were divorced after a stormy marriage, and my father dated heavily, married several times, and anointed me the head of the family when I was approximately 21 years old. He had abdicated the role of patriarch.

He was supportive of our being baptized and joining the Church of Jesus Christ of Latter Day Saints, and over the years attended the baptisms of our children and other events at the church.

To this day, I am still stunned at several pronouncements that my father made to me in the years after my baptism regarding the presence of religion in our family because of our choices.

First, that regardless of how late he had been out, or the activities he had engaged in, he always prayed each night before going to sleep. I was stunned to learn this fact. We had never had a family prayer of any kind except for the occasions where I would read the prayer to light the Chanukah menorah. Never at mealtime, or at any other time. He could not understand why I/we were all so surprised at this revelation.

Second, while we visited him in Sierra Vista, Arizona where he retired, we had occasion to sit with him along with the full-time missionaries, three stake missionaries, our two oldest children, and ourselves, and essentially conduct a 9-on-1 testimony meeting. I can still remember my daughter's tearful testimony of being baptized for her maternal grandmother and the impact it had on my father. Note: the senior stake missionary had even greater credibility because like my father, he too was a full colonel in the US Army. At the conclusion of that visit, my father declined our invitation to be baptized, but further shocked me by telling me to vicariously "do his work for him after he is dead." He believed!

Third, upon the death of his brother Eddie, he said to me, "I am so glad that my brothers are together again, and with my parents!" I was stunned and when I found my voice could only remind him that he was Jewish, and that the faith did not believe that was the case. He simply smiled.

In a later chapter I will recount how in a time of physical need he asked me and my home teaching companion for a priesthood blessing and would for the rest of his life tell anyone who was interested that I had healed him. No matter how many times I told him that I was merely a conduit, and not responsible for his medical cure, he would look me in the eye with the same paternal pride that accompanied all of my other temporal achievements, and try to convince me that I had done it.

What effect did my father have on my testimony and conversion? Obviously, I was not born into a family of faith, nor was I particularly encouraged to find it. I was neither encouraged or discouraged in my pursuit of truth and knowledge. I do remember having discussions with my father, during which I largely talked, and he would offer "commentary." I know that he was impressed by the spirituality of our family, and on more than one occasion shared comments reflective of his approval and favorable impression of how our children were turning out with the influence of the Church in their lives.

I still have many questions for my father and look forward to seeing him again on the other side of the veil.

CHAPTER 10

MOTHERHOOD

"Show me Latter-day Saints who have to feed upon
miracles, signs and visions in order to keep them
steadfast in the Church, and I will show you members ...
who are not in good standing before God, and who
are walking in slippery paths. It is not by marvelous
manifestations unto us that we shall be established
in the truth, but it is by humility and faithful
obedience to the commandments and laws of God."
Joseph Fielding Smith.

Perhaps the greatest of conflicts I continue to harbor as a faithful
Latter Day Saint is that I was not born of "goodly parents" like Nephi of
old. Mine is a different pioneer heritage through Ellis Island rather than
of handcarts across the prairie; but most importantly that I did not have
the type of relationship with my mother that most people can reflect
back on with feelings of pride, joy, security, and the knowledge that
they were loved. Further, that my *knowledge* of the eternal perspective
of motherhood has been acquired by my relationship with my paternal
grandmother Mary, as well as from observing my wife Susie as we reared

our five children, and now my daughters in their interactions with my grandchildren. I have a firm testimony that the greatest and most God-like thing we do in this life is to be a parent, and that there is an even greater stature associated with that of Mother.

My mother, Toby Lee Hefter, was born in Chicago, IL on February 4, 1938 the oldest of two daughters born to Joseph and Eunice Hefter. My mother graduated high school and shortly thereafter married my father at age 18. Toby was 20 years old when I came along, and she became a mother. I have good memories of interacting with my maternal grandparents and their families, but literally no day to day memories of faith being present in our lives either in our home or theirs.

As I was growing up and attempting to form my own beliefs, I would often share my insights with my mother, like reconciling Genesis and Darwin, and she would listen, usually without offering any insights. I suspect she was more intimidated by my fervor and desire for knowledge.

After my parents divorced, my mother immediately remarried a Jewish man who had studied for his own bar mitzvah and yet maintained no significant ties to the Jewish faith. Given that two of my brothers are eight and thirteen years younger, they could have been afforded the opportunity of being raised in the faith but were not.

My mother professed to a belief in God, and for many years professed to be a "Jew for Jesus" as some Jews with Christian beliefs were then known. Later in life, after the passing of her second husband, she joined the Methodist faith and received her confirmation in that faith, but I suspect that this affiliation was as much a social one as it was because of a fervent desire to immerse herself in the faith.

What did my mother contribute to my conversion and journey on the Path? In hindsight I realize that it was more her example as the antithesis of what I wanted to be as a person that drove me to find the Truth as I now understand it. For this, and obviously the gift of life, I am grateful.

CHAPTER 11

EARLIEST RECOLLECTIONS

"My dear friends, your faith did not begin at birth, and
it will not end at death. Faith is a choice. Strengthen
your faith and live to be deserving of the Savior's
approving words: "Great is thy faith." As you do, I
promise you that your faith, through the grace of Jesus
Christ, will one day allow you to stand with those
you love, clean and pure in the presence of God."
Neil L. Andersen

I was blessed with a good memory. We jokingly attribute it to my
Grandmother Mary. She had an incredible memory, and more often
than not our only defense to one of her memories (usually involving
the cost of a gas bill or some other mundane factoid from thirty or
forty years before) was to point out that there was nobody around
old enough to criticize her recollection. Well, I am quietly becoming
the institutional memory of the family though I can often pull out a
written journal to substantiate my recollections or resort to the Internet
for confirmation. As I am now getting a little older, I am finding that

while my short term memory is not as great as it used to be, the long term memories remain safely anchored in time.

My earliest memories are from around the time that I was 2-3 years old, and when I shared them with my parents years later, they were impressed by the clarity of the accounts as I shared them.

I remember my maternal great-grandmother Molly Mendelovitch and visiting her in a precursor to a nursing home on the Northside of Chicago. She was in her late 80s by the time I was born, and I remember looking at her translucent skin and wondering if we were all destined to look like that as we aged. More importantly I remember wondering then where she would go when she died. I remember the dimly lit, 25-watt lightbulbs on the stairwell up to her second floor room, and of course the smell of the facility – part age, part disinfectant, part ammonia. Inasmuch as smell is the greatest trigger of memory, I am taken back to that time every time I set foot in any long term care facility to this day.

The other great memory of my young childhood is of course November 22, 1963. I was home from morning kindergarten, having my peanut butter sandwich while watching Bozo the Clown (it originated locally on WGN out of Chicago) out on the enclosed rear porch of our second floor walk-up when the news came in that the president had been shot in Dallas. Walter Cronkite was in tears. At that time Walter Cronkite was the most trusted man in America, so his emotions impacted many his viewing audience. The president was gone. Where had the President gone? He was so young and vital. The torch of leadership had been passed from one generation to the next. He had challenged us to send man to the moon and to return him safely by the end of the decade. I remember wondering if he was now in a special part of Heaven because he had been the President. I wondered if I would have the opportunity to meet him. I wondered what happened to him when he was shot. While watching the videos that became available shortly thereafter, I wondered when *exactly* he stopped being the president. So many people shed tears over the next several days. The three major networks devoted coverage to his casket on display under an armed honor guard seemingly non-stop until his funeral a few days later. I distinctly remember wanting to look inside his casket to see *what* was in it. Did we stop looking like ourselves when we died? What happens to our spirit? I think Caspar the friendly ghost had something to do with that last question. These were heady thoughts for a five year old, and I know that they surprised my parents. Today I am experiencing the same degree of deep five year old questions from my own granddaughter who has wisdom that exceeds her years on earth. I guess it is another reason that I appreciate even more her accounts of nocturnal visits from the tooth fairy and things more appropriate for her age.

It was in this same time that my brother and I were featured in my father's business newsletter for AT&T wearing yarmulkes as we celebrated Passover. I always thought my brother's red hair was a real misnomer as he looked more like an Irish lad than he did a Jewish kid. To this day I am not certain why our family was featured that prominently given that we were largely non-practicing members of our faith.

Nearly three score years later, I can remember all those questions as vividly now as I pondered them back then. The difference being that I now have both peace and security in the beliefs around what happens when we die and move through the veil of mortality to that of immortality and eternal life. I am grateful that I had those questions, and that I was able to find my way to the light.

CHAPTER 12

HEBREW SCHOOL

"We can readily see that observance of the Sabbath
is an indication of the depth of our conversion. Our
observance or nonobservance of the Sabbath is an unerring
measure of our attitude toward the Lord personally and
toward his suffering in Gethsemane, his death on the
cross, and his resurrection from the dead. It is a sign
of whether we are Christians in very deed, or whether
our conversion is so shallow that commemoration of
his atoning sacrifice means little or nothing to us."
Mark E. Peterson

As previously noted, there was not a religious emphasis in our home while we were growing up. While both of my parents were presumably proud of their Jewish background, I think it is more a matter of their not having had the opportunity to learn about their lineage or the Jewish language that prevented them from more firmly embracing it. This was the case for my father. As previously noted, while his mother spoke eight languages when she came to America at age 10, aside from Yiddish (which has its roots in low German) and a smattering of Russian, by the time I came along, the others were long since gone for her. Donnie's dying in combat greatly altered life as my father then knew it, because gone forever was the banter and extroverted behavior that he remembers prior to that milestone. It is noteworthy that when I practiced my junior high school Russian or High School [high] German with her, we could communicate in our own language to which no one else was privy. I believe that our doing this gave my grandmother joy, and I know that it brought us closer to one another.

As children we never had any formal religious education until we moved to Aurora, Illinois where a wise and benevolent Rabbi encouraged my parents to enroll me in Hebrew School and to "pay whatever they could afford" towards the requisite tuition. I do remember hearing him say, "I want your boys in Hebrew School," and my father solemnly nodding his head to the arrangement. As I will explain in a subsequent chapter, this was monumental for my entire family at that point in time, and but for our being uprooted after only less than two years there, might have been a turning point for me in terms of my religious journey.

Other than that 18 month period of Hebrew School which I attended after school two afternoons each week, where I started mastering the language and the history, our formal religious education was limited to learning about Jewish traditions and of course the High Holy Days. I had the good fortune of being born on Rosh Hashana (the New Year) and we would often hear about some of the traditions from all our four grandparents.

Grandma Mary was always telling us to be proud of our heritage as the chosen people of God. I was not sure what we had been chosen for, given all the persecution that the Jews had endured throughout History.

It was during this period that I renewed my curiosity around death and where we go when we die. Again, my family, like most of the other Jews we associated with around us, believed strictly in the here and now and did not believe in life after death. On more than one occasion I was told not to worry about it, and that I should not even think about it "given all the wonderful years of life I have ahead of me." Naturally, that answer only fueled my curiosity. What were they hiding? Why could they be satisfied that when we died that we would get planted in the ground to return to dust and to trust that God would take care of us in some way? It simply did not make sense to me. The topic of death was definitely and completely verboten around my paternal grandparents. Donnie's death had taken a great toll on both of them. Wouldn't we have all been much happier knowing then what I know now?

Now before you start casting an image of me as a young *nebbish* (there's a great word meaning pitifully timid or submissive) resembling Woody Allen, rest assured that most of my curiosity was intellectually driven rather than out of a fear of the unknown or death itself. I simply wanted answers and to remain in control of my destiny...even as a child and teenager. Thank goodness I found them before I allowed temptation or fear to chart my course for me.

I have witnessed my grandchildren's reaction to death, and it is a healthy one. While they grieve the passing of a great-grandparent, they also rejoice in the celebration of their mortal life, and retain the innocent knowledge that they will see these people again in the next life because we are all part of an eternal family. It warms my heart to hear them talk among themselves about these issues, and to have answers that I so dearly I wish I had had when I was their age. This is another gift from our loving Heavenly Father for which I am incredibly grateful. Like balm on a wounded heart, the Plan of Salvation is truly the path for all of us to follow now and into the next life.

CHAPTER 13

THE BOY WONDER BEGINS

"You never totally move beyond faith as hope; it is not
a box we check off and say, "I am done." Rather, we
begin again and gain experience with a new principle.
It spirals upward as a helix, building and continuing.
Here is how that occurs. We move from level of faith to
level of faith through desire, a willingness to experiment
and act, and then receiving a spiritual confirmation as
evidence of things not seen. This process and experience
bolster our faith. Consequently, we exhibit an increased
willingness to experiment and receive an even greater
confirmation. Our confidence waxes stronger, line upon
line, precept upon precept, here a little and there a little."
David A. Bednar

For as long as I can remember, my father always referred to me
as the Boy Wonder. Certainly not because I was Batman's sidekick
Robin, but because he had high expectations of me, and I generally
always met or exceeded these standards and challenges as they were
placed in front of me. Being the youngest high school graduate in

the Northwest suburbs of Chicago certainly conformed with the high achievement drive that my father firmly fomented in me from the time I started reading at a high rate of speed and comprehension that merited attention of everyone in the school to include the principal with whom he insisted on confirming the results.

In hindsight, while I am grateful for the identification and recognition of my rudimentary talents, I also recognize that it was an incredible *burden* that I carried for a great many years well into my adult life. I can fully appreciate, "For unto whomsoever much is given, of him shall be much required: and to whom men have committed much, of him they will ask the more." (Luke 12:48).

When I asked my father *why* I had been the one raised so much differently than my other three brothers, his answer came quickly and quietly: "you were the one with the potential." While I was later forced and cajoled to share this with my brothers when we were gathered for our mother's funeral and looking back on our lives with our parents, I realized just how much of a burden it truly had been for me. The constant pressure to be the youngest; the first, the best and the brightest; to get there first and achieve the most, via the most difficult route with the greatest number of challenges, purely to earn his approval, well into my adult professional life, was both wearing and dumb on my part.

I remember learning that I was the *youngest* Captain in the United States Army when I was promoted to that rank, and that it meant so much more to my father than it ever could to me. We suspect that he was living vicariously through me and my achievements, going well beyond parental pride, hereinafter *nachas,* and bordering on the obsessive.

The bright spot is that the concept of being the Boy Wonder did instill in me the very *belief* that I was different. Not *superior* in any way, but different than my peers around me. I was never a great athlete, or musician, or artist (though I did win a Scholastic Art Award in 8th grade), and I generally identify the ability to work hard as my greatest talent. It did provide me with the confidence, desire, and belief that I could achieve anything that I set my mind to accomplishing. It allowed me to set high goals and aspirations for myself, and to ultimately live a life filled with achievements. It also has prompted us to want our children to be well-rounded, and not a superstar at any one thing.

This feeling of being different also fueled my desire to *know* all that I could about my *purpose* in this life. Why was I here? Where did I come from? What is my next stop after my mortal probationary period ends? What was I supposed to achieve? How am I to leave a credible legacy in this world? These were incredibly burdensome questions that I wrestled with for most of my childhood and into adulthood. If ignorance is bliss, then, again in hindsight, I may have welcomed a little more ignorance in my life.

Fortunately, the Gospel of Jesus Christ provides answers to <u>all</u> these questions in doctrine that is easy to grasp. It is elegant in its simplicity. I only wish that I could have had the benefit of it while I was growing up, and ever more grateful that my children and grandchildren <u>do</u> have it available to them, as life becomes increasingly fast, confusing, dangerous, disposable, and subject to temptation.

CHAPTER 14

BATTLE OF ANGELS

"I have been driven many times upon my
knees by the overwhelming conviction
that I had nowhere else to go."
Abraham Lincoln

It is ironic that as I outlined this book, the subject matter of this chapter became the fourteenth chapter of the story.

As previously noted, my father was one of the most logical men I have ever encountered. Beyond being a pragmatist, he was nearly a life-like image of *Star Trek's* Mr. Spock. Illogic, and the wasting of time and resources were maddening to him. By the same token, if there was an "angle" to be worked, a short-cut to be had, he was all in.

In hindsight I will confess that these first attributes can be used to describe me as well: a lack of logic or the failure to apply it, as well as the waste of time and money, to this day are still enough to agitate me. It is probably why I take pride in the epiphany I had when I was ten years old and throwing a ball against the house. I realized that an errant throw could break a window or other fixture, leading to serious and long-term indentured servitude for me. I can remember that day as clearly as if it were only yesterday, and I remember feeling as if the Spirit had taught me that lesson for a reason. I have passed it on to children and grandchildren as T-H-I-N-K, and have written about it before, and will allow this paragraph to suffice.

Back to Dad, aka Mr. Logic or Mr. No Nonsense. The man never had time for a baseball game or sports event on television, no time to throw the ball around with any of his four sons, because it was about being productive and making use of time. Unless the trumpet came out. Then he could be convinced to take time to lose himself in the music of Al Hirt and Herb Alpert. He worked full time, was a member of the Illinois National Guard and then the Army Reserves on weekends, and when he was home, he was a voracious reader, and was often engaged in correspondence courses to further his military career. If not those things, he would be busy doing "projects" around the house, which usually involved stints of apprenticeship service for me which is why I can do a lot of things around the house if I *choose* to do them. Within our immediate family, none of us can hear Harry Chapin's *Cat's in the Cradle* without thinking of my dad because sadly, it characterized his life.

Just as fear and faith cannot co-exist in the same sphere, logic and superstition are mutually exclusive forces... except in this instance. My father, Mr. Logic himself, was absolutely convinced that I was the subject of a near battle between the forces of good and evil, or as he would sometimes express it, "it's as if God and the Devil are fighting over you." Did that arouse some curiosity? I will tell you that the first time he said it to me it both scared and confused me. What the heck was he talking about? Why would you say that to a ten or eleven year old kid? As I am writing this and pondering this topic, I realize that for all the hype, all the stories, and all the times that we shared this account with friends and acquaintances over the years, that there may have been more to the story than met the eye.

We refer to this story simply as either the Curse or the Numbers, for this story is all about numbers. While I know some people are *all into* numbers. I never really gave them much thought until we started piecing this story together when I was a young teenager still living at home.

My Uncle Donnie for whom I am named was born in **1922** and died in combat at age **22** on October 30, **1944**. My father was **8** years old at the time. **Fourteen** years later, at age **22**, my father and mother became parents to me. **Eight** years later the **22**nd anniversary of my uncle's death, I was hit by a car chasing someone who had stolen my brother Michael's bicycle from our driveway. It was a bright Sunday afternoon, and my father was at Reserves, and was notified that there was an emergency at home and he legitimately assumed that it had something to do with the fact that my mother was **8** months pregnant, with my brother Mark, who is **8** years younger than I. In case you are not keeping up on the math, this is occurring in the year **1966.**

Thereafter for the next **fourteen** years, I had some type of accident on the anniversary of my uncle's death. Now before you go suggesting that it was merely a self-fulfilling prophecy that I fell into, let me assure you that I did everything but wrap myself in bubble wrap on that day. It also prompted my father, Mr. Logical, to remind me each year to be careful and to go so far as to call and warn/remind me to be careful even while I was on active duty with the Army and serving overseas in Germany! He was genuinely convinced that *something* was going on that we could not explain. These accidents ranged from sustaining a cut that required eight stitches on my finger when a fellow worker tossed me a price tag making gun while I was at work as a stock clerk, sprained ankles, to nearly being killed in a bunker blast at Fort Sill, OK.

The "curse" as we all referred to it as, lasted, you guessed it, **fourteen** years, until I was age **22**. It was not until 1981 when I was 23 years old, and had "outlived" Donnie, that the accidents stopped. At that time, I was back from Germany, stationed at Fort Sill once again, attending the Officer Advance Course, and carpooling with a fellow officer who by coincidence was a member of the Church of Jesus Christ of Latter Day Saints. We used to alternate driving so that at least every other day his wife had access to their VW mini-van. After the warning call from my dad the night before, I dutifully called my friend and asked him if it would be okay if he drove us to class the next day. Since it changed the order of days, and he was curious, I promised to explain it to him on the way in the next morning.

Well, I was no sooner in the van when he wanted to know what was going on. We had just driven through the gate that put us on the West Range road, a backway on to the main post, when I shared with him the whys and wherefores associated with my request that he drive us that day. I did not expect the reaction that I received from him. First, he slammed on the brakes, and pulled over to the side of the tank trail that we were driving on causing a great cloud of dust that swirled around the van. Next, he expressed the thought that he was not all that sure that he wanted to be anywhere near me that day. At first, I thought he was kidding, and then quickly realized that he was deadly serious. Imagine my shock when he then proclaimed that he thought that it might very well be a battle being waged for me between God and the Adversary. "Adversary?" I asked. "You know, Satan. The Devil. We refer to him as the Adversary."

I don't know if it was the look on my face in response to what he just said, or the feeling that came over me, but I felt great relief when he quietly asked if it would be okay if we had a word of prayer together. I was as shocked by that request, as by his previous pronouncement, and all I could think to do or say was to croak out an "okay" with a somewhat froggy morning voice. I don't remember the details of the prayer that he uttered, but I do distinctly remember the *feeling of peace* that came over me like a warm blanket being placed around my shoulders as he uttered a heartfelt prayer on my behalf. We arrived safely on post, attended all our classes that day, and I remember him dropping me off at home with a reassuring word that I would be okay for the balance of the day and night. When my father called me shortly before bedtime to make sure that I was okay, I recounted for him my experience with the prayer, and he quietly made some remark to the effect that it made sense to him. I wish I could say the same for me! While I was at peace with the prayer, and had genuinely *felt* something, I was still in the stage where I was questioning everything and trying to apply *logic* to a set of circumstances that did not lend themselves to pure logic.

In hindsight, I don't think I ever afforded my friend his proper due for his willingness to exercise his priesthood and to share a word of prayer with me in terms of what it contributed to my conversion to the Church of Jesus Christ of Latter Day Saints. Was it coincidence that of the 144 members of my class that I would choose to carpool with what I believe was the only member of the Church in the class? I know now that there is no such thing as coincidence and this good man was there to help me in my time of need.

So, what to make of all this number stuff. Over the years I have had any number of discussions with people who were intrigued by the story and how it evolved. I have even gone so far as to do a little research to see if there could be *anything* with which I could craft a *logical* argument or explanation for what I and my family had lived through with what I still lovingly refer to as the Curse.

From any number of sources to include the Internet "where everything is factual and true, I have learned that the number 22 is considered as one of the most powerful numbers, able to turn all dreams and desires into reality; that it is a number of precision and balance. In its full capacity, this number is the master builder, which means that it provides the power to achieve almost impossible things. Different angel numbers appear in various stages of our lives to convey to us the angels' messages for our current life situation. Further, that whenever they appear, they bring the guidance and advice we seek. The angels always try to help us accomplish our goals and achieve the ultimate success in life, and sometimes the angels will introduce the number 22 into our lives.

To recap, these are the number related to the curse:

22
1922 Donnie born
1944 Donnie died at age 22
1966 the curse begins 22 years later
1936-1958 – 22 years difference between my dad and I

<u>14</u>

Donnie was 14 years older than Erwin
I was born 14 years after Donnie died when my Dad was 22
The curse lasted 14 years until I was 22 and my dad was 44
I was born on the 14th of the month

<u>8</u>

Erwin was 8 when Donnie died
I was 8 when the "curse" began
The number of stitches required when I had to go to the hospital after having my finger sliced open.
My mother was 8 months pregnant with Mark when the curse began
I am eight years older than Mark who was born in 1966

CHAPTER 15

GUARDIAN ANGEL

"That is the God whom I serve, one who has
millions of angels at His command. Do you suppose
that there are any angels here to-day? I would not
wonder if there were ten times more angels here
than people. We do not see them, but they are here
watching us, and are anxious for our salvation."
Heber C. Kimball

Feeling different has not been a bad thing. Before I understood the
Godhead, and that I would be afforded the constant companionship
of the Holy Ghost as a protector and guide, I always felt like there was
something or someone looking over me as a guardian angel.

There were many occasions wherein I had chosen to take a specific
route to a destination or made a decision with which I harbored
reservations, and if I took a moment to pause and reflect, I would
often receive a very distinct impression as to what the proper direction
or course of action for me to follow was at that moment in time. To
this day, when faced with a choice between airline flights, I find myself

weighing the odds of one of them crashing, or simply wondering if I am tempting fate just by trying to get home an hour earlier. Some would simply chalk that up to superstition or being a fatalist, but for me it has always been far more than something that simple.

Prior to my baptism and the laying on of hands during which I received the companionship of the Holy Ghost, and most notably during the time that I was subject to "the Curse," I would often *feel* my uncle's presence and found it to be both comforting and reassuring.

In the 1980's when most of America was watching Tom Selleck portray *Magnum P.I.,* I was right there along with the rest of them.

I found it comforting to hear him refer to his "little voice" that would tell him how to proceed in dangerous situations. Those close to me used to compare Magnum's little voice with mine. While I never identified it as my uncle, I do know that on occasion that our paths have crossed, and based on other experiences of the last forty years, and the *knowledge* that I now possess, I have every confidence that our paths will cross again on the other side of the veil, and I look forward to that time.

CHAPTER 16

DRAG RACE

"Without death and the resurrection, we could not
be raised in immortal glory and gain eternal life."
Bruce R. McConkie

Not many ten year old kids are exposed to life and death in terms
of a drag race, but that was my experience. We were living in Des
Plaines in the very first home that my parents purchased. It was an
exceedingly small two bedroom, 1.5 bath townhouse that was part of a
larger planned unit development. Our unit was on the end of a six unit
building with another like building running perpendicular to it. Parking
for our building was at the opposite end of the building in an alley that
ran for the full length of the complex, or approximately half a mile.

The front of our building faced Ballard Road, a two lane road
with a posted speed limit of 35 mph. Aside from the front porch, the
living room with a bay window comprised of multiple smaller panes
of glass was the extent of our exposure to the road. A short flight of
stairs up took one to the two bedrooms and the full bath. A short
flight downstairs found the kitchen and family room. Six short steps

below the kitchen was the half basement that would over time become my bedroom. Once I moved down there, I essentially traded my two brothers as roommates for the furnace, freezer, washer, and dryer.

Ballard Road was ordinarily fairly quiet, and traffic was light enough that I was routinely allowed to walk my two younger brothers down the street to the 7-11 where we could purchase Slurpees and other desserts.

My father and I were in the alley doing something on the car when all of a sudden, we heard the roar of engines, two loud bangs, and then an explosion. The powerlines that ran along Ballard Road were swaying, and clearly something was terribly wrong. We immediately started running towards our house, and rather than running to the backdoor that ran between the buildings, we ran around to the front, and started running along the sidewalk in the front of the building that paralleled the road. A single car roared by us at a very high rate of speed, and when we arrived at the front of our unit, we discovered a car in the side yard of the building adjacent to ours, upside down, with three of its wheels spinning (the fourth wheel was missing, and I could have sworn that I saw it fly over the house), resting on the remains of the air conditioning compressor (the source of the explosion). Evidently the two cars had been drag racing down Ballard Road, and the car that was now in the yard had knocked over a telephone pole (causing the swaying of the power lines we had observed), run over a fire hydrant (partially snapping it off the ground and causing a geyser to erupt), gone airborne as a result of the hydrant, landing on the roof of the building next door before falling on to the air conditioning compressor blowing a hole in the brick wall of that unit.

As we arrived on the scene, we could smell gasoline, as the gas tank had ruptured and was leaking all over the ground. The risk of further explosion and fire were very real, but that did not stop my father from rushing to the car in an attempt to aid the driver who was still in the vehicle. He called me over to assist him, and between us we were able to extricate him from the vehicle. My recollection is that he was not wearing a seatbelt, which were still relatively a new thing, and not cool. The way his head swung freely clearly indicated that his neck was completely broken, and that he was most certainly dead.

People were screaming at us to get away from the car for fear that the gasoline would explode creating a fireball. We pulled the young man away from that yard on to the front lawn of our house. I believe my father attempted to administer basic first aid, but again, it was certain that he was dead.

We did not live far from a fire house, and it was not long before fire and police were on the scene and the incident sort of became a blur to me at this point. My brother and I were sent away, and we started walking down the alley. It was in the creek that pretty much equidistantly divided the subdivision that we found the fourth tire, some two blocks away from the scene of the accident.

I remember later in the evening a woman and her husband showed up on our front doorstep looking for my father and me. She was the [teenaged] driver's mother and wanted to know what we knew about the accident. I do not think I said anything of value and remember distinctly that she had an artificial hand and/or arm. That was over fifty years ago, and I remember that her mannequin-like hand appeared more ghoulish and creepier to me than had the shattered body of her son.

I remember distinctly looking at his broken body, particularly his open un-seeing eyes, and wondering what the moment of death had been like for him. Was it the telephone pole, fire hydrant, or exploding compressor that had killed him? What happened to him at the instant that his body suffered the blunt force trauma and snapped his neck? Did he die instantly? Was there a transition to the next life? Where was he at that moment? Would his mother ever see him again?

I do not remember receiving any additional attention after the accident, and it was quite a while before I could go to sleep without seeing the carnage associated with the accident. The questions I had about the boy who was driving persisted, and I began to pose them to my parents. Their answers began at the "I don't know" end of the spectrum, and as I persisted, graduated to the "nobody knows, and what does it matter?"

Seeing that boy dead on the front lawn made me think of our dog Bootsy who had died a few years earlier. While living in Aurora, we had gone to the local animal shelter and picked out a beagle much like

71

my Dad had had as a boy and brought it home. My brother and I were in love with this dog. Unfortunately this was when my mother was pregnant with my next brother, and the added burden on the household (her) was "too much" so after only a couple of weeks, they gave our dog away to a neighbor that did not take care of him. It was only a week or two after we had said tearful goodbyes that I was walking down an alley across the street from us, and I found Bootsy dead in the street. I had wondered then whether dogs have a soul and whether they can go to Heaven, but any mention of the dog was enough to cause fireworks to go off, so I quickly tabled any additional inquiries.

So many questions, so few answers until I did learn as an adult that death is not final; that it is in fact a transition or progression on the Path of eternity.

CHAPTER 17

BAR MITZVAH SEASON

"I am convinced that there is no simple formula or technique that I could give you or that you could give your students that would immediately facilitate mastering the ability to be guided by the Holy Spirit. Nor do I believe that the Lord will ever allow someone to conceive a pattern that would invariably and immediately open the channels of spiritual communication. We grow when we labor to recognize the guidance of the Holy Ghost as we struggle to communicate our needs to our Father in Heaven in moments of dire need or overflowing gratitude."
Richard G. Scott

My family was living in Des Plaines, Illinois in the early 1970s, and ironically enough, I went to school with a large number of Jewish classmates. In the two years leading up to my own thirteenth birthday I was invited to, and attended, at least fifteen to twenty bar mitzvahs. This included attending the ceremony in the synagogue where they would read from the Torah and then speak to the congregation, to participating in the sometimes very lavish party at a local hotel. For their mothers I trust it was a warmup to planning for future weddings. I remember that I had a pair of navy blue slacks and a charcoal gray blazer which I would wear with two interchangeable shirts (one red, one a pale purple) and ties, thus giving me two completely different ensembles to wear to the religious service and then the party.

Having attended my two older cousins' bar mitzvahs, I was keenly aware of the significance attached to this rite of passage. If I were to participate in my own bar mitzvah it would mean that I was thereafter responsible for my own actions, as I would become a man in the eyes of God. This was a pretty heady proposition but I realized that it was not in all likelihood going to be an option for me because of finances. This may sound odd, but like everything else related to this saga, there is a story.

Being a member of a synagogue requires payment of an annual membership fee, the purchase of "tickets" or seats for the high holidays of Rosh Hashana and Yom Kippur, as well as the payment of tuition for children to attend Hebrew School. In a word, my parents did not have the cash. As noted in a previous chapter, when we lived in Aurora, Illinois, the rabbi of that synagogue directed my father to enroll me in Hebrew School and to "pay what he could afford." It was an offer he could not refuse.

It was shortly after I had begun my lessons that we moved back towards Chicago to Des Plaines, Illinois, where the prevailing attitude was anything but what we had previously encountered in Aurora, and the family was not attending the synagogue much less Don attending Hebrew School.

We later moved out to Hoffman Estates, or the hinterlands as my grandparents initially considered it, only to find that that congregation there was actively soliciting funds from its members for the "building fund" so that they could in fact erect a building in which to meet. When they asked my father to take a second mortgage on our recently purchased house (one has to have equity to take a second mortgage, and we were sliding in on the proverbial shoe string), his response cannot be published here, and *that* was the end of any formal religious affiliation in our family. Period. Exclamation point. I was thirteen at this point, and clearly not going to be a Bar Mitzvah boy.

As I continued to attend all the bar mitzvahs to which I was invited, I started to question, "Why were they doing this?" Is this rite of passage going to make them a better person? Are they going to be any more knowledgeable about their faith? Will they have the answers to the questions that had already been fueling my fervent desire for knowledge. When I did talk to them, they all pretty much had the same answer: No. They did not feel any different, any more informed, or certainly not any more like a man. Most had done it to make their parents happy, or because it was a *tradition* in their family.

I felt like a man without a country. I was supposed to be Jewish, and yet I was hearing these things from my peers, and still laboring without any answers to the questions to which I so dearly wanted closure.

Was it ignorance on my part because I had not finished my own training? Should I feel inferior to my cousins and friends because of this shortcoming on my part? Was I destined to be something or someone less than they were? Would I ever be a man in the eyes of God?

When I asked my father about my bar mitzvah, he looked me in the eye and simply said: "I'll tell you when you are a man." He did this shortly after my thirteenth birthday but as I recall the moment, I found it somewhat unfulfilling and hollow.

It was simply another log on the fire as this desire to know and to acquire answers threatened to consume me. I wish that there had been someone I could have talked to during this critical time in my life.

CHAPTER 18

HAND IN THE GLOVE

"When we get to the other side of the veil, we shall
know something. We now work by faith. We have
the evidence of things not seen. The resurrection, the
eternal judgment, the celestial kingdom, and the great
blessings that God has given in the holy anointings and
endowment in the temples, are all for the future, and
they will be fulfilled, for they are eternal truths. We
will never while in the flesh, with this veil over us, fully
comprehend that which lies before us in the world to
come. It will pay any man to serve God and to keep His
commandments the few days he lives upon the earth."
Wilford B. Woodruff

I have only vague memories of my great-grandmother Molly
Mendelovich dying when I was three years old. Therefore my first
real exposure to death, aside from the drag race, was the passing of my
paternal grandfather Sol Levin, which occurred in November 1972
when I was fourteen years old, and now a man in my father's eyes, if
not in God's eyes as well.

In the waning months of his life, my grandfather literally wasted away as the cancer with which he was afflicted slowly ate away his body. In an effort to help him and to provide some measure of respite to my grandmother, it became very common for someone to drop me off at their home in Chicago after school on Friday afternoon, and to leave me there until Sunday evening and at age thirteen I had my first experience with being a caregiver, and ultimately, with death. It also filled me with a plethora of questions that would not be satisfactorily resolved for another thirteen years.

When my grandfather finally died, I had the realization that one minute he had been a living human being, and in the next minute, he was gone. To this day, this is an image that still absolutely intrigues me. Fortunately, I now have answers that are satisfying to me spiritually and intellectually. Unfortunately, in 1972, I did not. Therefore, the questions that permeated my very soul at that time focused on Where did he go? Where was the essence that had made Sol Levin, bare knuckle boxer, my grandfather? What would happen to me when it was my turn to pass from this Life?

I asked these questions to my father who simply said, "he didn't go anywhere. He is just gone." I could not accept that answer. Aside from being completely illogical, it filled me with an array of emotions that ranged from anger and frustration to fear and foreboding. As an answer it seemed so incomplete and uninformed, and so final and filled with sadness.

Oblivious to the fact that my father had just lost *his* father, I was relentless with my questions. Surely, Grandpa had gone *somewhere!* No, he was just gone. He no longer existed. His time on Earth had come to an end, and now he was gone. I was not buying it. I *knew* that he had gone somewhere.

It did not make sense to me that we were here without a purpose and that we would then arbitrarily die. Where had I come from, why was I here, and where was I going to go when it was *my* turn to die? For once, my seemingly all-knowing father did not have answers for me. I asked other family members and they too merely shook their heads, shrugged their shoulders, or brought their hands in front of them showing me their palms.

A few of them attempted to minimize my concerns by sharing that it really does not matter; that what mattered is the kind of life we live while we are here on this Earth. This argument was even more mystifying to me, because what does it matter how good or bad, we are if all bets are off as soon as our bodily functions cease? If there was no "heavenly reward" waiting for us, what was the incentive to be good? Simply to avoid *punishment* in this life? Where were the checks and balances? Where was the science behind that theory? I had already learned in science class that for every action there is a reaction, which in turn had led me to learn and to believe that everything has an opposite.

One family member listened to my questions and thought that I "might be on to something" but could not offer me any validation to my thought that Grandpa still existed and that he was merely in another place, his [physical] body and spirt now separated from one another.

My persistent questions on the subject of death were somewhat worrisome to my parents, because they assumed that the questions were motivated by some sort of fear of dying on my part, rather than an intellectual curiosity of what actually happens when we die and our spirit leaves our body much like a hand leaves a glove.

Ordinarily I would have talked to my grandmother, but her grief at losing her husband of fifty years was palpable. In fact, I was standing next to her, holding her hand at the direction of my father, when she dropped my hand and literally threw herself on my grandfather's corpse as we filed passed his open casket. She genuinely believed that her beloved Sol was lost to her forever, much like her darling son had also been ripped from her so many years before.

It was a gray, rainy raw November Chicago day when we buried my grandfather. I remember helping to carry his casket from the hearse to the gravesite, with so many questions running through my mind that I was distracted from the rituals being celebrated as we proceeded to say our final farewells.

In as much as I was the same age at this point as Joseph Smith was when he had his First Vision of God the Eternal Father, and His Son Jesus Christ, in hindsight I imagine it is why I was able to embrace the account of a fourteen year old boy being visited by Celestial beings so much easier than many investigators to the Church.

I remember the emptiness that accompanied these questions for so many years of my life, and I am grateful today to finally have to have the answers to those questions of "where did I come from, why am I here, and where am I going."

CHAPTER 19

A NEW BIRTH CERTIFICATE

"Faith is like the muscle of my arm. If I use it, if I
nurture it, it grows strong; it will do many things.
But if I put it in a sling and do nothing with it, it will
grow weak and useless, and so will it be with you.
If you accept every opportunity, if you accept every
calling, the Lord will make it possible for you to
perform it. The Church will not ask you to do anything
which you cannot do with the help of the Lord."
Gordon B. Hinckley

I had just started my freshman (ninth grade) year of high school
when my father asked me if I wanted new clothes for school. Given
that I had grown seven inches in height over the last year, and was now
standing a proud 5'6, and had the growing pains in my knees as proof,
I naturally said yes.

Imagine my surprise the next day when he came home from his
office and handed me an envelope. It was flat, so unless there was
one bill with Ben Franklin or Ulysses Grant on the front, I was not

expecting much in terms of a new wardrobe. I nonetheless opened it with great anticipation only to find my birth certificate inside. Thud.

Upon closer examination, my father proudly pointed out how he had rather cleverly converted an 8 to a 6 in the birth year, and I was now officially sixteen years old and eligible to work in a public place, thus able to "start paying my own way in life." I honestly think this was well-intended on his part, another rite of passage, but in hindsight, I realize that this was all part of the plan to "maximize the potential" he obviously believed that I possessed, and, kept a few bucks in his own pocket as well.

The next thing I knew he announced that he had found a job for me, and I was working roughly 35-40 hours over the course of the weekend or from immediately after school on Friday afternoon until the wee hours of Saturday, pretty much all day and evening Saturday, and all day Sunday, as a busboy in a local delicatessen. This was the first in a succession of jobs that took me from bussing tables to installing carpet (really hard on the knees) to my final high school/college job of stock clerk in a Target-like store...all courtesy of the bogus birth certificate. Throw in the part-time security guard job, as well as ROTC, and I was well-rounded by the time I graduated college.

Unfortunately, fourteen year old boys need sleep, and I was so exhausted after the weekend that more often than not on Monday, despite my best efforts to the contrary, I typically slept through half of my classes at school! This job also effectively put an end to my Boy Scouting progress. At age 30 it led me to being a tongue-in-cheek charter member of the Order of the Almost Eagle Association, my bittersweet reconciliation to the fact that this job and the ones that followed had largely cost me the last years of my childhood and the opportunity to earn this coveted award. In the big scheme of things it didn't kill me not to be an Eagle Scout, but it was something that I used to dream about and I remember aspiring to becoming the Junior Assistant Scoutmaster like the very mature seventeen year old [shaving] Eagle Scout in my troop had done. I am proud to say that both of my sons are Eagle Scouts, and all three of my sons-in-law are as well. Upon receiving his Eagle Scout Award, my younger son presented me with a handmade certificate declaring me an Honorary Eagle Scout in recognition of all the assistance and support I had provided to him in achieving his own award. It was the ultimate validation as a father, and a bright memory.

One of the perks of working in a restaurant is that you typically get to eat free from the menu, and I very quickly worked my way through the menu of offerings. The absolute best perk was working with a group of four young ladies who were waitresses there, all in high school, and simply some of the nicest people I have ever known. Three of the four were nearly six feet tall, and the fourth, well, she clocked in at about an even five feet, so it was much easier to see eye to eye with her. Over the months I would share meals with each of them while on break, feeding the juke box, as well as talking about a wide range of things, to include, oddly enough, religion. It was fascinating for me to hear their different beliefs about God, Life, and most notably the next world. They all offered to introduce me to their priest, pastor, or minister, but that is the subject for another chapter. These conversations continued to open my mind and soul, and to fuel my desire to find the Truth. We quickly became friends, and it was not until two of them asked me for a ride home after work one night that my true age came out, but that did not change our relationship. I worked this job for about six months, and it was truly an eye opening experience for me as these girls shared the doctrines of their various faiths and fueled the growth of my ever increasing number of questions.

I could end this chapter right here and now, but the saga of the bogus birth certificate did not end there. In fact, it was some years later when thinking it was long gone that I thought it had reared its ugly head again.

After graduation from the Field Artillery Officer Advance Course, I was permanently stationed at Fort Sill, OK. I was assigned to the general staff for the Post, responsible for training and inspection of all the tactical nuclear artillery units stationed within III Corps. I could not have selected a better job for myself had I been given the opportunity. The plan was for me to be in this position for eighteen months before assuming command of an artillery battery within III Corps.

I was in my office in McNair Hall when my phone rang, and I answered it with a crisp and confident, "Nuclear Surety Branch, Captain Levin, this line is not secure," when a voice on the other end identified himself as Major So-and-So of the Artillery assignments branch of the Army Personnel Center (ARPERCEN) located in Alexandria, VA, and began what was a very nerve-wracking conversation for me.

"Captain Levin, how old are you?" he asked.

"Twenty three Sir," I replied, unclear why he would be asking such an obvious question given that he had my Military Personnel Records Jacket (MPRJ) on his desk.

"You're certain," was his next question.

"Uh, yes sir. I am twenty three years old, and will turn twenty four in a couple of months," I somewhat stammered, "Why do you ask?"

"Wait one," he said, and placed me on hold.

This was when my imagination really started taking over. At this point, my heart started palpitating, and I had an image of the bogus birth certificate surfacing, and the implications of it starting racing through my mind. Would I lose my security clearance because this was construed as a false entry on my DA Form 398? Would I receive a reprimand? I silently cursed my father at this moment.

"Twenty three years old huh," he asked when he came back on the line.

"Yes Sir."

"Well, a few of us were sitting around reviewing the results of this year's promotion list, and we were startled to see that you were already a captain and only twenty three years old, and so we started doing some digging, seeing as how most of the other younger captains are at least twenty *five* years old. We were assuming that your stated age must be a typo of some kind or that something *hinky* was going on."

"No sir, no typo, and nothing hinky," I said, feeling sweat forming on my upper lip.

"So how is it that you are nearly two years younger than the rest of your newly-promoted peers," asked the Major. "By our calculations, a 17 year old plebe at West Point will graduate at age 21, and four years later be promoted to captain. How did you beat the curve," he asked?

Once I realized that I was in no danger of being in trouble, I explained how I was sixteen when I graduated high school, seventeen by only a few days when I signed my ROTC contract, and nineteen when I graduated college and received my commission. Four years later, and here we are having this conversation.

"We thought maybe you lied your way into the army or used an older brother's birth certificate," he said with a snort. "Congratulations. You young man, are in fact the youngest captain in the US Army as of this moment."

I mumbled something, and quickly ended the call. Later that day when I shared that bit of trivia with my father, I could again hear his vicarious pride and *nachas* when he was quick to label me the Boy Wonder. I then asked him to destroy any copies of the bogus birth certificate that he may still retain in his possession.

CHAPTER 20

FIRST FIGHT

"The viewing of signs or miracles is not a secure foundation for conversion. Scriptural history attests that people converted by signs and wonders soon forget them and again become susceptible to the lies and distortions of Satan and his servants. In contrast to the witness of the Spirit, which can be renewed from time to time as needed by a worthy recipient, the viewing of a sign or the experiencing of a miracle is a one-time event that will fade in the memory of its witness and can dim in its impact upon him or her."
Dallin H. Oaks

It was my freshman year of high school and I found myself in gym class with guys literally twice my size. Because our PE lockers were assigned alphabetically, I found myself dressing between two members of the football team. These guys looked like grown men compared to me. One of these guys thought it was my responsibility to supply him with toiletries, i.e. he had no qualms about grabbing my Brut aerosol spray deodorant and applying it liberally to the two tufts of hair growing under his massive shoulders until the day I substituted Brut hairspray, and the damage was done. Let us just say that a quick spray or two, and he put his arms down, and could not lift them again. Since he could not prove that I had done anything wrong, and was embarrassed by the mistake, he quickly put his shirt on and left the locker room. The only thing better than that was when another one of my [smaller] classmates who was being tormented by this same gentleman, surreptitiously filled an unwashed athletic supporter [that he had previously been forced to wear on his face] with Nair – the then-fashionable hair removal product favored by a number of the cheerleaders. Those in the know stuck around for what would be revealed after a tough two hour practice. It was worth the wait to see yet another bully get his just desserts.

To this end, I will freely admit that at this point in my life I did have a chip on my shoulder. I did not like be being bullied, and I was also keenly aware that as a Jew that ours was a history of persecution. In some ways I guess I wore it as a badge of honor. Hearing from my grandmother how my Uncle Don had had to fight anti-Semitism in the army and my Uncle Ed the same discrimination in the US Marine Corps, I resolved that I would never tolerate it.

We were on the athletic field one morning, enduring a 45 degree PE class wearing nothing but our regular PE clothes and a sweatshirt, and I was in no mood for any bull from anyone. I hated playing flag football with the behemoths in the class who viewed the contest as just a regular football game without pads and helmets.

I was just coming off the field, when one of my classmates bumped me and, adding insult to injury, called me a "dirty kike." I had heard that term before but had never had it directed at me. *Kike* is a word derived from the Hebrew word for circle, which is the mark that many Jews who did not read and write English made on their immigration papers as they came through Ellis Island and other ports of entry into the US. They made this mark to distinguish between the 'X' that many other immigrants made. They did this because the 'X' looked too much like a crucifix. The term "kikers" or "kikes" came into usage by immigration officers who used it as a short-hand slang for a group of Jews on a manifest. I remember my grandmother teaching me that I should be as insulted if I were to hear that word directed at me as much as an African-American were to hear the 'N' word directed towards him.

With grandma's words ringing in my ears, I turned around and grabbed "Pete" by his sweatshirt with my right hand, whirling him around, and immediately threw a left hook that caught him right in the mouth. Contrary to what you see in the movies, a punch like that hurts... to receive, and to deliver. My knuckles were on fire. I would have sworn that I broke my knuckles as well as the rest of my hand. Well, Pete fell backwards, and I immediately jumped on him and straddling his chest, started flailing both lefts and rights on to his face. We were quickly hidden by a ring of classmates, and I had thrown maybe an additional five or six punches when out of nowhere, the gathering crowd parted and this hand, attached to a very meaty arm, grabbed me by the scruff of my sweatshirt and *easily* lifted me and my [maybe 95 pounds] off of Pete.

Our PE teacher, Merv Miller, who we all affectionately referred to as Marine Merv behind his back, roared, "what the hell is going on here?" You could have heard a pin drop. Merv was in fact a former Marine, (I know, there is no such thing as a former Marine), with biceps bigger than my thighs. He looked like a Marine and when he barked, we jumped. It was not uncommon for him, on the spur of the moment, to "drop" the entire class and demand 25 or 50 push ups from us, because "we all want to grow up to be Marines."

As I hung suspended in the air by the top of my sweatshirt, Merv looked from me to Pete, and back to me. I should note that Pete was a successful and talented cross country runner, blonde, tall, good-looking, and popular, or in other words, someone that any self- respecting nerd like me could simultaneously envy and hate.

To his credit, Pete stood up, and while holding a bloody nose, owned up to having used a derogatory term that had not set well with me. I had calmed down by this point, and was now fearful that I was about to be handed a three-day suspension for fighting, when Merv dropped me to the ground, and with the wisdom of Solomon, directed us to shake hands and to get back to playing football. Pete and I looked at one another, shook hands, and determined that playing flag football was a much better alternative than visiting the Assistant Principal's office. Word quickly spread around the school what had transpired, and that certainly did not hurt my reputation any. I dare say that I received more than a few nods of respect from some of the other guys.

Naturally, my father was proud of my antics, my grandmother horrified as to my fighting, but then proud of me when my father told her *why* I had fought. My bare-knuckle fighting grandfather was in the process of dying, and he too was proud of me for sticking up for myself and "getting my licks in."

To this day I do not know why I started that fight, particularly with someone bigger than I was. While I am not excusing it, I do recall the anger that flared at hearing that word; I also know that it smoldered until a number of years later when I was newly assigned to my army unit in Germany, but more on that later. Maybe in some deluded way I was defending the honor of the six million Jews who had perished in the Holocaust. Maybe it was for all those people with number tattoos on their arms that I viewed on Oakton Street in Skokie while I was growing up. Maybe it was to make my grandfather proud of me. Maybe it was just my own anger welling up at having taken so much guff from other bullies over the years.

I neither condone nor recommend fighting, and in hindsight am simply grateful that I did not hurt Pete by breaking his jaw or his nose, and that we both avoided a deserved suspension for fighting. I am relating this story not because I am proud of it but rather to illustrate where I was in terms of my religious path at this critical juncture in my life.

At the end of the school year I transferred to the new high school built near my house, and I really never saw Pete again after that school year until some fifteen years later when I was at the YMCA with my two older children who were taking swim lessons. I was in the waiting area, and after the kids had come out of the pool and we were gathering up school bags and other paraphernalia, who walked out of the locker room in a very nice and presumably expensive tailored suit, but my former foe Pete. Now an inch or two passed six feet in height, with the same blonde hair, white teeth, and tan, he could have been a movie star.

Our eyes met, and the first words he said were, "you're not going to hit me again are you?"

Pete and I shook hands, exchanged a few words in passing, and then he turned to my son and said, "listen to this guy. He is tough. He cleaned my clock when we were in school together." To say that my son was shocked would be a gross understatement. It was a good day in the Dad department.

CHAPTER 21

SEDER

"Many years ago, this conference heard of a young man who found the restored gospel while he was studying in the United States. As this man was about to return to his native land, President Gordon B. Hinckley asked him what would happen to him when he returned home as a Christian. "My family will be disappointed," the young man answered. "They may cast me out and regard me as dead. As for my future and my career, all opportunity may be foreclosed against me."

"Are you willing to pay so great a price for the gospel?" President Hinckley asked.

Tearfully the young man answered, "It's true, isn't it?" When that was affirmed, he replied, "Then what else matters?" That is the spirit of sacrifice among many of our new members."

Dallin H. Oaks

I was speaking with my brother yesterday asking him if he could recall any memorable religious moments in our lives from when we were young. He recalled for me the several times that we would attend a Passover Seder ceremony at the home of our Uncle Eddie and Aunt Eleanor, and how inadequate (he used the word 'stupid') he felt because of a total lack of knowledge of what was going on. He also referenced the inadequacy of reading from the book. He did not recall what it was, but I still remember. I still remember enough of the ceremony and the significance of each element, to be dangerous, and over time have come to appreciate more and more the symbolism attached to the ceremony. Later, while serving as bishop of a YSA ward, our activities committee chairman persuaded me to conduct a Seder for one of our weekly Family Home Evenings, just as she and her family had done while she was growing up.

My skepticism was dissipated by her enthusiasm, and it ultimately became an annual tradition that grew in numbers over the years until we filled the cultural hall with many tables. We invited the Stake Presidency and other members of the three stakes from which our members were drawn, and it became quite the event. We economized where we could – Mr. Coffee filters with which to cover our heads– so that we could afford to feed everyone with more than just a taste of the lamb that we would roast and serve. As the bishop I was asked to be the reader and Head of Household. It was a privilege and a joy to share in this experience.

The Seder is a ritual performed by a community or by multiple generations of a family, and essentially is the retelling of the story of the liberation of the Israelites from slavery in ancient Egypt. The Seder itself is based on the Biblical verse commanding Jews to retell the story of the Exodus from Egypt: "You shall tell your child on that day, saying, 'It is because of what the Lord did for me when I came out of Egypt.'" (Exodus 13:8) Traditionally, families and friends gather in the evening to read the text of the Haggadah (the book my brother could not recall), an ancient account that contains the narrative of the Israelite exodus from Egypt, special blessings and rituals, commentaries from the Talmud and special Passover songs.

Seder customs include telling the story, discussing the story, drinking four cups of wine (we used grape juice for our FHE version of the Seder), eating matzoh (unleavened bread), partaking of symbolic foods placed on the Passover Seder Plate, and reclining in celebration of freedom. The Seder is the most celebrated Jewish ritual, performed by Jews all over the world, and is one of the most vivid memories I do possess from childhood.

One of the reasons I remember the Passover Seder as well as I do is that while many Jewish holidays revolve around the synagogue, the Seder is conducted in the family home, although communal Seders are also organized by synagogues, schools and community centers, some open to the general public. It is customary to invite guests, especially strangers and the needy. The Seder is integral to Jewish faith and identity. In the Haggadah, it is explained how if not for divined intervention and the Exodus, the Jewish people would still be slaves in Egypt. Therefore, the Seder is an occasion for praise and thanksgiving and for re-dedication to the idea of liberation. Furthermore, the words and rituals of the Seder are a primary vehicle for the transmission of the Jewish faith from generation to generation. Attending a Seder and eating matzoh on Passover is a widespread custom in the Jewish community, even among those who are not religiously observant which probably explains why my family participated in the ceremony.

At the home of my aunt and uncle, we would take turns reciting the text of the Haggadah, with my cousins doing it in the original Hebrew and rest of us in a translated version. Again, this is the book to which my brother was referring that intimidated him. It is traditional for the head of the household and other participants to have pillows placed behind them for added comfort.

Probably the thing I remember and have come to appreciate the most are the six items on the Seder plate which included:

- *Maror*: Bitter herbs, symbolizing the bitterness and harshness of the slavery which the Jews endured in Ancient Egypt. For *maror*, many people use freshly grated horseradish or whole horseradish root.
- *Chazeret* is typically romaine lettuce, whose roots are bitter-tasting. In addition to horseradish and romaine lettuce, other forms of bitter lettuce, such as Endive, may be eaten in

fulfillment of the mitzvah, as well as green onions, dandelion greens, celery leaves, or curly parsley (but parsley and celery are more commonly used as the *karpas* or vegetable element).

- *Charoset*: A sweet, brown, pebbly paste of fruits and nuts, representing the mortar used by the Jewish slaves to build the storehouses of Egypt. The actual recipe depends partly on ethno-cultural tradition and partly on locally available ingredients. Ashkenazi Jews, for example, traditionally make apple-raisin based charoset while Sephardic Jews often make date-based recipes that might feature orange or/and lemon, or even banana. I do remember that this was one of the better parts of the plate that I did enjoy!
- *Karpas*: A vegetable other than bitter herbs, usually parsley but sometimes something such as celery or cooked potato, which is dipped into salt water (Ashkenazi custom), vinegar (Sephardi custom), or *charoset* (older custom, still common amongst Yemenite Jews) at the beginning of the Seder.
- *Zeroa:* A roasted lamb or goat bone, symbolizing the *korban Pesach* (Pesach sacrifice), which was a lamb offered in the Temple in Jerusalem and was then roasted and eaten as part of the meal on Seder night.
- *Beitzah*: A roast egg – usually a hard-boiled egg that has been roasted in a baking pan with a little oil, or with a lamb shank – symbolizing the *korban chagigah* (festival sacrifice) that was offered in the Temple in Jerusalem and was then eaten as part of the meal on Seder night.

Upon reflection, I can say that participating in the Passover Seder was important to me and was probably when I most *felt* like a Jew. It was humbling and when I felt truly *connected* to my family.

I have a cousin who is two and one-half years older than I and has a wonderful sense of humor. Unfortunately, my aunt did not appreciate it as much as I did, when, while we were college students and sitting at her table for that year's ceremony, we proposed that we only conduct the Passover Seder on leap year. Our humorous irreverence was not appreciated and we both received a bemused reprimand from our grandmother.

CHAPTER 22

DATING

"Your trust in the Lord must be more powerful and enduring than your confidence in your own personal feelings and experience.

To exercise faith is to trust that the Lord knows what He is doing with you and that He can accomplish it for your eternal good even though you cannot understand how He can possibly do it. We are like infants in our understanding of eternal matters and their impact on us here in mortality. Yet at times we act as if we knew it all. When you pass through trials for His purposes, as you trust Him, exercise faith in Him, He will help you. That support will generally come step by step, a portion at a time. While you are passing through each phase, the pain and difficulty that comes from being enlarged will continue. If all matters were immediately resolved at your first petition, you could not grow."

Richard G. Scott

So, I am working like a fiend in order to be largely self-supporting, going to school, playing chess "professionally" at tournaments, and finally, dating. I was dating before I had a car but living in the suburbs where public transportation largely does not exist was definitely a crimp in my style. Fortunately, my father was very anxious to procure a driver's license for me and we attempted to do it the night *before* my sixteenth birthday. Who knew that you had to actually be sixteen? Not me. I had [successfully] completed and passed the road test when the examiner realized that I was about twelve hours early, and was all set to put the kabosh on the entire thing until my father gave him a hard luck story on why I really needed the license that night. I don't know if he bought my father's line of malarkey or just felt sorry for me, but when he signed the report, he "inadvertently" dated it the next day, and even the clerks inside failed to catch it. I was officially a licensed driver…just as soon as I gave my father the cash differential for adding me to his State Farm insurance policy. I remember stopping by to visit my aunt and uncle who were flabbergasted that I had somehow managed to acquire the license the day before my birthday, but they wished me and my father *good nachas* any way.

Apparently *nachas* is what my parents would receive from me as I achieved things that would make them proud and provide bragging rights with their friends. On television we often hear Jewish parents bragging about "my son the doctor," or "my son the Harvard graduate." That is nachas. Clearly a very Jewish thing. As I look back on that concept I realize that I fell into it with both feet. Although I believe that the purpose of one's life has to be something beyond being a source of nachas to one's parents. But, to be fair, I obviously have benefitted in terms of achieving things academically and professionally by being spurred on by this concept even if I was not fully aware of what the heck nachas was all about. I think it may have been this concept that was such an influence on my father to drive me to be better and better so that he could live vicariously through my achievements. Yikes.

I had a car – again, as soon as I plunked down cash on the barrelhead and bought my grandfather's car from my father – and with insurance in place, I was ready to start doing some serious dating. Even in the mid-1970s, having a set of wheels was something that placed one on a different social stratum.

My approach to dating was quite simple in that for every "no" (or six) there was a "yes" just waiting to be discovered. When word spreads that you are a "nice guy" and a "gentleman" dates become more plentiful. I dated mostly older girls because I just related better to them, and again, having a car was a real distinction. One of the reasons I enjoyed dating was getting to know girls and listening to what they thought about and believed. This was helpful as I continued down my path of religious enlightenment. The week of high school graduation I had nine dates with that many different girls. It was fun and helped me discern the qualities that I was looking for in a companion.

One of the girls that I dated for a while was in fact Jewish. Lori even crocheted me my own yarmulke and a "man purse" to carry it in. I still have it some 45 years later with a cute note inside that reminds me of the pursuit of knowledge in which I was engaged. She had a very nice family who took a shine to me – after all I was Jewish then too, and there were not a lot of us in the high school – and they were always inviting me to dinner or to tag along on family trips to include a ski trip to Wisconsin. These activities never occurred in my family, so I thought it was wonderful. We would have interesting conversations about Judaism, and they were "understanding" of my lack of a bar mitzvah. I was introduced to their Rabbi with whom I had several conversations. Unfortunately when I raised my trifecta of questions, i.e. where do we come from, why are we here, and where do we go when we die, the Rabbi tried to placate me with "does it really matter where we came from or where we are going? The important thing is that you are here and now, and we need to make the most of that experience." But why? What does it matter how good we are in this life if there is no accountability or tangible reward? In my mind it was like playing sports and not keeping score. The deeper I wanted to dig, the more evasive the rabbi became with his answers. I was disappointed and felt even more isolated from the very faith that I was supposed to be embracing.

Dating Pam was fun. A lively spirit, up for just about anything, she was also the daughter of a Lutheran Pastor who also enjoyed having religious discussions with me. Whether it was at his church or in their living room, we would sit down facing one another, he would slap both of his hands down on his thighs, and court would be in session. When I posed the same type of questions to him regarding the trifecta, he became very animated and said that he was "delighted that I was exploring my religious options and welcomed the opportunity to be a steward to me while I was on my spiritual journey." With this attitude, I felt more confident that I would finally begin to get some answers, but he too dismissed my questions as "the mysteries of life." What? Come on. Mysteries of Life. Why would so much of the world be satisfied with answers that were not really answers?

Kathy was smart, gave me a run for my money in several classes at school, and was cute too! I liked her a lot. She was a good Catholic girl, and she would very liberally share the tenets of her faith with me. When I agreed to meet with her priest, she was ecstatic. I was guardedly optimistic that I would finally get some insights into my questions. Imagine my surprise and ultimately frustration when the bulk of the answers I received were cloaked in a blanket of answers such as "you don't need to know" or "you'll find out."

At this point I was really wondering whether any religion had the answers to the questions that were perplexing me. In hindsight it may have been their collective way of keeping it simple for me, but all it served to do was to push be farther down the path with no resolution in my heart but a growing determination to find a Truth that simultaneously satisfied me intellectually and imbued me with faith. I wondered what a guy had to do to get some answers. These were learned men, and nobody was helping me. I was not looking for a burning bush or for an angel to visit me, but some *guidance* upon which I could start building a foundation of faith would have been nice. I once again felt like the ten year old attempting to reconcile Genesis and Darwin.

I largely kept this pursuit of Truth to myself, as nobody else in my family seemed particularly bothered by this lack of knowledge [and faith] in their lives, and I viewed it as a part of what made me different than the rest of them and the world. As I talk to my grandchildren now, it is gratifying to me that they do have this spiritual foundation; that they *know* why we are baptized and the significance of receiving the Holy Ghost as a companion; and are both excited and filled with the wonder of doing work vicariously in the temple for our ancestors. I often wonder how different and yes, maybe even better, my life would have been had I enjoyed the luxury of this knowledge when I was their age.

CHAPTER 23

GRADUATION

"Three things are necessary in order that any rational
and intelligent being may exercise faith in God unto
life and salvation. First, the idea that he actually exists.
Secondly, a correct idea of his character, perfections, and
attributes. Thirdly, an actual knowledge that the course
of life which he is pursuing is according to His will."
Joseph Smith

But for the fact that I was chosen to speak at my high school commencement, odds were running high that I would not attend it. Up until that notification, I do not think anyone really had expressed any desire to see me walk across the stage in the auditorium. The move to the newly built Hoffman Estates High school at the start of my sophomore year afforded those of us in the class to essentially rule the school for three years, only eleven of us opted to graduate after our junior year. As a result, when I was identified as having the top GPA of the eleven of us, I was the top 9% of the class all by myself and awarded the dubious honor of speaking on behalf of the graduating class. Ironically, we were not recognized as the first graduating class of the school, with that honor resting with the remainder of our class that did attend as seniors. Even more ironic were the number of parents who did not even consider them to be the first graduating class, feeling that the class that started at the school as freshman were in fact entitled to claim that title. Did you see both the eye and head roll as I wrote that last sentence?

In any event, I was given the honor of sharing a smattering of the wisdom that I had acquired during my two years of education at the new school and realized that for as momentous as high school graduation is supposed to be, I had nothing. In fact, I had less than nothing. I was still so befuddled by a lack of answers to my trifecta of where did I come from, why am I here, and where am I going. As a result, I filled my talk with the usual platitudes and obligatory thanks to parents, faculty, and staff. I also attempted to capture some of the highlights of being alive in 1975, and all the promise contained in the future as most of us looked forward to marching off to institutions of higher learning in the Fall.

I was interviewed by a reporter from the Daily Herald who was very enthusiastic to hear about my plans to go into politics in an attempt to change the world around me and was completely enthralled by the fact that I was only sixteen years old. I was the youngest graduate in the Northwest suburbs of Chicago! One would think that this would constitute more *nachas* for the parental units ... and one would be wrong! My reward for graduation, the National Honor Society, and of course being #1: one-half a sports coat. One half you say? It goes something like this: "Would you like to go to the mall tomorrow night for a sports coat?" Absolutely. "Good, I'll pay half." There is no record of another gift from the other parent. This is not a work of fiction.

CHAPTER 24

SUICIDE IS NOT PAINLESS

"During difficult experiences often filled with
pain and suffering character is built, hearts are
purified, and souls are enlarged as individuals
gain experience and spiritual tutoring."
David A. Bednar

Contrary to the lyrics of the song made popular in the movie
M*A*S*H, suicide is not painless to the survivors who are forced to deal
with the aftermath of what is probably the most desperate of decisions
anyone can make for themselves in this life.

The summer of graduation also was the end of my parents' marriage,
and my mother's re-marriage the very next day. It meant that my mother
and three younger brothers moved out of the family house and into a
townhouse with her new husband about five minutes away. I was not
invited to the party. As it was, my plan had been to move into Chicago
and to live with my grandmother and commute down to school from
there. I had arranged a transfer from the suburban store in which I had
worked for a couple of years courtesy of the bogus birth certificate to a

store in the city, when my grandmother suggested that I stay at home with my father so that he wouldn't be lonely, and commute to the city via the train. More so to please her, I acquiesced, and we were going to be "two wild and crazy guys" living together. It did not quite turn out that way, because while Dad was like a kid turned loose in a candy store dating lots and lots of women, I was busy. Busy juggling three jobs, 24 hours of credits each quarter, and commuting three hours round trip each day. The good news is that I was able to live there rent free, in exchange for doing a litany of household and yard chores.

I was busy. So busy. A college student trying to get through school as quickly as possible so that I could get on with life on my own terms. I was so busy that I fell out of contact with my three best friends from high school. In hindsight it is ridiculous that this happened because we had largely been inseparable for our high school years. They were all [still] seniors at Hoffman Estates High School and still lived less than 1-2 miles away from me. In fairness, I was also dating and frankly, the idea of being with a girl was a lot more appealing than hanging out with the guys. Oh, how easily deceived and blinded I was by feminine wiles.

Mark and I, along with twins Larry and Doug were the four musketeers. Nothing that was crazy or outrageous was beyond our capability. We would venture out to Woodfield Mall (then the largest mall in the country), and confound security guards by draping fishing rods off the upper level to the fountain below, or visiting the 1890's themed Farrell's ice cream parlor dressed as the Marx Brothers – Groucho, Chico, Harpo, and even Zeppo. We all need a straight man in life. Much to the delight of the management, we packed them in. The kids did not know who we purported to be, but their parents did. We filmed homemade movies and constructed audio "nut tapes" that featured Mark's 1928 Model A Ford, conducted tormenting raids to teachers' homes, as well as entertaining our fellow students with our antics. We had more or less been the high school nerds that amused everyone but did not fit in anywhere. We would motor on by Dunkin Donuts in either Mark's car or mine, plunk down a dollar and walk out with a dozen hot donuts to consume while cruising on a Saturday night.

My friend Mark had moved from Chicago's inner city to live with his grandparents in the suburbs because of some "trouble" with the gangs in the high school he was attending. His parents would visit on the weekend, and that became the norm. Mark was almost a year older than we were, far more worldly, and even had sideburns and the vestiges of a moustache before the rest of us. By far the most eccentric of the four of us, based on his manner of dress and antics, he was in some ways a real creative genius.

Twins Larry and Doug were quiet, reserved, and musical. The perfect straight men for some of our zany antics. I remember meeting them in junior high and realizing that I could be myself around them. Throw in crazy Mark, and we indeed made an interesting foursome.

There are probably a handful of chapters contained in this memoir which are more poignant than the rest; in hindsight there is no doubt in my mind and my conversion was complete that this entire episode provides one of the cornerstones of my faith and why I am the person I am today.

It was the end of Spring Quarter, 1976, and I was finishing my third quarter of college, and it was finals week. I was juggling my jobs, cramming for finals, and still traveling downtown via the train to take my exams. It was an exhausting time, and I was looking forward to a couple of weeks off from school and only having to work before the start of summer school and an abbreviated and compressed term.

It was Tuesday morning, and I was home studying before having to work a 1:30 – 10:00 shift at my stock clerk job. Tuesday was the day that we received our shipments and engaged in a major effort to re-stock the shelves on the retail floor, as well as organizing our overflow in the backroom. It was actually one of my favorite days because as the quasi-assistant manager of the department, it was always left to me to organize the other clerks and to ensure that the work was completed in a timely manner. Even then...

I had just completed my studying when my girlfriend Kelly came by the house. She too was scheduled to work the same shift as I, but in a different department of the store. After hanging out for a while, she suggested that we leave for work early and go to one of our favorite hot dog joints and have of a dog and a beer. I should mention that while I was only seventeen at the time, I did have the luxury of a full beard which enabled me to buy the brews when called upon. I was not unreceptive to the idea, but nearly simultaneous to this suggestion, the *thought* popped into my head that I should instead go visit Mark at lunchtime at his grandparents' house. I do not know why that thought popped into my head other than the fact that I had not seen him in quite a while. I am not certain he would even be there, but the thought came to me at least three times, each time with increasing intensity. *Go see Mark. GO see Mark. GO SEE MARK!*

I mentioned this thought to my girlfriend and she dismissed the idea, and again encouraged lunching on a dog and a brew. As you can imagine, I acquiesced, and off to lunch we went, and clocked in at work a few minutes before 1:30.

It was about 7:30 that evening, and the work of re-stocking the shelves in full force, when a store-wide page over the intercom announced that I had a telephone call. Personal calls were frowned upon, so I was anxious to find out which of my family or friends was violating this rule. I immediately went to the multi-line phone mounted on a pillar in the men's department and punched in the blinking light. After saying hello, I was met by the tear-filled voice of my former girlfriend Lori of whom I have previously written. We were still good friends, and I knew her well enough to know that something was seriously wrong. What I did not know or realize was the lasting ramifications of this phone call.

"Hi Don, it's Lori. I know you are at work, but I just heard something and thought you should know about it as soon as possible," as she began sobbing. My heart started racing, and I could feel the adrenaline being released into my bloodstream. I also wanted to comfort her for whatever was upsetting her.

"What happened," I asked, as I placed one hand on the pillar bracing myself for what I assumed was going to be something awfully bad.

"Mark killed himself today," she said, and then was unable to say anything else for I do not know how long. Time more or less stood still for me. I remember getting a bit dizzy and thinking that I might even throw up. The silence on the phone line was paralyzing.

"How, when," was all I could find enough voice to croak out as my throat became constricted.

"He sat in his car in the closed garage with a tube hooked up to the exhaust pipe on the car," she said, with more sobs.

I am not certain, but my heart may have skipped a beat. "When," I repeated my question of earlier.

"They are saying that it probably happened when he was home for lunch from school this afternoon," she said. I nearly fell when I heard her words and realized that I was going to have to shoulder some of the blame for his death.

"I'm so sorry Don. I just thought you should know," she said, sobbing anew. I do not think I will ever forget those last six words.

"Thank you for thinking of me," I said, grateful for her kind spirit.

"Let me know if there is anything I can do for you or for Mike's family," she said, as I felt my heart completely imploding on itself.

"I will. Thanks again."

"Bye."

If there are moments that forge our character as if in a refiner's fire, then this was one of mine. As I hung up the phone, I could scarcely breathe. I was conscious of the blood pounding in my head and in my heart, and I realized that there was nothing I could do to change the outcome. I had majorly screwed up. My lack of action had killed my best friend. Something spiritual had reached out to me and I had ignored the call. I had figuratively refused the charges on a collect call in the name of lunch. It was my fault that he was dead.

While logic would say that I did not kill my friend and that had I ventured over there that day and even stopped him somehow, surely, he would have made another attempt in the future. The tortured heart and soul of a seventeen year old kid was not going to abide by logic, and it was probably fully twenty years before I fully understood this to be true.

I was so full of *shame, fear, embarrassment* and consumed by *guilt*. The fear of failure that had so neatly been engrained in me by my father completely enveloped me. I had failed in the most momentous of ways – in a life and death situation -- and I would never see Mike again. I had been a terrible friend, and because he had felt abandoned, he took his own life. Was it him communicating with me that morning? Was it an angel? Was it some form of extra sensory perception that my mother was always claiming that she possessed and may have passed on to me? Whatever it was, I had ignored it, and Mike was dead at age 18, before his life had even begun. So talented, yet so tortured.

My grandfather dying a few years before had been a blow, but he was an old man suffering from the ravaging effects of cancer. It had been a blessing when he was released from his suffering. Mike on the other hand had not even graduated high school or embarked on the journalism career about which he was always talking. Oh, why, why, why, didn't I go over there? I *would* have heard the car running in the garage. To this very day, I can still hear the distinctive sound of that 4-cylinder 24 horsepower engine. Every time I hear that sound at a car show or on the road, these very same albeit muted feelings return.

I would have broken into the garage or the house and I would have stopped or saved him. But I did not. I went for a hot dog, fries, and a beer. I had been weak, maybe even cowardly, because I did not do what I presumably *knew* to be right.

I just realized as I was completing this chapter that these feelings may have been encapsulated in the scar tissue of passing time, but they are never completely gone. I will candidly admit that simply re-living that telephone conversation was enough to strip away the scar tissue and to re-expose the raw emotions of that experience in ways that I have not considered for a good number of years.

I finished my shift largely in silence and solitude as I "faced" shelves, and swept floors. I did not trust my voice, and my heart was pretty much in my throat. As I recall, I did not tell my girlfriend Kelly what had happened until the store was closing and we were getting ready to head home. Even though she was 18, and out of high school, she still had a strict curfew because she lived at home but obtained permission to follow me to my house given the extenuating circumstances.

I remember driving home *extremely fast*, followed in an ever increasing gap by Kelly in her own car. I walked in the door, dropped my stuff on the floor and sat down in my [fashionable] bean bag chair and in a scene nearly out of a M*A*S*H episode when Hawkeye has a concussion and is afraid of falling asleep and lapsing into a coma, proceeded to deliver a four hour soliloquy interspersed with tears of sorrow, guilt, anger, and remorse. I must have eventually run out steam and fallen into bed after Kelly left for home.

I could have prevented it. The Boy Wonder had failed. I ignored my little voice or whatever had attempted to communicate with me. In the early 1980s when Tom Selleck brought Magnum, P.I. to the small screen, he always referenced hearing a little voice that was like a conscience or personal compass. At that point in my life I was very receptive to this concept. But that was several years in the future, and for now, I was severely wounded, and more than prepared to harshly punish myself.

That was Tuesday. I believe it was Wednesday morning that I started cluing in people (to include my family) that Mark was gone. I am thinking that it may be a blessing that I really do not remember what happened that day. I may have had another final, which I think I did. With that many courses, I was jammed with exams that week. I do not recall sharing my experience of the previous morning with anyone else. I did not know if doing so would make me culpable in some way. Crazy thoughts go through the mind of a grief-stricken seventeen year old.

Late Wednesday afternoon/evening was the viewing. I remember putting on my graduation present [half] sport's jacket and tie and venturing into the funeral home on rubbery legs. I do not recall who was with me. I suspect that it was Larry and Doug, mercifully I just cannot recall. I do recall being nearly overwhelmed when I spied Mark's dad standing next to the casket stroking the face of his dead son. I was completely without breath when I walked up to him, and he put his arms around me in a fatherly embrace. I hugged him back and said that I was sorry, so deeply sorry, but do not believe that I shared with him my culpability in his son's death.

Some of the "beautiful people" from school who used to ridicule Mark were all there as if this was the social event of the season. Their presence angered me so deeply that I nearly lost all vestiges of self-control. Ultimately, I went to Mark's Dad and the funeral director and identified which of these "phony friends" needed to be escorted out of the premises. In other words, I had them thrown out as a final gesture of loyalty to my dead friend. I was feeling so guilty at not preventing this tragedy that I could not allow them to make it even worse by making a mockery of this opportunity to say goodbye and to honor him.

Friday was the funeral. I don't remember how I did it, but I had secured permission from my professor to take the final exam scheduled for that day at some future date, but my dad was pretty adamant that he didn't think Mark would want me to mess up my exam schedule on his account, so I went down to school to take the exam rather than attending my best friend's funeral. Unbelievable. In fairness to my dad, he may have been attempting to help me focus on something other than Mark's death but as long as we are heaping it on, let's add a few more logs of regret, remorse, anger, and frustration for that stupid decision on my part.

When I did get together with the twins, they too shared feelings of guilt over Mark taking his own life. They told me that they too had harbored concerns about Mark, mainly because he had become more and more withdrawn in school, and ultimately from them. While their guilt could not come even close to the two ton weight that I was carrying around with me, they too felt a degree of responsibility for his death. It might have been their own Jewish guilt rearing its ugly head.

That was forty four years ago. In accordance with my Jewish roots, there has not been a year that has gone by since then that I have not thought of Mark on either December 10th, his birthday, or on April 20th, the day that he died. If I were still a practicing Jew, I would light a Yahrzeit candle on both of these days or leave a single light bulb burning for the day, as a sign of remembrance. I do not do either, but I do always say a prayer for him, and take solace in the fact that he is in a better place. To brighten April 20th, the Lord saw fit to present us with a beautiful grandson with a sweet spirit born on that day.

I still think of Mark on both of those days not only to remember him, but to remind myself of the importance of always heeding the promptings of the Holy Ghost, which I now understand was the source of the *thought* that was being communicated to me. To this day, I never allow myself the indulgence of ignoring a prompting of any kind, regardless of how seemingly insignificant it might appear to my own pea-sized brain with its limited knowledge of the bigger picture.

He is the Comforter, Revelator, and Messenger of the Father and the Son, and I know that His companionship is the greatest gift that we can enjoy as mortal men. I am grateful for this companionship and I know that it has saved me from many trials and tribulations in my own life, and I pray that I am always deemed worthy of this gift.

CHAPTER 25

HIGHER LEARNING

"What are the three most important decisions?
First, what will be my faith? Second, whom shall
I marry? Third, what will be my life's work?"
Thomas S. Monson

Unlike my wife and kids who have fond memories of sororities, parties, Institute, and campus life, college was pretty much a blur for me. Juggling a full-time job (stock clerk), part-time job (security guard – great homework time), ROTC (clerking job and regular training activities), an average of 24 credit hours, as well as a three hour commute each day to the University of Illinois – Chicago Circle (UICC), I was not as consumed with a thirst for spiritual knowledge. It basically boiled down to a complete lack of time to dwell on it, but it was never completely off my radar screen.

School was challenging, but largely a joy for me as I was intellectually stimulated, earning good grades, and having new horizons opened for me. Complete semesters of Solzhenitsyn, Hesse, Vonnegut, on top of double majors in Political Science and Criminal Justice, minors in

History, German, and Military Science, provided lots of opportunity to read and process different perspectives on life. I was quite literally a sponge and enjoyed learning.

Over the years many people have asked me why I had denied myself the college experience that most people enjoy and chose to attend a commuter school in the city of Chicago especially when so many friends went downstate to Champaign-Urbana, Bloomington, or Macomb. I really could not give them an answer. I do remember attending college night at Fremd High School and checking out all the schools in Illinois. I was excited that DePaul University and Loyola University, both located in Chicago, had programs that had interested me, and I had made application and been accepted to both schools. I had even thought that I could live in the city at my grandmother's house and it would be a short commute by car. So how did I end up at UICC, much less in the ROTC program rather than at either DePaul or Loyola where I would ideally explore religion to a greater degree?

It was probably some twenty years later that I finally learned the truth on how I ended up electing to attend the University of Illinois-Chicago Circle (UICC) rather than my first two choices of DePaul University and Loyola University. I was going through some papers at my Dad's Illinois home in my role as caretaker for the house while he was out west at Fort Huachuca, Arizona during Desert Shield. After I had attended college night and came home with information from all the different universities all located in Illinois, and really fired up about DePaul and Loyola Universities my father inserted himself into my plans. In his guise as Major Levin, he then took it upon himself to write to the Professor of Military Science at UICC about what an outstanding candidate I would make for the ROTC program at the school. Pretty soon, gone were the financial aid forms for the two private universities, and I was being encouraged to compete for a State of Illinois ROTC tuition waiver which I won. I largely attended college for the cost of my quarterly student fees as well as books. The rest we say is history. But we digress.

Reading the complete works of Alexander Solzhenitsyn in one ten week semester meant essentially the reading of one phone book, I mean novel, per week. I distinctly remember the weekend when I had to read *Cancer Ward* cover to cover to stay current. Oh my gosh, life in a Russian hospital cancer ward. Forty three years later I can still tag it as one of the most depressing weekends that I have ever spent. It did stir something inside of me as I considered the very nature of our existence. The human body is truly a marvelous work, and to this day, I stand all amazed at the elegance and simplicity of it. In a later chapter I will talk about birth and reproduction, but even after five children, nineteen grandchildren and one great-grandchild, I am astounded by it. The billions of possible permutations would seemingly make it impossible for us to have normal healthy babies and yet we do it every day. Likewise, one permutation of one gene, and cancer forms, potentially metastasizing to major organs and killing us.

Is it random chance? Does there have to be an external catalyst for cancer to form? Why are some families prone to it while others remain immune? And as life slowly ebbs out of a cancer-ridden body, as I have watched with several of my own family members, what impact does it have on the soul? When life leaves the body, like a hand exiting a glove, and all that is left of a person is his or her spiritual essence, what is that transition like? Is it something to be feared or welcomed? These were the questions that continued to plague me as I firmly entered adulthood, seeking for Truth that would provide me answers.

CHAPTER 26

CROSSROADS

"The spiritual rebirth described in this verse
typically does not occur quickly or all at once;
it is an ongoing process not a single event."
David A. Bednar

The only advantage to taking so many credits every semester is that the agony ends that much sooner. I think I was conscious of the fact that my life was difficult what with my parents' divorce, their subsequent re-marrying of other people and the introduction of step-parents and siblings, the lack of financial support for my college expenses, and general feeling of solitude. I had not shaken the feelings of guilt associated with Mark's death, and I was ready to move on to whatever life had to offer in terms of career, graduate education, and greater financial stability.

While I started college as a declared Political Science major – what better place to study politics in the 1970s than in Chicago with the original Mayor Daley orchestrating the movements of the Chicago Machine – I came to embrace Criminal Justice in my second trimester.

A film, *The Glass House*, based on the book by Truman Capote, starring Alan Alda and Vic Morrow, scared the daylights out of me, and I promised myself, at age 17, that I would never place myself in the position of facing prison. Talk about being scared straight!

I wrote a paper on the film which obviously impressed my professor (hard to believe since there were at least two hundred students in that class) because eighteen months later as I was preparing to wind down my college career and move on, he suggested that I attend graduate school in the Criminal Justice Department, and became a mentor to me. With his encouragement I took the Graduate Record Examination, and within a week or two of the school receiving my test scores, I was accepted into the graduate program for the following Fall term.

I was sitting number one in my ROTC military graduating class, declined a Regular Army commission, and planned on going into the Army Reserves (hopefully into the Military Police Corps) while also looking at a management position in retail to temporarily make ends meet while in grad school.

Imagine my surprise when one of my ROTC classmates met me in the cafeteria while I was enjoying my $0.70 early bird special breakfast and said "Congratulations. You're going to Germany!" I immediately set him straight on what my plans entailed, and he said, "No. It's posted up on the bulletin board. You are going on active duty and headed to Germany branched as a field artillery officer."

As soon as I got over the urge to throw up my breakfast, I dashed up to the seventh floor of the Science building where the Military Science Department was headquartered, and sure enough, there were the announcements that my friend had referenced. Another classmate of mine, also a Criminal Justice major desirous of assignment in the MPs, had the identical orders branching him as an artillery officer with orders for Germany. Seemingly the needs of the Army that year dictated the commissioning of a lot of field artillery officers and their deployment to the Federal Republic of Germany.

It is important to note that the Professor of Military Science (PMS) was both a Lieutenant Colonel, and a Latter day Saint. I did not know this at the time, and my interaction with him had no religious overtones.

He had independently determined that I was the "caliber" of officer (no pun intended) needed on active duty today and had changed my request for duty from reserve to active duty without consulting me. After learning this from the Sergeant Major, who did confide that I could get it changed if I were willing to push the issue, I was furious, and stormed off to consider all of my options. Clearly, had I opposed this request for active duty I could have avoided the duty, but it would have been a less than stellar way to start my military career.

I went to visit with my Criminal Justice professor/ mentor, who after hearing my case, quietly said, "You know Don, you are only 19. Three years in the army would make you the right age for graduate school. It would also give you a different perspective. You got into grad school once, you can get in again. Go in the Army." I was shocked. This was 1978 and Vietnam was still a fresh scar on our Society.

Needless to say, Dad was thrilled. He even bought me a brass cannon while he was honeymooning in the Grand Caymans. The Boy Wonder had provided him with *nachas* yet again. I was still torn as to what to do.

Grandma Mary had been okay with my largely financing my education courtesy of ROTC and of going into the Reserves here in Chicago, but when she heard that I was going on active duty she was beside herself and began showering me with counsel consisting of, "we have one dead hero in the family. You come home a live coward." Upon learning that I was going to Germany, the very land that had produced the killer of *her* Donnie, she pleaded with me not to go. When she realized that I didn't have a lot to say about my assignment, she relented, and would send me letters while I was in stateside training and overseas in Germany, always repeating the above counsel, as well as reminding me to "remember who you are, not to disgrace the family name, to be a good man, and a good Jew." I always thought it was interesting that she reminded me to be a good Jew when most of the time we were growing up, she never talked about our religion except to disparage God for "turning his back on her and taking away her Donnie."

It only recently occurred to me that but for that change in my request for orders, my life could be unrecognizable from what it is today.

I likely would not have gone on active duty, much less be stationed for three years in Germany, have met my future wife Susie, and surely would have missed out on all the Latter Day Saint contacts that I had throughout my early military career. It may have meant that I may or may not have found the Truth for which I had been seeking.

Given my belief in miracles, and the level of faith that I have acquired, I no longer have the luxury of chalking all these life events up to coincidence. It may even be as Deepak Chopra expressed in <u>Synchrodestiny: Harnessing the Infinite Power of Coincidence to Create Miracles:</u> "The coincidences or little miracles that happen every day of your life are hints that the universe has much bigger plans for you than you ever dreamed of for yourself."

CHAPTER 27

FORT LEWIS

"When you are converted, you not only know what you
should do but you also desire to do the right things.
It's not enough to just avoid doing wrong because you
are afraid of getting caught or punished. When truly
converted, you really want to choose the right."
Dieter F. Uchtdorf

After sweating out a computer programming class that I elected
to take pass/fail to complete the 20 hour math requirement that I had
for my Liberal Arts degree, I was declared a graduate of the University
of Illinois-Chicago Circle. The commencement ceremony was held at
the old Chicago Stadium, where the Bulls and the Blackhawks played
their home games. I did not attend. As I recall, there was zero desire or
support expressed by my family to attend the ceremony (so much for
nachas,) and the idea of sitting in the Old Barn (as it was known) for a
couple of hours in the heat of summer without any air conditioning with
thousands of graduates to walk across the stage didn't make sense to me,
so I blew it off. I do remember my Grandmother saying that she would

attend – she had been driven to Peoria, IL by my aunt and uncle for both of my cousins graduations from Bradley University – and claimed that they were two of the happiest and proudest days of her life – *nachas*. But it was a non-event for me.

Shortly after that non-event, I was off to Fort Lewis, WA to attend my six week Advanced Camp to complete ROTC. This was good news, because every year up until this one, our school was always assigned to the camp at Fort Riley, KS where it was always hotter than blazes. We had heard horror stories from the classes ahead of us about the grueling conditions. As a result, going up to the Pacific Northwest sounded like, and turned out to be, a real blessing.

Ordinarily this camp is attended during the summer between one's Junior and Senior year and determines leadership assignments within the cadet battalion for the senior year. Because I was already a graduate, I was designated a "Commissionee" and would receive the gold bars of a Second Lieutenant at the conclusion of the camp. The good news about being a commissionee is that I was told by my platoon evaluators that I would have less leadership assignments during the camp as well. Unfortunately, that was not the case, but is not germane to this story.

We lived in two-story wooden barracks leftover from World War II, with two ten-man squads per floor in bunk beds. With only one latrine with communal toilets and a single large shower room, privacy did not exist on any level. Because it was summer, there was no heat at night, and when the temperatures dropped to around 50 degrees, it was cold in the barracks, and we made use of both of our issued wool blankets and often slept with socks and a field jacket.

We were on the hand grenade range, and after hearing the mandatory safety briefing, we then watched the captain who was the officer in charge, violate his own safety rules, and attempt to dispose of a live grenade that had not exploded as planned. The result was that he literally blew his own body in half killing himself immediately, and severely maiming the NCOIC who was attempting to assist him. This happened in front of our company of approximately 120 cadets. It remains one of the more horrifying experiences I encountered in twenty five years of military service. Naturally, we were all offered counseling services, but this remains an instance of arrogance replacing common sense and safety and I did not feel the need to "talk" to anyone.

It did however prompt me to have a flashback to the kid who had died on my front lawn, my grandfather's departure from this world, and all of the same questions came flooding back to me. What happened to the captain when he died? Where did he go? What was that moment of transition like from mortal existence to whatever he was subsequently experiencing? This is where a true tender mercy occurred.

I should note that I met my first avowed Mormon during this six week period. He was a BYU student, a return missionary, and already married. I remember he was in the squad across the bay from me, and I noticed that he was wearing what I believed to be long underwear. I thought it a bit strange that he was going to wear it during the day, because we were experiencing an unseasonably warm *and dry,* summer in Washington State (it was 99 degrees on the 4th of July) and while I could see wearing it at night after the sun went down, it certainly did not make sense to wear it during the day.

One of the guys noticed my curious looks and laughingly informed me that it was not long underwear but rather a "Mormon Flak Suit." When I asked what he meant by that, he shared that it was a religious garment that was worn by most of the church members, and offered some level of protections to the wearer, hence the term. I categorized that as an oddity, but having known a few orthodox Jews over the years, did not really object to it, especially since it was apparently worn *under* regular clothing and not ordinarily noticeable.

It was shortly after the incident on the grenade range that I had walked up to the crowded snack bar, and I spied Allen sitting alone at a corner table. When he saw me with my tray of pizza, he waved me over and offered to share his spot. It was not long before the conversation turned to religion. I was surprised at how open he was, extremely comfortable with, and more than willing to talk about, his faith. I had already noticed that he did not drink coffee (I did not either), did not drink Coke, much less knock back a beer. And he was so confident. He was SO certain. I admired that. I was even a bit envious.

I recall another night at the snack bar when our casual conversation took on a more serious timber, and he talked to me about the concept of eternal families, marriage for time and eternity, and *testified* to me that I would have the opportunity to meet my Uncle Don in the next life. All that sort of made my head swirl, but for the first time, someone was providing me with answers to my three questions. I was intrigued.

I must admit that at first, I was a little stunned and maybe a little skeptical. However, when I asked additional questions, he could answer these questions and back it up with references from his very worn set of scriptures. I was impressed.

Our six weeks together quickly came to an end, and on August 2, 1978, I raised my right hand on the parade field of North Fort Lewis and received my commission. Later, at a reception at the Officer's club, my platoon evaluators arranged for me to have my gold bars pinned on by General Donn A. Starry. August 2 happens to be my father's birthday, and he often thereafter said that while he was not present to witness it (there was a surprising number of parents in attendance), my commissioning was the best birthday present he has ever received. More *nachas!*

It is funny how close you can get to people in six weeks. We had a good group, and we said our goodbyes. Allen was going back to Provo, Utah to finish his last year of school and to receive his commission in a year. I have a vague recollection that there may have been a baby on the way as well, which nearly cooked my brain because I could not imagine being married while in college, much less expecting a baby, but Allen was an old man at 24. I on the other hand would report to Fort Sill, OK on August 28, to begin at least four years of active duty with the Army.

Was it a quirk of fate that sent me to Fort Lewis rather than Fort Riley? It was the only year that Illinois schools went any where other than Riley. Was it an accident that Allen was in my platoon? I believe that there were approximately three thousand cadets on post during the two cycles, and yet our paths crossed. I have often heard that it takes seven contacts with the Church before a lot of people will feel the spirit and complete their conversion process. I would like to think that Fort Lewis, and Allen, were one of those requisite contacts.

CHAPTER 28

THE BUNKER

"Line upon line and precept upon precept, gradually
and almost imperceptibly, our motives, our thoughts,
our words, and our deeds become aligned with
the will of God. This phase of the transformation
process requires time, persistence, and patience."
David A. Bednar

I have compiled a list on my cell phone that identifies all the times
over the years that but for the grace of God, I would already be dead. I
don't know if everyone can readily identify as many times as I can (I am
now up to fourteen), but let's just say if a cat has nine lives, that may be
another explanation for why that was my nickname ("Cat")in the office
softball league down at Fort Sill. Some of the instances are run of the
mill car accidents and tornadoes. Others were arguments with grenades
and artillery shells or being shot at by enemy soldiers.

As a new field artillery lieutenant, I could expect to direct off-shore
Naval gunfire, Air Force Close Air Support, and of course indirect fire

of field artillery cannon batteries and Infantry/Cavalry mortar platoons. Over the years I had the pleasure to do all of it except for Naval gunfire.

I was on the West Range of Fort Sill under the tutelage of our gunnery instructor, Marine Gunnery Sergeant Nowicki. Gunny Nowicki could make "sir" sound like a four letter word. Even though we all outranked him, there was no doubt as to who was in charge both in the classroom and most notably out on the range. He would chew his tobacco, and spit near the tip of your boot, but never hit it. His job was to train a bunch of green, wet-behind-the-ears second lieutenants to direct artillery fire on the battlefield, and he was good at it.

One day, we were conducting what is lovingly referred to as the bunker exercise. The idea was to draw the fire closer and closer to our position and ultimately drop the rounds on top of the bunker which consisted of seventeen feet of steel reinforced concrete. The front of the bunker had a slit through which we could use our binoculars to direct the fire onto the targets. This slit consisted of six 3/4" thick panes of glass. The intent was to expose us to the potentially devastating destruction of our weapon systems, but also to instill confidence in the safety that a fortified bunker would afford us.

A number of us had successfully conducted our fire missions – it is a lot of fun to call in fire and to blow targets up – and we were getting close to the end of the day. One lieutenant was being a bit timid in his corrections, and literally dragging out the exercise, and more importantly delaying happy hour for all assembled. "Come on Sir, come on. We are going to be over run," screamed the Gunny in an attempt to extract some urgency out of Adam. A bold correction was not quite as bold as it needed to be, and rather than landing on top of the bunker as a number of rounds had already been placed throughout the afternoon, resulting in nothing more than a steady stream of concrete dust dropping form the ceiling, Adam's rounds "skipped" off the *front* of the bunker, and the war went up for grabs after that and chaos was king.

As an aside, Adam, the lieutenant in question, was viewed as being a little odd by the rest of us. He was always reading from the Bible and was a poster child for what a straight arrow was all about. He was subject to a fair amount of ridicule, and in hindsight I am glad that I never directly subjected him to some of the harassment that he tried to take in stride. My most vivid memory of him was when he was working in the fire direction center and refused to repeat the target descriptions from the forward observer directing the artillery fire and the righteous indignation with which he dressed us all down with for laughing at "school bus of children and nuns in the open, fire for effect." In his mind it was nearly sacrilegious to want to blow up children and nuns. That was Adam.

On the fateful day in question, we had been firing 81mm mortars, 105mm artillery, 155mm artillery, and on occasion some big-boy 8" (203mm) main gun corps artillery. Adam's mission *should* have been picked up by the [larger, more dangerous] 155mm or 8" battery with their 98 or 200 pound projectiles, and had it, we would have all been dead. Instead, the 105mm battery was quick on the line and pumped their 33 pound projectiles out super-fast alas just a tad shorter than planned.

When the rounds skipped off the face of the bunker, they cut all our telephone landlines and shattered four of the six panes of viewing glass. The concussion of the blast inside the bunker was intense, and ruptured a lot of ear drums, and even caused a few concussions. My ear drums did not rupture, but I was pretty much stone deaf for about twelve hours which was pretty scary. The sheer force of the impact gave me an enormously powerful and healthy respect for the damaging power that was at hand whenever we sent rounds out of our tubes. It also provided me with perspective for when I watched war movies and artillery rounds or aerial bombs would land and literally throw people around like rag dolls.

Needless to say, when the landlines were cut, and the fire direction center and the various gunlines could not communicate with us, they feared the worst, and Range Control followed protocol and scrambled wheeled (ground) vehicles and air med evac helicopters assuming that we had suffered mass casualties or been killed. We were all subjected to a trip to the hospital, and I was immediately discharged with the guidance to "go home and rest and wait for my hearing to come back. I was advised that I could take aspirin if my ears hurt me in any way."

As I wandered around my BOQ room, and the halls, not being able to hear much of anything up until the time I finally went to bed out of boredom, I became aware of just how much for granted I had always taken my five senses. We all take it for granted that we can see the sunrise, hear the birds chirping, smell breakfast cooking, taste the goodness of a fresh chocolate chip cookie fresh and warm from the oven, or experience the touch of a baby's newborn skin. I resolved that night never to take any of that for granted again, and said a prayer asking that my hearing would be restored. Since I could not watch television, or listen to music, and after a couple hours of reading and some homework, I was done for the day, I repeated my prayer and went to bed.

The next morning, I woke up, and before I remembered that I had gone to bed not being able to hear, I *heard* the sound of guys running and carrying on in the hallway outside my BOQ door. While my first thought it was too early for them to be making so much noise, my second thought was a prayer of gratitude when I realized that I was in fact *hearing* the noise from the hall. While most people could and would probably say that the restoration of my hearing was just Nature taking its course, I was willing to concede that it might have been an answer to prayer.

We had a fun-loving and sometimes irreverent chaplain attached to our school who would often entertain us in leadership class and at the Officers Club with his view of Life, the Army, and the role of God in our lives. After the bunker incident, he was very quick to point out that our survival was nothing short of a miracle and that we should all be grateful to be alive, and to forever be aware that God had a special work in mind for each of us. While delivered somewhat tongue in cheek and with a twinkle in his eye, he was also profoundly serious.

I for one was intrigued as to the concept of the entire incident being a miracle rather than a series of mishaps and miscommunications, and offered to buy the fine chaplain a drink or two at the club in order to hear more of this thoughts. During these conversations, the chaplain made a strong case on the topic of miracles. As he pointed out, who is to say that the issue of which gun battery actually "owned" that fire mission was not really a miracle rather than a mistake or confusion or coincidence. It may have been intervention by God that spared all our lives. Since I did not have the ability to prove a negative, it was definitely food for thought.

He challenged me to reconsider the entire concept of coincidence and to realize that while God does not care what we do day to day, he does retain the final authority to intervene on our behalf. Again, for the second time in three months I was hearing about the notion that there is no such thing as coincidence.

Chaplain Billy's further challenges did make me question my Purpose in life that day and embedded an attitude of gratitude that I like to think remains to this day. He also asked me to never take life and all its splendor for granted. I am reminded of how whenever we have a malady as simple as a sore throat, we pray that it will go away and promise to never take *not* having a sore throat or stuffy nose for granted ever again, until we do, and then we get sick again and make that promise anew. To this day, I will walk around our beautiful yard or inside the house and simply marvel at all the beauty and bounty that we are enjoying.

I have a good friend, Teddy, who is always saying, "Today is a gift, that's why it is called the present," and he would be correct.

Albert Einstein was clearly a man of science, but he conceded that "There are only two ways to live your life. One is as though nothing is a miracle. The other is as though everything is a miracle." I am good with that as a premise.

CHAPTER 29

WE DON'T DO THAT HERE

"Miracles, or these extraordinary manifestations
of the power of God, are not for the unbeliever;
they are to console the Saints, and to strengthen
and confirm the faith of those who love, fear,
and serve God, and not for outsiders."
Brigham Young

After five months and two schools at Fort Sill, and some leave spent in Chicago en route to my first duty station, I was off for what would prove to be the biggest adventure of my short life.

I was met by my sponsor and his wife at the Rhein-Main Air Force Base in western Germany, about three hours from our post down in Bavaria, and after a quick stop at the Sight and Sound Shop – it was Sansui Dollar Days – we were off for Bindlach, West Germany. Everybody I knew in Germany bought themselves a big and powerful stereo system. In fact, it was not unusual to walk into a four-man room in the billets and to find that each occupant had their own mega system. Often, they were reduced to having to listen to their music through stereo headphones, but it was just too good a deal not to take advantage of the [cheap] prices offered in these government sponsored outlets. Over the years as we have moved around the country, professional movers who have come in to pack up the stereo will instantly ask "Germany or Korea" because they themselves may have purchased a like system during their own period of overseas military service.

It would be some six weeks before I received permanent quarters to live in, and for that entire time, my five large cartons containing my newly-purchased sound system sat like a mountain in the middle of the floor of the transient officers quarters located next to Richard Wagner's *Festspielhaus* near downtown Bayreuth. The Festspielhaus, home of the Bayreuth Festival was built by Richard Wagner with primary funding provided by King Ludwig II of Bavaria. It opened in 1876. By placing my name on a waiting list when I first arrived, I was finally able to see a performance about thirty months later.

Our post, Christensen Barracks, was an old Luftwaffe base left over from days of old, located in Bindlach, West Germany. It was home to only 1st Squadron, 2nd Armored Cavalry Regiment, with the organic Howitzer Battery to which I was assigned located downtown on the Hans Schemm Kaserne which we shared with the Engineers and Military Police. At the very end of my tour they were constructing billeting and motor pool space for our unit up on The Rock as the post was lovingly known.

There were not many amenities on the post. A simple commissary about the size of an oversized 7-11, a tiny post exchange (PX), snack bar, recreation center/gymnasium, a one screen theater, a Class VI store where alcoholic spirits and cigarettes were sold, and a community club. There also was one chapel in which parishioners could choose between weekly Catholic or non-denominational Protestant services.

I arrived in Bindlach on Saturday evening, and after dinner with other battery officers and their spouses, I explored the post on Sunday, and on Monday after the obligatory in-processing, I departed for Grafenwoehr to join my unit in the field for what would be the first of many many field deployments. We were down there for about two weeks and when we returned, I was once again walking around the post when I happened to encounter the Squadron Chaplain. He was a good-natured Southern Baptist who prided himself on meeting the spiritual needs of the squadron's personnel as well as of their families.

I will never forget how he gazed at my name tag, and said in his southern accent,

"Levin. Levin? You're Jewish…. We don't do that here. If you want Jewish services, you have to go to Nuremberg." I was a little taken aback by that, and then he laughed, and said that I was welcome to attend the Protestant services if I did not want to make the trek to Nuremberg. He also indicated that there were only about four other Jews assigned to the command near as he could recall.

For as strange as I thought that was as a welcome to the community, imagine my discomfiture when later that very weekend at our monthly squadron officer Hail & Farewell party I was approached by the squadron interpreter. Herr Schneider, a German civilian, approached me, clicked his heels, introduced himself, and then uttered, "You're Jewish." There was something about the man that gave rise to my taking an immediate dislike to him. I later found out that he had been a Nazi during the war, but like most Germans employed by the US Army "only fought the Russians."

My initial impressions of people are correct about 95% of the time, and this was no exception. I later learned that he was still very anti-Semitic, and often did not hide it well. As my dislike for him increased over the time I was stationed in the squadron, I would often alter the route of our two mile battery run so as to pass the apartment building he owned and in which he lived, and with 160 voices strong, serenade him with our favorite running "jody" of the day at 0600 once or twice a week. This was easy to do since the building was literally around the corner from our Kaserne, and all of a two minute walk door to door. I ultimately got the last laugh on him, when one of my friends who rented an apartment from him offered to let me stay there for the ten nights that I would be in garrison the last six months that I was in country. Because I was gone so much on training and field exercises, it was silly to maintain my own apartment out in Bad Berneck (where Hitler used to go for the therapeutic baths) I took advantage of Bruce's offer, and

135

thoroughly enjoyed sleeping there, knowing that our esteemed landlord was probably beside himself at the knowledge of having a Jew sleeping under his roof. Pyrrhic victories can be just as sweet!

How did I know that he was still a Jew-hating Nazi? The Squadron had a good friend in the Chief of Detectives of the Bayreuth Polizei. A lovely man, he had been a Displaced Person (DP) after the war and assigned to the camp that was located in the training area immediately across from our main gate. A fellow Jew, he had welcomed me warmly to the squadron. In anticipation of the annual Bayreuth Festival Ari would show up at Squadron Headquarters with buckets laden with wooden tokens for free beer at the festival. As officers we were encouraged to take as many as we could and to share them with our troops. He was as kind-hearted as he was generous, and as I said, was a good friend to the squadron and would often help us out when on pay day weekends some of our boys might get a little rambunctious in a gasthaus or other establishment.

Apparently it was at one of our monthly Hail & Farewell parties back around 1960 when an inebriated Herr Schneider got in Ali's face, and casually pronounced with a sneer, "it's a shame we missed you when we had the chance." Needless to say, there was still no love lost between them some twenty years later, and Ali and I became allies against Schneider. I was once again, proudly wearing that Star of David chip on my shoulder, prepared to do anything to fight against the bigotry.

CHAPTER 30

THE DISAPPEARING COKES

"I am not asking you to pretend to faith you do not have.
I am asking you to be true to the faith you do have."
Jeffrey R. Holland

After my experience at Fort Lewis with my platoon mate Allen, I knew that LDS people lived by a strict dietary code referred to as the Word of Wisdom. I knew from his example that "moderation in all things" was more than just a catch phrase for him. I also knew that LDS people did not drink tea and coffee, or alcohol, and as I would quickly learn, caffeinated soft drinks.

Truth be told, because of the hard demands of a very high training tempo, I think it would be fair to say that a good number of the Army personnel assigned to the squadron lived on coffee and to a lesser degree Coke both in garrison and most notably while in the field. Long days, short nights, or often no nights left us needing that caffeine jolt. After working a full regular duty day, I would routinely report to Squadron Headquarter at 1700, receive a briefing on ongoing activities, and then spend the entire night awake as the Staff Duty Officer in the often cold

Squadron Headquarters building, presumably with authority to act in the Squadron Commander's name, or to handle emergencies as they arose. Regular trips out to check on sentries and post facilities would break up the night, but I can still remember that groggy, grimy feeling just as dawn was approaching. Depending on the day of the week, I would then leave to join my unit for PT or grab a shower and shave and return to my desk, ready to then work the new day as if nothing were amiss. I found this easy to do because of my college schedule, but multiple sleepless nights strung together could make it tough to stay awake without some assistance.

My second duty position was that of the Battery Fire Direction Officer. The duty title is quite descriptive of your duties as the FDO. It is a great position for an artillery lieutenant and certainly one to aspire to because it was your voice and command that would launch the rounds from the gun line. As the FDO, I ruled the roost in the Fire Direction Center (FDC) which was located in the tall, armored command track that had a tent extension that could be erected if additional space was desired and if we were going to be in spot long enough to justify the labor in erecting it. As the FDO I was responsible for the data that would be computed and passed to the gunline so that the rounds fired would land where desired.

The FDC was extremely crowded, especially if a crew of 4-6 young men were all gainfully employed around the 1950's era field artillery digital automatic computer (FADAC), the manual firing chart, as well as manning the radio, and calling down fire commands to the gunline via the telephone landline that we would always install upon occupying a firing position. Because space was at such a premium we also pulled a ¼ ton trailer upon which we had constructed a plywood enclosure in which to store and keep dry all of our duffle bags, extra fuel and oil products, as well as our cache of Coca Cola and pogey bait.

It was during my first field trip as the FDO when I noticed that if a crew member put down a cup of coffee or a can of Coke, it would quite often get spilled or nearly as often simply mysteriously disappear. Needing to balance the importance of keeping the computer and firing charts as well as the radios and telephones free of liquids with that of creature comforts for the crew, this could become a real issue. I never imagined that it would be as big an issue as it seemingly was, given that we were presumably all adults not in need of sippy cups.

Whenever I drank a Coke I would usually mark the can with my name or with the initials "LT" so as to prevent anyone else from taking a swig, or worse, spitting tobacco juice into it, as there was absolutely no smoking of any kind near any of the vehicles, particularly when we were firing artillery rounds with thousands of pounds of gunpowder and high explosives around us. When it happened that several of my drinks disappeared, I quietly investigated the phenomena and discovered that one of my best and brightest FDC crewmen, Spec4 Eddie, was the culprit. His motivation and ultimate excuse in extenuation and mitigation when I busted him: he was LDS and it made him uncomfortable to see us consuming so much caffeine when his faith's Word of Wisdom warned against the harmful effects.

After counseling him on why he did not have the right to "inflict" his beliefs on those around him, I let him off the hook after he promised to discontinue the practice. Unfortunately, while I [good naturedly] directed the crew to forgive him as well for his trespasses, the crew later exacted their revenge when during a family day back in garrison, they learned that Eddie was going to show his young blushing bride where he worked while in the field. The FDC track was looking pristine and very organized, but when Eddie opened up the trailer to show her where we sometimes took turns sleeping on a piece of plywood placed over several ten gallon cans of petroleum products, the plywood walls of the trailer were covered in some of the guys' favorite Playboy pinups. Poor Eddie. Did he ever have to do some quick talking to get himself out of that jam.

It was also around this time that another officer in the squadron and his wife began sharing their LDS faith with me, and Susie, encouraging me to read from the Book of Mormon, and to meet with the young American missionaries that would occasionally visit their quarters on post. This will be the subject of a later chapter.

Years later I also discovered that my battery commander was a *lapsed* Mormon, meaning that he no longer followed the tenets of the faith. The nearly two gallons of coffee and three packs of cigarettes he consumed in lieu of food each day while we were in the field would otherwise have been a real tip off.

In hindsight, I must admit that it was quite refreshing to find a young man like Eddie as passionate and committed to living his faith seven days a week, and not merely paying lip service to it. A model soldier, he was also a good husband and father, and another person I appreciate as I consider all the people who influenced my conversion to the Church of Jesus Christ of Latter Day Saints.

CHAPTER 31

GAS CHAMBERS

"Conversion does not normally come all at
once. . . . It comes in stages, until a person
becomes at heart a new person."
Dale E. Miller

It was while I was stationed in Germany that ABC aired a mini-series on the Holocaust. It was particularly poignant to me after having visited the Dachau concentration camp located in a suburb of Munich. My grandmother's sister died in Auschwitz, which over the years had also fueled my sometimes anger directed at those who either refuted the existence of the Holocaust or the barbaric behavior of the SS Death Squads or simply decided to be anti-Semitic with an extraneous "dirty kike" comment.

In the course of one of my infrequent calls home to the family back in Chicago, I had mentioned to my dad how much "fun" our recent annual sojourn to the gas chamber training area down in Grafenwoehr had been, particularly for my black troops who suffered from *pseudo folliculitis barbae.* With a doctor's note, this allowed them to skip shaving, and to essentially grow beards, but <u>not</u> to be excused from the annual gas chamber exercise. With the presence of the beard, they were unable to secure a tight seal with their gas masks, and as a result each enjoyed a lung full of gas and one heck of a good cry as it burned their eyes as well.

After graduating from yet another school in which I became certified as a Nuclear, Biological and Chemical warfare officer, or as we used to refer to it "Bugs and Gas" and being afforded several more opportunities to spend time in the gas chamber, I had had my fill of the adventure.

One of the things we loved to do after time in the chamber, was to go to one of the community clubs and to stand at the bar. At some point someone from our unit would walk past one of us fresh from the chamber and casually slap us on the back or the shoulder. Doing so would send up a cloud of invisible gas particles that had impregnated our clothing. People at the bar would start to cough and have watery eyes and wonder what the heck was going on. The challenge was to maintain a straight face and to hold our breath until the crisis had passed.

On our most recent outing, and after completing my turn in the chamber as the Officer in Charge, I made the casual comment that there had to be something in the Army Regulations or the Geneva Convention that would make it illegal to require a Jew to voluntarily spend time in a gas chamber located in Germany. I said it in my inimitable dry wit, and for whatever reason, I was never required to attend any of the sessions scheduled during my last year in country.

That may have been a shameless but unintended attempt to manipulate the system, which was for naught, because on the last day that I was in Germany, literally leaving for the airport from yet another field exercise at Grafenwoehr, I had just stepped out of the command track when the battery's NBC NCO, SGT Jim, yelled "hey sir, catch," and tossed me something from the commander's hatch on the top of the track where I had spent so many hours during road marches. It turned out to be an activated gas canister that immediately engulfed me as soon as it hit my hands. I had one last good cry in country.

CHAPTER 32

SACRED GROVE

"Conversion is an enlarging, a deepening, and a
broadening of the undergirding base of testimony. It is the
result of revelation from God, accompanied by individual
repentance, obedience, and diligence. Any honest seeker
of truth can become converted by experiencing the mighty
change of heart and being spiritually born of God."
David A. Bednar

Despite spending an inordinate amount of time away from garrison either on field exercises or in training areas perfecting our craft, I was also attempting to spend as much time as I could reading, studying, and praying about the truthfulness of all the religious counsel received and materials I had been devouring.

Because I had for so long wondered, "which church is true?" and had engaged in a largely similar investigation of the various sects available to me, it was not hard for me to embrace the account of a young Joseph Smith retiring to the Sacred Grove and praying for guidance as to which church he should join and attend.

Already believing that God had communicated with man throughout the scriptures going back thousands of years, it was not hard for me to embrace the concept that he would continue the practice in these the latter days. If He had spoken to us in the times of Moses and Noah, why would He stop communicating with the faithful who were seeking the truth and light that accompanies being disciples of Jesus Christ?

By definition, prophecy refers to the inspired utterances of prophets. Believing that prophecy comes to the prophet by power of the Holy Ghost, I was quickly warming to the concept that I could readily find the answers to my questions by listening and heeding the words of the men who had been ordained apostles and of course the prophet of the Church of Jesus Christ of Latter Day Saints, and in my immediate corner of the vineyard, the missionaries with whom I was sporadically meeting.

The Seventh Article of Faith states that "we believe in the gift of tongues, *prophecy*, revelation, visions, healing, interpretation of tongues and so forth." When I first read that article of faith it resonated with me, and I had a partial witness that my investigation and pursuit of truth would soon bear fruit.

CHAPTER 33

CLEANLINESS

"Whenever I hear anyone, including myself, say, "I know the Book of Mormon is true," I want to exclaim, "That's nice, but it is not enough!" We need to feel, deep in "the inmost part" of our hearts, that the Book of Mormon is unequivocally the word of God. We must feel it so deeply that we would never want to live even one day without it. I might paraphrase President Brigham Young in saying, "I wish I had the voice of seven thunders to wake up the people" to the truth and power of the Book of Mormon."
Russell M. Nelson

One of the first lessons that really resonated with me as taught by the missionaries was the importance of being clean because the Spirit will not dwell where it is not clean. While this denotes spiritual and moral cleanliness as opposed to simply physical cleanliness, I was enough of a literalist that I always insured that I had washed my hands and was physically clean as well before I picked up my scriptures. I have always treated all books, but particularly my scriptures, with respect – some of my kids would even say that I border on the maniacal about avoiding cracking the spine of the book, or shudder, bending and folding pages around while reading a paperback book.

As part of a "front-line" unit with an active mission of patrolling the West German/East German/Czechoslovakian border, service with the Second Armored Cavalry Regiment also presented me with a lot of "field" time in general. Regular rotations to the major training centers in Germany, most notably Grafenwoehr [famous for Rommel's training the Afrika Korps on these very same tank trails] kept me away from home over 80% of the time. It was nearly like being deployed overseas with an occasional opportunity to check in with my family that just happened to be in country with me.

I was on one such training rotation at Grafenwoehr, supporting Level I gunnery for the Cavalry troops, essentially living out on Firing Point 621, tucked away on the Northwest corner of the reservation. As either the Fire Direction Officer or the Officer in Charge of the firing point I was pretty much stuck out there living in the muck of February, for the better part of the entire exercise.

After ten days of living out on the range, it was finally my turn to rotate to our Tent City located near main post, and again, I began to think about the significance of being clean if I was serious about reading and studying the Book of Mormon.

This thought was absolutely reverberating in my mind as my driver steered our jeep in from the range where I had just spent those ten days without seeing the insides of a shower or a mess Hall. Ten days of bathing and shaving out of my helmet and having hot chow brought out to the firing point in giant metal containers had definitely altered my priorities as we drove on the muddy tank trail heading for what in my mind had taken on the epic proportions of Nirvana. I could already feel the sting of the hot water on my skin, and was breathing in the steam that was going to envelope my body as I treated myself to a much needed extended stay under the shower as well as some real food from the burger bar.

At the same time, I realized that in addition to these creature comforts, I was going to be afforded the opportunity to crawl into my sleeping bag on my cot and read select portions of the Book of

Mormon and ponder them as I had been challenged to do by the missionaries with whom I had been meeting. While I had endeavored to read my scriptures several times while out on the range, the constant interruptions had made it pretty much an exercise in futility.

Therefore, my quandary was whether I should read or shower first. On one hand, I was afraid that by not showering and becoming [physically] clean that the Spirit might not touch my heart as I hoped it would, and on the other, I knew that the only thing keeping me upright after ten hard days in the field with long days and very short nights was the dried sweat and grime of the range; I was afraid that by showering it off that I would be too tired and too relaxed to read and that I would miss out only my opportunity to study.

I wrestled with this choice the entire way back to Camp Normandy. Upon arrival there I was still undecided and determined to say a prayer to resolve the question. I had no sooner sat down on my footlocker and cleared my mind, when I received a very distinct and powerful impression, almost a whisper that ran through my heart and mind, that it was important that I shower first, so as to strip away the dirt of the world before I began my study of the Book of Mormon. I quickly gathered up my toiletries and a clean uniform and headed for the concrete shower house about one hundred yards from my tent.

As expected, the hot water of the shower was absolutely delightful, and I literally felt the cares of the world being washed away. Ironically, I had the shower to myself, as most of the camp was attending a movie, and I stood there under the water for a long while. I had literally just turned the water off when I heard and felt a large explosive thump that seemed unnaturally close in both severity and volume. Mind you, we would often hear artillery and tank firing going on around the clock, so this was not unusual. I learned how to sleep through it! However, the severity of the impact of this round however made it feel different, and definitely up close and personal. Sensing that something might be amiss, I quickly dried and dressed myself, and headed back outside.

Imagine my surprise when I discovered that the source of the explosion had been an errant 8" artillery round from an adjacent training area that had completely missed the range impact area and had actually landed in our camp, with my tent near the center of the blast radius! Having already experienced the bunker blast and hand grenade debacles, it was somewhat surreal to walk over to the remains of my tent and to view the damage that the shrapnel from this 240 pound shell containing about 21 pounds of TNT had done to cots, sleeping bags, foot lockers, and the concrete pad on which it all rested.

Personnel from Range Control, the post medical detachment, as well as military police all converged on the area because this incident was a big deal, and probably meant that more than one or two heads were going to roll before all was said and done. While we jokingly refer to such incidents as an "oops" the potential for loss of life is great. Over the years I was party to several such incidents in various training areas in the US, fortunately always with the same result and no loss of life. In fact, I have shrapnel sitting on my desk from such an oops....

Miraculously, no one was injured, but there was a lot of personal gear and equipment destroyed by the exploding round, to include my footlocker and everything in it. I literally was left with the clean clothes on my back and the few personal items that I had taken with me to the shower house until I was sent to Quartermaster Sales the next day to have my personal uniforms and equipment replaced courtesy of Uncle Sam. It is the only time in my military career that I did not pay for my personal equipment as is required of commissioned officers.

Later that night after all the brass had left the area and my tent mates and I had found ourselves a new tent in which to spend the night, I settled into my sleeping bag on my cot, and began to say my nightly prayers. It was not until that moment that I had the stark realization that had I not heeded *and acted upon* the impression to take a shower *before* performing my study and reading, I could very well have been in my tent at the time that it was destroyed.

That revelation was enough to release a large dose of adrenaline into my system, and had I not already been lying down, I probably would have had to sit down. All four of my limbs instantly felt as solid as Jell-O and I could feel myself beginning to perspire and my respiration to quicken. It was probably a good 15 to 20 minutes that this condition persisted, and I was able to regain control of my body.

As the years have passed and I have shared that story on a limited basis, the reaction to it has largely been the same. Those with faith have been quick to point out that I was *blessed* because of my desire to be clean before I read from the scriptures. Others have said that I was *lucky* and that this experience is proof that "timing is everything." With the passage of forty years, the benefit of 20/20 hindsight, and the acquisition of knowledge during this period, I know that *luck* had nothing to do with my survival, and that it was my desire to be *obedient* as well as my heeding the prompting of the Holy Ghost that was the true basis of my avoiding harm.

Candidly, the impact of this lesson has become more and more significant to me as the years have passed. Back at the time of it happening, but for the realization in my sleeping bag of just how close I had come to potentially being killed, the spiritual lesson was somewhat lost on me, for it was another four years before I entered the waters of baptism. Maybe I am a slow learner after all.

CHAPTER 34

INTERREGNUM

"Our Heavenly Father seeks those who refuse to allow the
trivial to hinder them in their pursuit of the eternal. He
seeks those who will not allow the attraction of ease or the
traps of the adversary to distract them from the work He
has given them to perform. He seeks those whose actions
conform to their words those who say with conviction,
I am doing a great work and cannot come down."
Dieter F. Uchtdorf

By definition, an interregnum is a period when normal activities of
a government or regime or reign are suspended. Some will use the term
to denote an interval or pause. I had returned to the United States from
Germany, attended the Advance Course at Fort Sill, Oklahoma (where
the curse ended), married Susie, became an instant Dad, and moved
back to Chicago. I finished my graduate degree from the University of
Oklahoma by transferring three classes from Roosevelt University in
Chicago back to OU.

While being a weekend warrior, I was Mr. Mom during the week
and after finishing a semester of three night classes, I was prepared to

151

spend the winter and spring studying for my Comprehensive Exams and writing my Master's Thesis while enjoying the company of my daughter in the morning before her attendance at afternoon kindergarten. As a result, this did not leave a lot of creative time to pursue additional spiritual learnings.

Susie and I would engage in religious discussions sporadically, usually focusing on how we wanted to raise current and future children as well as what we wanted for ourselves from whatever faith we settled on.

Susie had entertained occasional visits from full-time missionaries before we married, but during the Interregnum we were largely left to our own devices.

Adding to the tumult of being newly married, forging bonds as a family, going to school, studying, writing, and still maintaining military proficiencies, we decided that it made sense to give up the apartment and to have a larger duplex built for ourselves.

Oh yeah, this was also when we determined that since no local municipalities were hiring people with MPA degrees, and the other types of jobs available in the civilian market were not a match for what I had done in the Army, we decided that Susie would continue to work at the American Red Cross and I would go to law school full-time. If you google the word CRAZY, our pictures come up especially when we decided that we would also add to our family by having a baby.

CHAPTER 35

IT'S A WONDERFUL LIFE

"A person may get converted in a moment, miraculously. But that is not the way it happens with most people. With most people, conversion [spiritual rebirth and the accompanying remission of sins] is a process; and it goes step by step, degree by degree, level by level, from a lower state to a higher, from grace to grace, until the time that the individual is wholly turned to the cause of righteousness. Now this means that an individual overcomes one sin today and another sin tomorrow. He perfects his life in one field now, and in another field later on. And the conversion process goes on until it is completed, until we become, literally, as the Book of Mormon says, saints of God instead of natural men."
Bruce R. McConkie

The one notable exception to my somewhat stalled religious progression during the Interregnum is that during the Christmas season of 1983 I was introduced to what would eventually become my favorite holiday movie and take on significant importance at different times of my life over the next 35 years.

Good friends of ours introduced me to Jimmy Stewart as George Bailey in the Frank Capra classic *It's a Wonderful Life*. Somehow, I had gone through twenty five years of life without ever viewing this timeless classic.

After getting over the frustration of how poor George never escapes from Bedford Falls in order to see the world and to build tall buildings and bridges, and how somehow he becomes responsible for Uncle Billy's absent-minded loss of the huge cash sum of $8,000 (equivalent to about $110,000 in 2019), and Mr. Potter's unfair enrichment by this same untraceable amount, I came to an appreciation for what a wonderful life George actually had led and why he truly was the richest man in town.

I was intrigued by the role Clarence Oddbody plays as George's somewhat hapless guardian angel. When George wishes he had never been born, Clarence shows him a timeline in which he never existed. Bedford Falls is now Pottersville, a town occupied by sleazy entertainment venues, crime, pawn shops, violence, and amoral people. With this alternative universe as a backdrop, Clarence then shows George all the lives he has touched, and how different life would be for his wife, family, wartime personnel, and community had he never been born. I found myself really wondering about, and wishing for, the presence of angels in our every day lives. My ever growing experience with my own guiding "little voice" was making me incredibly curious about this potential reality.

A big lesson for me is how we all are related to one another and that our actions seemingly cause ripples that effect countless others. For example, the *ripples* of the decision of a couple to end an unhappy marriage not only impacts their two lives, but also those of any children, grandchildren, siblings, parents, grandparents, cousins, friends, neighbors, co-workers, fellow parishioners, etc.

Who can fail to see the seeds of the Adversary in the soul of Henry Potter, as he lives a lonely and "twisted" life?

Viewers can see in great evidence the emblems of service, kindness, selflessness, love, forgiveness, and redemption.

The film is one of the most beloved in American cinema, and has become a tradition in our household, because it is not Christmas until we have viewed *It's a Wonderful Life*.

CHAPTER 36

LAW SCHOOL

"Our behavior is nothing more than a reflection
of the depth of our conversion to Jesus Christ."
Ed. J. Pinegar

In addition to a time during which I was purportedly trained to think like a lawyer, law school was also a period of great spiritual growth for me. There were so many lessons learned, practiced, and even time tested.

The first lesson I learned was of the importance attached to keeping the Sabbath day holy. This has been interpreted in many ways and were we to survey a thousand people it would not surprise me to receive nearly that many different definitions on what it means to honor the Sabbath.

After being told that my 4.0 GPA in graduate school meant *nothing* in law school, and being reminded of the fact that all of us sitting in the opening day class largely represented the top ten percent of our respective classes and now 90% of us would no longer be in the top 10%, they had my attention. We were instructed, nay commanded, that we would be required to study and prepare three hours for each credit hour of class time. Since I was taking the standard load of fourteen hours, some quick math dictated 42 hours of study time every week. Yikes, that is like a full-time job in its own right. After factoring in my train rides to and from the city that I could devote to study and prep, time after the kids went to bed, as well as requisite library time, and having committed to never use a "canned" or prepared brief, but to do all of them on my own, I was prepared to be the ideal first year law student and to dedicate myself to this regimen which out of necessity would unfortunately require me to study seven days per week. I did this for both semesters of my first year, and aside from a couple glimmers (only one of four A's handed out in Real Property to a class of 450), my first year was only mediocre at best. I was solidly in the upper middle third of the class, and that was not acceptable to me.

So, it was at the start of my second year that I said a prayer, seeking guidance, and received the impression that I needed to take control of my life. I had always been a good student. My performance in graduate school beyond a perfect GPA had included being the first student in seven years to have both my Comprehensive Exams and Thesis deemed acceptable on the first go round. So why the heck was I allowing law school to change my study habits and undermine my confidence? In my zeal to be part of the pack, I had inadvertently thrown the baby out with the bath water. I had thrown away twenty years of solid proven study habits to be something that I was not. That stopped after I received that impression.

As we were seriously talking about baptism into the church at this time, and because we had determined that if we were going to take the plunge of baptism, then we were going to do it all…. Word of Wisdom, Tithing, and keeping the Sabbath day holy. At that point I decided that I was no longer going to study on Sunday. I started "book briefing" my cases rather than laboriously writing them out long hand, I spent a lot of time underlining and highlighting cases in my text books, writing in the margins, and also working smarter by incorporating insights from the commercially available "canned briefs" into my text book margins.

and literally cut my study time in half. Ironically, my GPA rose one full point. Coincidence? I think not.

Aside from performing my Army duties on the Sundays that I had to be away, whenever I was home, we did observe the Sabbath, spending time as a family on worthy pursuits, and I found that my mind was clearer on Monday morning, and that I was less burned out overall. This day away from study allowed me to be present for my family, to attend Church, and to be a more well-rounded person. I can only draw the conclusion that the rise in GPA was a tangible reward of this obedience to make the Sabbath Day different from all the other days of the week.

During this same period, Rick and Sally, our friends from Germany who had really spent a lot of time introducing us to the Church, would make the seven hour drive to Chicago from Fort Knox, KY and spend long weekends with us. We would attend church with them, have wonderful spiritual discussions, and really feel the Spirit. Of course, they would leave, and Monday morning would dawn, and we would revert to our "heathen" ways which included the consumption of coffee by Susie, iced tea by Don, the drinking of wine from the collection that I had assembled in the time that I was home from Germany, and caffeinated soda. These were not acts of rebellion, but merely ongoing habits about which we had not really formulated any firm resolve to change.

A tender mercy for our conversion occurred when we learned that Susie was pregnant with our daughter Katie, and all of a sudden the smell of coffee brewing in the big urn at the American Red Cross office was enough to make her sick to her stomach. No longer did the stake president's wife who was a volunteer nurse in the office, have to spill out the coffee with guidance as to why it was bad for her to consume. No withdrawal, and no desire to go back to it after pregnancy. Coincidence? I think not.

CHAPTER 37

TITHING

"This is a gospel of great expectations, but God's
grace is sufficient for each of us if we remember
that there are no instant Christians."
Neal A. Maxwell

Neither my wife nor I can do anything at less than 110%. To this end, as we debated on whether we should be baptized and how we were going to live *all* of the commandments of the Church, a major concern for me as the paymaster, was how we were going to literally take 10% off the top of our meager gross household revenues to pay a full and honest tithe. It was not a lack of desire to meet this requirement, but rather the harsh reality that we were living so close to the edge, that I did not have $0.50 for bus fare in the bad weather downtown. When the bone chilling wind came off of Lake Michigan allowing Chicago to live up to its moniker of the Windy City, I was dashing between the lobbies of the various skyscrapers in an effort to spend as little time as possible exposed to the elements. There were times at the end of the month that we would have to "time" the mailings of our bills to prevent checks from clearing too closely together. Needless to say, the idea of living on only 90% of what we were currently bringing in posed a real logistical challenge, and it became a real quandary for me as I wrestled with this dilemma, wondering how other people can do it and make it look so easy.

In addition to my multiple weekends with the Army Reserves, I was also a graduate assistant to a professor down at the law school, as well as an Assistant Reference Librarian in the law school library, both of which paid *bubkus* – *or* a rather inconsequential amount of money, but money nonetheless, and more importantly, provided much needed additional law-related entries for my law vitae.

I knew the Director of the Library by sight, and could wave to him at the end of the day but had never engaged him in conversation until one fateful day when the phone on reference desk rang, and his secretary indicated that the Director wished to see me in his office. For whatever reason, the thought process that went through my mind was along the lines of "oh well, I can always get another job." I do not know why I thought this, especially since my work had always been rated as excellent to this point.

When I knocked on his office door, he was seated at his desk reviewing some documents, and when I walked in, he removed his eyeglasses and stood up, directing me to a chair located in front of his desk. He then sat down, folded his hands on his desk in front of him, and announced with a big smile, "I understand that you have some questions about tithing."

Given that Chicago is not Salt Lake City, and there is not a Mormon on every street corner, I suspect my confused look gave me away. He then laughed, and said, "let me introduce myself. When I am not here at the school as Professor Parkinson, I am actually *Bishop* Parkinson of the Naperville Stake. You are in the Schaumburg Stake. You know what a stake is, right? I understand you have some questions on tithing."

Because I had retained my Chicago roots, and was still pretty scrappy, or simply still young and stupid, I figured that a good offense would make a good defense, and with polite bravado replied, "No questions, just concerns about how I am going to pay it given that you folks don't pay me a whole lot of money, and we are living danger close in terms of finances. I am beginning to think that we may have to wait to be baptized until after I graduate in a couple of years and am gainfully employed again so that we can afford to pay tithing."

"Uh huh," he said, sitting back in his chair. "Would it help you to hear how certain University of Chicago economics professors have explained the basic premise of tithing," he asked, leaning forward toward me across the desk.

Since U of C professors were regularly bringing home *Nobel Prizes* in economics, and certainly constituted a solid authority on finances, I was definitely intrigued and standing up from my chair, I asked if I could go and retrieve my note pad so that I could take notes. He waved me back into my seat with both of his hands.

"Are you ready," he asked.

"Yes."

"Just do it, it works," he said, and donning his glasses, resumed reading the papers on his desk. Sensing that I had been dismissed, I mumbled a quiet 'thank you' and walked back to my desk. I finished my shift, clocked out, walked to the train, all the while letting *just do it, it works,* roll around in my head. I was distracted from my studies while on the train and resumed my deliberations on the drive home in the car.

When I arrived home, Susie greeted me at the door with a hug and kiss, and a genuine "how was your day?"

Having rehearsed this conversation in my head on the way home, I nonetheless blurted out, "Mormons are squirrels," and proceeded to recount the mysterious, if not darn right strange, conversation with my boss. While I was expecting Susie to agree with me, she threw me a real curve ball when she said, "He's right. Tithing is not about money. It is about faith. We just need to do it."

My brilliant retort was something along the lines of, "Oh no. *Et tu Brute?* You drank the caffeine free Kool Aid," which earned me a hairy eyeball and additional commentary about how because "we know that the Gospel is True, and we are committed to doing everything else, that we simply need to exercise our faith that we will have sufficient for our needs and pay our tithing."

This was an argument that was so illogical on its face, that I could not believe that we were even discussing it, so I opted to employ a different strategy. "Okay, so pick," I quietly said to her, lulling her into a false sense of security.

"Pick what?"

"Pick which kid is not going to eat this month, because that is the only way we can peel 10% off the top and still keep the lights on," I said somewhat triumphantly, snapping shut the trap.

Again, the hairy eyeball, and another chorus of how tithing was all about faith and not about money. While not in direct sales herself, my wife can be very persuasive when she is passionate about a subject.

Needless to say, we were baptized shortly thereafter, and dutifully wrote our tithing check before any others, and inevitably we would be the beneficiary of an extra Reserve weekend, expense money check, a tax refund, a bonus check, birthday money, or some other form of income that would in fact help us meet our needs.

Since the Lord is bound to deliver promised blessings if we are obedient, and to withhold them in the event of our disobedience, I have never had to think twice about writing our tithing check. Hearing how we are robbing God when we do not pay our tithing also made an impression on me.

When I explained the concept of tithing to my father after he had attended our baptism, he was true to form, surprised that we would willingly part with ten percent of our income, especially when money was so tight for us. I will also never forget his somewhat impassioned, and very stereotypical Jewish-accented *"gross?"* in hopes that maybe I only had to contribute a sum based on our net income.

I did make an effort to explain to him that we genuinely believed that all of our income came from God, and that we were allowed to retain 90% of it. Further, that with all the blessings that were being showered down on us, it would be selfish not to *return* the mere 10% that the Lord was directing.

Over time, he would add that he too tithes and would explain his concept as follows: "I throw all my money into the air; God can keep as much of it as he wants, but all that falls to the ground is mine."

I may have been a slow learner, but I do have a testimony that Tithing does not have anything to do with money, and everything to do with faith. We have been full and faithful tithe payers for 36 years now, and never question or regret writing the check. This experience also provided me with a great story for Tithing Settlement when I was bishop of my own ward. In hindsight, I would not have traded the experience for the world.

CHAPTER 38

THE MIRACLE OF LIFE

"A testimony is spiritual knowledge of truth obtained by
the power of the Holy Ghost. Continuing conversion is
constant devotion to the revealed truth we have received—
with a heart that is willing and for righteous reasons."
David A. Bednar

I will candidly admit that there have been times in my life where I really thought I had things figured out. I knew that hard work paid off, and that being mindful of the laws of Nature and Science was also a prerequisite to success. I had enjoyed success as a commander in the Army really by simply doing my job. Because there were so many of my peers willing to make me look good by not doing their own, it was as if I had the recipe for the secret sauce. I had mastered graduate school – no pun intended – and was slowly but surely figuring this church thing out after ten years of methodical study.

Then I was exposed to the Miracle of Birth, and everything that I thought I *knew* went out the proverbial window. While I was in control enough to be a support and birth coach to my wife, and to successfully cut the umbilical cord, that singular experience in my near twenty-six years of life taught me that I did not know squat about anything.

Any doubt that there was a higher power far superior to all of us was put to rest for me when I witnessed the birth of my daughter Katie. It was a magical experience, and when I left the hospital in the wee hours of the morning to go home and catch a few hours of sleep before taking a law school final exam later that day, I was left to ponder the miracle I had just witnessed. Yes, miracle.

I am not a medical person, but I do have great admiration for the human body. The inner workings, the complexity, the simplicity, the unexplainable aspects of what makes it all work the way it does has always fascinated me. But, watching my own child being born was enough to put me over the moon.

The odds of having a normal healthy baby are quite astronomical because of the *billions* of permutations that are possible. One zig instead of a zag, one strand of DNA going slightly askew, and you could end up with something sporting a tail. Yet, every day, these little miracles join us, capture our hearts, and forever change our lives.

So, while it sounds a bit trite, I can honestly say that the birth of each of my children, and subsequently, my grandchildren, has been a quiet reinforcement for me that God lives, and that we are in fact his spirit children. I find great reassurance in this knowledge and cannot really get my arms around how people can find peace of mind in *not* believing.

TAKING THE PLUNGE

"It is not an easy thing to become a member of this
Church. In most cases it involves setting aside old
habits, leaving old friends and associations, and stepping
into a new society which is different and somewhat
demanding. With the ever-increasing number of
converts, we must make an increasingly substantial
effort to assist them as they find their way. Every one
of them needs three things: a friend, a responsibility,
and nurturing with 'the good word of God.' It is our
duty and opportunity to provide these things."
Gordon B. Hinckley

So the baby is nearly two months old, the fall term of law school has
resumed, the older kids are back to school, and we are developing a new
normal as Susie resumed working, I was still in the Reserves, juggling
the two part-time jobs, and now in the afternoons as much as possible,
playing Mr. Mom to three kids as well as starting dinner.

We were still living in our duplex, had just fed and bedded the baby,
and it was nearly 11:00 on Sunday night, with the alarm set for 0500

so that I could catch my train downtown and start the week anew. I had just switched the lights out when a small still voice on the other side of the waterbed quietly said, "would it be alright with you if I am baptized?"

The lights went back on, and *three* hours later, went off with the decision made that we would both be baptized as soon as possible. The timing of this decision may have had something to do with the fact that good friends Rick and Sally had driven the seven hours from Fort Knox and spent that weekend with us, and what we didn't know, had pretty much agreed on the long drive home that while they would remain our friends, they were done trying to be missionaries with us. Sally cried most of the way home to Fort Knox because clearly, we were *progators,* a term that full-time missionaries used to label people as professional investigators, i.e. those who know the truth but will not enter the waters of baptism.

When we called them to invite them to come back to Chicago for another weekend soon, they were reticent to making the trip...until they heard the purpose. The whoops were audible all the way from Kentucky without the phone.

Since it was a "double baptism" Rick explained that in their Stake typically the husband is baptized first, confirmed "poolside," ordained a priest in the Aaronic priesthood, and then baptizes his wife. I was pretty stoked about that until our Stake President said not only no, but heck no. I was thrown by this because if the Church is the Church, and true everywhere, why would the "rules" vary so much from congregation to congregation? This issue troubled me enough that I nearly pulled the plug on being baptized. I can remember even being angry about it until it was pointed out to me that anger had no place in this decision <u>and</u> that Satan would be on high alert and doing anything possible to prevent us from being baptized to include filling our heads with questions, doubts, challenges, as well as temptations. I found this warning to be quite sobering, and we agreed to be place ourselves on high alert for any of Satan's further high jinx.

Our economic circumstances had not improved, especially since we were back into Pampers and baby formula, and I still found myself walking to school from the train station downtown. On days of rain or inclement weather I usually wore my trusty Dingo cowboy boots with a pair of white tube socks inside them. When I was not wearing them, they would typically sit on the floor of our closet directly under the pants that hung from the clothes rod.

A rainy Monday prompted me to grab the trusty Dingos and when I inserted my foot into the boot, and started walking, there was clearly something in the boot. When I removed it and held it upside down, out fell a shiny new dime. I did not think anything of it, put on the boot and off to the train I went. When the very same thing happened two days later, I realized that this was beyond coincidence because I never have loose change in my pants pocket because to this day I carry a change pouch, a habit I developed in Germany because the mix of US and German coins would wear holes in my pockets.

So, what is the big deal about loose dimes? Well, back in the day when the missionaries used standardized lessons with which to teach investigators, the picture card used in the lesson on tithing depicted nine dimes lined in a row, with a tenth dime, representing the tithe, falling aside. When I found a *third* dime in my boot three days later, it gave me pause to reconsider the entire struggle I was having about how logistically difficult tithing was going to be for us until I had graduated from school.

When we discussed this with Rick and Sally and with one another, we decided that this was Satan's last ditch effort to dissuade me from doing what I knew was the correct thing to do. We had met the challenge and overcome it.

That might have made a good ending to this chapter but for the fact that on the day of our baptism the missionaries realized that they had not completed all of the paperwork for Susie. When they called her into the foyer at church, and sat down in one of the sofas in order to complete the paperwork, she stood in front of them and looked down, and right up against the toe of her dress shoe was...you guessed it... another dime. It so spooked her that she picked it up and begged them to take it away. They naturally thought she was losing her mind because they were not privy to what had transpired in our closet over the past week. When we later shared that story with them, they in their natural exuberance, thought it was cool. Rest assured, that was not our reaction.

We were nonetheless baptized, with Rick doing the honors for both of us.

CHAPTER 40

THE HOSANNA SHOUT

"You know you are becoming converted when you
start to live the higher law, the gospel of Jesus Christ.
You live the spirit of the law as well as the letter of the
law. You live the gospel in all aspects of your life."
Dieter F. Uchtdorf

In the spring of 1985, a matter of only six months or so since we had
been baptized, the Chicago, Illinois temple was dedicated. Presiding at
the ceremony was President Gordon B. Hinckley of the First Presidency.
Our oldest had also been baptized in the interim, and he too was able
to attend the dedication.

While we did not fully grasp the significance of having a temple
in our midst and how important this temple in particular would be to
our eternal progression, we were content to "go with the flow" and to
attend one of the dedicatory sessions.

Being a student of both history and tradition, I was intrigued by,
and thoroughly enjoyed, the entire process. The dedication of a temple
is in fact an incredibly significant event, and up until recently typically

represented great sacrifice by the members who would thereafter be attending the temple.

Historically, the Kirtland, Ohio, Nauvoo, Illinois, and early Utah temples like St. George, Logan, Manti, and Salt Lake City were built by the members themselves in the form of contributed funds, materials, and labor. While we had not had to do any of this, I can still remember the feeling I had as we entered the temple.

At the conclusion of the ceremony we all participated in the traditional Hosanna Shout, following the same tradition established by the Prophet Joseph Smith at the dedication of the Kirtland Temple. While standing, ordinarily facing East, and waving white handkerchiefs with each word or phrase of praise, the united congregation says with a firm voice:

> *Hosanna, Hosanna, Hosanna,*
> *To God and the Lamb;*
> *Hosanna, Hosanna, Hosanna,*
> *To God and the Lamb;*
> *Hosanna, Hosanna, Hosanna,*
> *To God and the Lamb;*
> *Amen, Amen, Amen!*

While that rite was a little mystifying to me, what I do remember vividly from that day was when President Hinckley passed us, and we were able to shake his hand. While he was a mortal man just like me, I could *feel* that he was in fact a man of God and I had a very definitive witness that he would someday become our prophet and President of the Church of Jesus Christ of Latter Day Saints. The man emanated love for us, and I experienced feelings of warmth, comfort, and belonging. I was where I was supposed to be, progressing on the path.

CHAPTER 41

ORDINATION

"People can change. They can put behind them
bad habits. They can repent from transgressions.
They can bear the priesthood worthily. And
they can serve the Lord diligently."
Thomas S. Monson

It was with great anticipation that I was ordained to the office of Elder within the Melchizedek Priesthood. The Holy Priesthood after the Order of the Son of God is called the Melchizedek Priesthood to avoid using the name of Deity too often. The priesthood is an everlasting precept and existed with God in the pre-existence and will forever be part of eternity. The priesthood is designed to enable men to gain exaltation in the highest Heaven of eternity. Through this priesthood men become joint-heirs with Christ, receiving and possessing the fulness of the Father's kingdom.

As pertaining to man's existence on this earth, priesthood is the power and authority of God delegated to man on earth to act in all things for the salvation of men. It is the power by which the gospel is preached and by which the ordinances of salvation are performed so that they will be binding on earth and in heaven.

The concept of being ordained and subsequently imbued with this power and authority to act in God's name was simultaneously unique and overwhelming to me. The very idea that I would be able to be the *voice* through which blessings could be pronounced upon the faithful was humbling and a bit frightful. My ability to be this conduit was predicated upon my own faithfulness and obedience. I recognized the great responsibility that accompanied my accepting this priesthood by an oath and covenant.

It was easy for me to relate the oath and covenant of the Priesthood with the same oath and solemn promise that ended with "So help me God," when I received my commission in the Army. I have always regarded both of these solemn undertakings as two of the greatest decisions of my life. To this day, my line of Priesthood authority hangs on the wall of my study immediately above my commission as an Army officer with my charge as a grandfather representing the third element of this valued troika.

I remember the moment that I was ordained and received the power and authority of the priesthood. I felt the power course through my body and did not take it for granted. I have endeavored never to be complacent or to not be worthy to exercise this power and authority for the good of others by the laying on of hands. I have appreciated every opportunity to lay hands upon my children in times of need, at the start of school years, when they were sick, or seeking spiritual guidance. I am genuinely grateful for every opportunity through which I have been allowed to magnify my priesthood. I am always saddened when men *choose* not to exercise this authority for their own family members as well as those around them.

It always warms my heart to see young boys exercise the authority they have through the Aaronic Priesthood also known as the preparatory priesthood. I have never been able to bring myself to refer to it as the lesser priesthood, especially since it is through the Aaronic Priesthood that I was ordained a Bishop. The priesthood is about love, service, and the choice to follow God.

CHAPTER 42

YOU ARE SPECIAL

"Adult converts to the Church often have a
better understanding of this transformation
because they feel the contrast as they come out
of the world into the kingdom of God."
Robert D. Hales ""

It was shortly after we had joined the church and I was attending a Fast and Testimony Meeting which I rarely was able to do because the first weekend of every month was typically my regularly scheduled Army Reserve weekend. As a result, when I did attend church, I tried to pay close attention to what other people said when they bore their own testimonies, and I would mentally compare it to my own.

I can remember attending church one weekend with Rick and Sally before we were baptized when Sally stood up and let everyone know that she had known Susie in the pre-existence. That was enough to leave both of us scratching our heads because the implications of it were enormous as we continued our own search for the truth.

On one occasion after I had mustered the courage to bear my

testimony, I had left the stand and resumed my seat in the congregation and at the conclusion of the meeting I was in the process of picking up Cheerios off the bench and the floor when this older member of our congregation shuffled up to the bench behind me and tapped me on the shoulder. When I stood up, she thrust out both of her hands. When I offered my right hand, she grabbed it in both of hers and proceeded to tell me that my testimony had been wonderful and had really touched her heart. Well, I had been in the Church long enough to know that faint praise for all is praise for no one. I also had already figured out that people are not going to seek you out and tell you, "wow, that was really lame," or "boy, I could barely keep my eyes open during your talk," even if that is the truth. Further, that civility more or less required us to say things like, "good talk," or "I enjoyed your testimony," so the cynical Chicago attorney in training prompted me to say a simple "thank you," and attempt to retrieve my hand. No such luck.

"You are so special," she began, and with a bit of false modesty, I replied that I could get her several counter opinions. I then realized that she had more to say to me.

"You are so special," she began again, and then proceeded to tell me that as a convert to the Church, I was indeed special because unlike her, I had not "had my testimony spoon-fed to me from the time I was knee-high to a grasshopper." She then let me know that she has always been impressed by converts, especially adults from other faiths, who have the courage to question what they have always known and even more courage to embrace something new. As she continued to talk, she was making me feel differently about myself.

"You discovered your testimony all on your own, in a very scary world. My mother used to take me to the pulpit and whisper my testimony to me in my ear. I didn't see anyone whispering in your ear," she said with a nod of her head in affirmation. With that, she patted my hand, released it, and shuffled off to Sunday School.

Over the years I have thought about that exchange and wish I had been more profuse in my thanks to her. I have repeated her words and the sentiment attached to them to other converts that I have encountered, especially when I had the opportunity to interview them in my office as bishop.

In essence we are all converts and have to develop our own testimonies. I have worked with missionaries assigned to our ward who found their testimonies while serving as a missionary. I have known other people who have discovered or "solidified" their testimony after some life-altering event.

Being a disciple of Jesus Christ requires more than just following the tenets of the Church; it requires us to live the Gospel. It is more than just "following the rules" but embracing the covenants we make and revering the ordinances in which we participate.

While I am sometimes jealous of my children and grandchildren for having had the benefit of growing up in the Church, more and more with the passage of time, I am grateful for my conversion and the capacity I have to compare and contrast life with and without the church *and the Gospel*.

Ironically, not too long ago, one of our children asked us what it was like to live without the Church and prompted my wife and I to both answer the question with as much detail as possible. I knew he was looking for answers with depth, and well past the typical discussion of what it is like to watch R-rated movies, drink alcohol and caffeine, and to have a more cavalier attitude towards life. Answering him required me to really pause and take stock of how different my life is today than it was thirty five or forty years ago, and why I am so much better off because of the decision I made to be baptized and to become a disciple of Jesus Christ.

The big takeaway from that discussion for me is that being a faithful member of the Church of Jesus Christ of Latter Day Saints goes well beyond adhering to the rules; it is about embracing a life style that if adhered to on a daily basis in all aspects of our life affords us the opportunity to claim a great inheritance that results in our living once again with our Heavenly Father.

This discussion also afforded me the opportunity to recount for him my experience with that dear sister so many years ago, and why while difficult at times, the process of conversion had been well worth the effort. It also made me feel good about myself and to realize that she had been correct in her assessment: I am special.

CHAPTER 43

SEALING

"Faith is like spiritual oxygen. As we allow faith to freely
flow within us, it awakens and enlivens our spiritual
senses. It breathes life into our very souls. As faith flows,
we become sensitively attuned to the whisperings of the
Spirit. Our minds are enlightened, our spiritual pulse
quickens, our hearts are touched.
Faith fuels hope. Our perspective changes; our vision
becomes clearer. We begin to look for the best, not the
worst, in life and in others. We gain a deeper sense of life's
purpose and meaning. Despair gives way to joy."
David S. Baxter

A year to the day after we were baptized, we were in the temple to
receive our endowments and to be sealed to one another and to Katie.
We arrived at the temple at 4:30 in the afternoon, and Katie went down
to the nursery. Approximately four hours later she was brought up to the
sealing room dressed in white and was very calm. Even though Katie
had been a great baby, very even tempered, and pretty flexible in terms

of schedule, at not quite fifteen months of age, we didn't know what to expect after her time in the nursery, being well passed her bedtime, etc.

While that was a momentous day for us individually, as a couple, and of course as a family, much to my wife's dismay, the thing that I remember most about the day is the look of peace, serenity, *and complete knowledge* of what we were doing there under the authority of the priesthood that was present in Katie's big brown eyes. I will remember until the day I die the look of assurance and confidence that she flashed me when they brought her into the room and quietly set her down on the altar between us.

So many times, since that night I have wished that she had the power of speech and the ability to convey what she was thinking as we were united for time and eternity. I have every confidence that she knew *exactly* what we were doing, and probably had an even *greater* understanding of what we were doing because her memories of the pre-existence were probably still present in her mind. Oh, the stories she could have conveyed and the education and insights she could have imparted to all of us in that room that night.

To this end, I often wonder what it would be like if we could have, if only for an instant, a momentary glance of our life in the pre-existence. How much better equipped would we be for handling the trials and tribulations of our mortal existence? How much further could we advance the work? How much better as people would we be during our probationary period in mortality? I suspect that the very reason we do forget about life in the pre-existence is to "wipe the slate clean" and to make this mortal probationary period the test of agency and acquisition of knowledge that is required of us.

Nonetheless, the look in Katie's eyes that night in the temple was a source of great reassurance to me that we were definitely on the correct path, and I felt the "concrete" of my testimony set a little firmer after that night.

CHAPTER 44

PATRIARCHAL BLESSING

"Your patriarchal blessing, with its declaration of
lineage, will link you to these fathers and be more
meaningful to you. Your love and gratitude for your
ancestors will increase. Your testimony of and conversion
to the Savior will become deep and abiding."
David A. Bednar

The Scriptures have always been a source of mystery and intimidation
to me. Even though I have been an avid and voracious reader from the
time I was young and first started school, I have never *mastered* the
scriptures like so many people that I know and admire. In this regard I
am genuinely envious of all of my children because of their exposure to
them while growing up in Primary, four years of intense study during
High School while attending early morning Seminary, Institute classes
in college, and in the case of our sons, the total immersion into the
scriptures and the Gospel during two years of missionary service.

To this day, I marvel at people who can readily recall and quote
passages of scripture that are germane to the discussion or issue at

hand. While I made a commitment to myself to become as versed in the scriptures as possible, and have read all four of the standard works (the Bible -- Old Testament and New Testament, Book of Mormon, Doctrine and Covenants, and Pearl of Great Price) several times each over the years, and on occasion can recollect a pertinent story or actual passage of scripture, I largely remain a non-scriptorian of little repute.

When I was ordained and set apart as a bishop I was directed to "remain close to scriptures, most notably those of the latter day prophets as contained in General Conference and other latter day utterances," and this I have done. I was pleasantly surprised at how empowered I was with a command of this direction from our latter day prophets, especially while serving as a bishop.

For a long time, I was jealous of those to whom the scriptures spoke to on an individual basis, and that was the beauty of receiving our personal patriarchal blessings at the hand of our stake's patriarch.

We believe that nearly every member of the Church is a literal descendant of Jacob who gave patriarchal blessings to his twelve sons, sharing what would happen to them and their posterity if they remained faithful and obedient. From the time I heard of this I was excited at the prospect of receiving a revelation that could serve as a personal road map for me as to what direction my life could take, predicated on my own worthiness.

In the 1950's the First Presidency explained that "Patriarchal blessings contemplate an inspired declaration of the lineage of the recipient, and also where so moved upon by the Spirit, an inspired and prophetic statement of the life mission of the recipient, together with such blessings, cautions, and admonitions as the patriarch may be prompted to give for the accomplishment of such life's mission., it being always made clear that the realization of all promised blessings is conditioned upon faithfulness to the gospel of our Lord, whose servant the patriarch is. All such blessings are recorded and generally only one such blessing should be adequate for each person's life."

We believe that these personal revelations are private and to be shared with only immediate family. I have consulted mine many times over the years, and while it is not intended to serve as a roadmap or provide inflexible direction or serve as a checklist, it has provided me with guidance, general direction, and inspiration. For it to do anything more would surely remove our agency from this life. I have also learned to think of it as a great jewel or treasure, and like the luster of a gem it can change in appearance depending on the angle with which I gaze at it.

CHAPTER 45

PRIESTHOOD MIRACLE

"As you ponder how to serve, consider where
you can best participate in the steps that must
unfold for a family or an individual to receive
enduring conversion and full gospel blessings."
Richard G. Scott

Miracles. By definition are those events which are beyond the power of any presently known physical power to produce. They are occurrences which deviate from the known laws of nature and which transcend our knowledge of these laws. A surgeon who professes to having had his hands guided during surgery in a manner that he knows he has never been able to perform in the past – that would be a miracle.

Extrapolating that idea would mean that one hundred fifty years ago jet airplanes would have to have been considered a miracle because they defied the existing knowledge of Man at the time because manned flight was an occurrence that was wholly beyond the power of man to perform or to control.

I do not know too many people who do not appreciate the concept of miracles and find themselves uplifted by movies that build on this as a theme. For most people who are in distress and seeking divine intervention, miracles become a viable alternative to their present situation. Knowing what I know now, I feel that miracles are a part of our world, but most importantly, are predicated upon the faith of those seeking the miracle, as well as how that miracle "fits into" the master plan. I do not believe that there is anything random about them.

I know that there was nothing random associated with my education and growth as a priesthood holder and new convert to the Church of Jesus Christ of Latter Day Saints. I have no doubt that the Lord provided the very people I needed at various stages of my journey along the path. I can almost visualize each of them as if their faces on mile markers along the highway. For this I am eternally grateful.

We determined to spend Christmas 1985 with our friends Carl and Becky out in Sycamore, IL, a tiny hamlet, but the county seat with a regal old courthouse that dates from the 1920s. We headed out there on Saturday, Christmas Eve, filled with anticipation and grateful for the short break from law school before beginning the studying associated with preparing for the two-day bar examination.

When we arrived, Carl was actually putting on a suit which was a shock to me, and in a very serious tone announced that *we* had to go and administer to a sister in his ward for whom he had responsibility. I quickly changed my clothes and off we went. It should be noted that while I was a newly ordained elder, and had given a few father's blessings to my children, I had never been in a position to administer to a sick person.

On the way over in the car, Carl and I reviewed the proper procedure for anointing a person with oil that has been consecrated and set apart for the healing of the sick, as well as the procedure for sealing this anointing as well as the proper process of pronouncing the blessing as if the Lord was saying it. It was at that moment that I realized that I was going to be responsible for one of these two actions and was a bit nervous at the prospect. I also assumed that because of their relationship that I would be asked to anoint, and that Carl would be the voice of the blessing.

We knocked at the front door of this small but well maintained older house, and a young boy invited us into the warm and brightly lit home. The woman we were there to administer to was reclined in a large chair with several blankets over her large heavy bathrobe. With one look at her flushed face and glistening forehead it was quickly evident to me that this woman was sick. As she coughed, I could *feel* the rumble of her bronchial spasms in my own lungs. This woman was really sick.

Introductions were made, and I quickly learned that she was a single mom of two young children and worked as a registered nurse in the local hospital Emergency Room. My thought was that was where she belonged. Almost as if he could read my mind, Carl informed me that Mary had been seen by a doctor at the hospital who had wanted to admit her for treatment, and but for a total lack of family in the area and someone to take care of her children, as well as the upcoming holiday, she would probably be in the hospital being treated for her double pneumonia. After a few moments of small talk, we prepared to administer to Mary.

My heart nearly stopped when Carl asked Mary who she would prefer to anoint her and which to bless her, and she indicated that she would like me to be the voice of the blessing. Carl smiled, and to this day I wonder if he had not set that up ahead of our arrival. Nonetheless, he anointed her, and then it was time for the two of us to administer to her. I was confident on what to say in terms of the sealing but was at a complete loss as to what would happen after that was completed. It is one of the few times that I was conscious of the words coming out of my mouth and can remember telling/blessing her with "immediate relief and restoration of her health." Since that is subject to interpretation, I pretty much determined that it probably meant over the course of antibiotic treatment and a week or better of bedrest. When we were finished, we shook hands with her, exchanged Christmas wishes, and said goodbye.

Our Christmas eve with Carl and Becky and their son was a lot of fun, and after watching *It's a Wonderful Life* we drove home in a white-knuckle blizzard, stuffed some stockings, and went to bed.

The next morning, we had enjoyed presents, stockings, and a large breakfast feast when the phone rang with an incredible phone call from Carl and his family.

Apparently about an hour before, their doorbell had rung, and Carl's son answered the door and quickly returned to the living room with Mary and her two boys in tow. Mary looked like a new person. No fever, color in her cheeks, and both of her lungs clear of congestion. At first, they had all wondered if she was not a healthy twin sister of the person we had visited yesterday, but it was Mary.

Mary went on to recount how almost immediately after we left, she began to feel a change in her body. Within a couple of hours her fever broke, and the congestion in her chest began to noticeably clear. By the time she went to bed after her own Christmas preparations she was feeling better than she had felt in ten days and had a restful night's sleep. When her boys woke her early the next morning, her cough was gone, and she felt like her old self, and *knew* that it was the result of the priesthood blessing that we had administered the previous afternoon.

I was stunned to hear this account. Absolutely stunned. Having had pneumonia several times as a child, and having observed her obvious discomfort less than twenty four hours before, I knew that she rightfully should have been in the hospital and that her current condition *was* miraculous, but was it a miracle? Carl and Becky could not have been more pleased, and Susie looked at me quizzically because Mary's condition certainly did not conform with what we had reported the night before upon returning from her house.

Mary had felt so much better after getting up and celebrating with her children that she had baked Christmas cookies as thanks to us, and quickly departed to make some additional deliveries.

Needless to say, the four of us had a very animated discussion. I should note that Becky had visited Mary two days before and in her capacity as a nurse had confirmed the diagnosis, so it was not a fluke or misdiagnosis. Carl was so excited at the outcome and was about to bust a button or two off of his vest and had near-paternal pride in my "first blessing effort."

Clearly this woman was up and about and had recovered in less than eighteen hours from what I would have said was one of the worst cases of double pneumonia that I had ever observed. Coincidence? Clearly not. Did Carl and I heal her? No. It was a miracle based on the faith of all those who participated in that blessing. This experience certainly became some sophisticated tutelage, a great and dramatic testimony builder, and example of faith to me and greatly strengthened my testimony.

A few months later on a Sunday afternoon, my father called me and in a very firm and somber voice informed me that he had gone to the doctor two days before and had failed a stress test. The doctor was concerned enough that he had ordered an angiogram for Monday, and if the results were not to his liking, they could be proceeding to an angioplasty procedure on the spot. I was more dumbfounded because our family did not have a history of heart issues and while my father was not an athlete, he was still passing his Army Physical Fitness Test (APFT) each year, at least on paper....

He then shocked me by inviting me and my "friend" (home teaching companion) to come to his house and to give him a blessing and to "heal him." While I was more than happy to do so, I explained to him that we did not have the "power" to heal him, but that any restorative blessing would be predicated on his faith as much if not more than on ours. He was amenable to that, and I immediately called my companion Jon, and we ventured over to my father's house.

In addition to being friends and neighbors, Jon and his wife Tammy had been our escorts in the temple and Jon and I would later serve in the Elders Quorum Presidency together. I also knew that Jon would either insist or persuade my father that I should be the voice of the blessing, and this disturbed me. I did not want to be the voice of doom and forever have to live with an undesired outcome. When I expressed this sentiment to Jon, he looked me square in the eye, and said, "where's your faith Brother? It's going to be fine."

As expected, and after a knowing smile and nod of confidence from Jon, my father was delighted with the idea of my being the voice of the blessing. Jon proceeded to anoint him, and I sealed the anointing and pronounced a blessing that directed that "his body would rebuke the current affliction and heal itself." Hearing that, my father was convinced that we had in fact healed him, and he was looking forward to seeing the doctor the next day.

I went home as nervous as the proverbial cat on a hot tin roof, because if he had not been healed it would give rise to all sorts of recriminations about "my" church and the priesthood. Recognizing that the procedure involved was routine anyway, I was prepared to work from the assumption that the "repudiation and healing" could be interpreted as requiring the necessary surgical procedure.

The next day my bar exam study was interrupted by my father. He had just left the doctor's office with a completely clean bill of health. The angiogram had proven normal, and the doctor had dismissed any further talk of surgery and was "frankly mystified by the difference in test results between Friday and Monday." I do not recall if my father shared with him that he had been healed by the power of the priesthood, but would forever after that, tell anyone interested, that I had healed him. No matter how many times I told him that I had nothing to do with it other than being the *conduit* between Heaven and his body, he remained convinced that his "boychick" had healed him. More *nachas*.

Coincidence? I say not. While false positives and false negatives can impact any number of tests, from what I later learned, the doctor was convinced enough that my father's condition warranted the procedure that they had already scheduled it for later Monday morning. Given that as evidence, I do not think it was a fluke or misdiagnosis on Friday that created this opportunity for me to instruct my father through priesthood action, why my faith was so important to me.

That was nearly thirty five years ago, and I remember it as if it were only yesterday. Again, Jon's is another face on the milestone marker along my journey's path.

In a later chapter I will share perhaps the greatest miracle with which I have ever been associated, the story of our grandson Walter.

CHAPTER 46

THE BAR EXAM

"Follow the example of Joseph Smith and the pattern
of the Restoration. Turn to the scriptures. Kneel in
prayer. Ask in faith. Listen to the Holy Ghost."
Robert D. Hales

We all suffer from those recurring nightmares where we are late for class, forgot our homework, or cannot find a classroom or location. During my life, there have been many such nightmares that still plague my sleep to this day.

Unless they are lying, I suspect that every attorney who has ever sat for the state Bar Examination that this too must be one of their nightmares. After four years of undergraduate work and degree, and three years of law school and degree, there is still one more hurdle that threatens to prevent an attorney at law wannabee from practicing law: the bar exam. Two days in duration, it is one day of 200 multiple choice questions on a core of five subjects, followed by a second day of sixteen essay questions drawn from any of thirty-two topics, some of which the examinee may or may not have had the opportunity to study while in school. That certainly seems prudent.

The exam is given only twice a year, and the results take approximately 2.5 months to be reported. If one fails either part of the exam, it is a no-go, and one has to wait until the next semi-annual test offering to take the entire exam anew.

There are now several bar review courses that the attorney-in-waiting can sit through in addition to the intense independent study that is required. Making the study (cramming) even more stressful is considering that job offers can be withdrawn in the event the exam is not passed. That ugly fact coupled with the prospect of having to endure another cycle of study and testing makes viewing the negative a horrible alternative. In some states the pass rate is as low as 38% which means that there is a lot of pressure attached to this final hurdle.

My heretofore written about personal fear of failure, instilled in me by my father as I progressed through the Boy Wonder stage, was absolutely raging, as I had to contemplate this added bit of humiliation if lightning were to strike. Add to that the fact that Susie was also pregnant with our fourth child, and the pressure was slightly off the scale for me to pass the exam and go to work! These are all thoughts that attacked me prior to, and immediately after, taking the bar exam.

I was studying morning, noon, and night. I had too much riding on this blasted exam to leave anything to chance. If I was not studying, I felt guilty and that I was potentially letting my family down. I know that I was heaping a whole lot of pressure on myself, but I just assumed it went with the territory. Finally, amid all my final preparations to take the exam that someone suggested that I receive a priesthood blessing. At first, I rejected the idea because I honestly still believed that these blessings were more intended for people who were ill or battling *real* issues. I was quickly set straight on this and was wisely taught that the ability to both give and receive these blessings was in itself a blessing from our Heavenly Father. From that experience I became converted to the idea of always providing blessings to my children at the beginning of each school year, before big exams, and any other time that they requested one. It is the aspect of my church membership and worthiness as a priesthood holder of which I am most proud and grateful.

I do not remember who I asked for the blessing but was somewhat nervous at the ideas of what the blessing could say to me. It might just be the Lord laughing at me and preparing me for failure. Nonetheless I did receive a priesthood blessing prior to going downtown to sit for the first day of the exam. The blessing promised me that my "mind would be clear and active, and that I would be able to recall the things that I had learned and that I would be able to put forth my best efforts...." Not exactly a promise of success or that I would pass the exam, but since I had studied hard, attended the bar review class without fail, and took to heart everything our instructors said to do in terms of preparation, it filled me with more confidence and made me feel better about my chances of taming this beast. Sleeping and eating in the days leading up to the examination simply did not occur, and so by the conclusion of the second day of testing my body was in outright rebellion. Coming home on that second day I realized that the marathon was over...at least for now. I felt like I had done well, but with essay questions and answers it all depends on the perspective of the reviewer.

The days turned to weeks, and the weeks slowly and agonizingly into a couple of months. I continued my preparation to hang out my own shingle as a sole practitioner, and whenever I thought about the potential of failure, after my stomach would literally do the same flips it would do as if I were on a rollercoaster, I would take a deep breath, remember words of the blessing, say yet another prayer, and wish that I was still a drinking man... not really.

I remember the day that the examination results arrived. Susie was at work, the older kids were at school, the baby was napping, and I was at home making preparations for opening my open law office (we were still thinking positive if for no other reason than the alternative was too horrible to contemplate) when I saw the mailman fill the community box with everyone's mail. Having been disappointed every day for the last two weeks, I had little confidence that we would ever see the results.

Sure enough, the letter with the return address of *Attorney Registration and Disciplinary Commission* (ARDC), the same addressee that would strike fear in the heart of every Illinois attorney for the rest of their career even when simply receiving their annual license renewal (it got me every time), was sitting there in the box along with a couple of bills. I felt my pulse quicken, and my heart started pounding as if I had just completed a half-marathon. My face felt two sizes too big for the skin, and feeling a bit light headed and even a bit queasy, I walked into the house, took my pulse to find that my heart was beating 165 times a minute, and I called Susie at the office.

"They're here," was all I could manage to croak out between the lump in my throat and a mouth that had lost every vestige of moisture. "Well?" she asked. "I don't know, I haven't opened them yet." "So, open them!" she nearly screamed.

I nearly passed out with the first word: "Congratulations." I slowly slid down the wall and sat on the floor. I quickly read the entire letter aloud as it informed me that I would be sworn in at McCormick Place, down in Chicago, with all the other mopes who had successfully negotiated this minefield, approximately three days before our baby was born, about a month from that day.

Interestingly enough, my emotions at that moment were not those of elation but rather simply relief. I had done it! It was not a matter of my having conquered the beast, but rather I had survived a kill or be killed situation. I could get rid of the bar exam manuals, notebooks full of notes, and crib sheets, and memory aids because the nightmare was over. Though in reality, I kept them all in a box for many years until safely into my new career.

The day of the bar admission ceremony and *major nachas* quickly arrived, and Susie was joined by my dad and my grandmother in the audience. As I recall, I heard "my son the lawyer....," more than a few times that day.

Even though I have not practiced law for over twenty years, and am very content with my chosen career, one of my recurring nightmares has me in law school for the second time, just for fun this time. In the course of the dream I will be late for class, usually because the elevators between the multiple linked buildings don't stop on all floors AND because I can't remember where the class is supposed to take place, and to complete the trifecta, I have not prepared my briefs for class. At this point I can usually remind myself that I have already passed the bar exam and I can walk away from this boondoggle anytime I want. Freud would have a field day with that one!

The priesthood blessing that I received did not promise me that I would pass the exam but that I would be able to recall all that I had learned, and squarely put the responsibility for success on my shoulders. In the years that followed, I often thought about that and realized that I could not have asked for anything more.

CHAPTER 47

THE TEMPLE

"We become converted and spiritually self-reliant as
we prayerfully live our covenants—through worthily
partaking of the sacrament, being worthy of a temple
recommend, and sacrificing to serve others."
Robert D. Hales

When people ask me where I learned the Gospel, I am quick to respond, "in the Temple." For the countless number of members who did not have the good fortune as we did to have a temple literally twenty minutes away, I now understand why they were willing to make the countless stories of sacrifice we have heard about.

The Temple has been the cornerstone of our faith, and because of our devotion to the temple, our children were able to feel it as well. For over thirteen years I worked at the Chicago Temple every Thursday evening. But for our moving to Cincinnati, this service would probably have continued. At various stages during this tenure of service the temple was a classroom, a vineyard of labor, and ultimately a sanctuary for me.

Don Levin

Walking into that building I came to fully appreciate how much it *is* the Lord's House, and that the grounds of the temple are indeed hallowed. So many times, over the years when I have ventured to the temple I have found answers to questions as to what to do in my personal life, professional career, and while serving as a bishop and common judge in Israel.

Entering the temple was indeed an opportunity to shed the affairs of the world and to be as close to Heaven as one can be while on the Earth. It was in the temple that I learned so much about the Gospel, and our purpose in this mortal life.

On more than one occasion when the temple was either closed because of maintenance, weather, or it was a holiday, it would genuinely freak out the kids to have us home on a Thursday evening. It simply did not feel right to me if I was anywhere else on a Thursday night.

I have had many wonderful spiritual experiences that I cannot write about in the context of this work, but it was in the walls of the temple that I worked on increasing my testimony and conversion. I know that being gone every Thursday night was sometimes a hardship on the family but by the same token, it was through this effort that our children garnered an appreciation about the importance of the temple in our lives and why it is so important to always be worthy of a temple recommend.

For me, the beauty of the Gospel rests in its simplicity. It is nothing short of elegant in the straightforward manner in which it is constructed around discipleship of Jesus Christ. It was in the temple that I could fully embrace this aspect of the Gospel and incorporate it as an integral part of my life. It was also wonderful to share this aspect of th Gospel with Susie, who also worked in the temple for many years.

CHAPTER 48

AND BABY MAKES SEVEN

"Faith in the Lord is trust in the Lord. We cannot have true
faith in the Lord without also having complete trust in the
Lord's will and in the Lord's timing. As a result, no matter
how strong our faith is, it cannot produce a result contrary
to the will of Him in whom we have faith. Remember
that when your prayers do not seem to be answered in the
way or at the time you desire. The exercise of faith in the
Lord Jesus Christ is always subject to the order of heaven,
to the goodness and will and wisdom and timing of the
Lord. When we have that kind of faith and trust in the
Lord, we have true security and serenity in our lives."
Dallin R. Oaks

Life was genuinely treating us right. The new law practice was
growing on a monthly basis, Susie was a stay at home mom, everyone
was healthy, our regular church and temple callings were going well,
as was my [Army Reserve] military career as I was wrapping up a very
successful three year command tour. We seemingly had everything, and
I could not imagine how life could get any better.

Don Levin

I was driving our mini-van full of our older kids and some of their friends to church for a Saturday night activity when I had a bona fide vision that drove me to tears. To this very day, some thirty two years later, I can remember exactly where we were on Freeman Road, and the vision that I saw: our youngest daughter…in what turned out to be her annual birthday photo taken at age two… in the very dress and pose.

I don't know what prompted the vision, or what the segue in terms of train of thought may have prompted it, but all of a sudden I felt the strongest of impressions that we were supposed to have a fifth child. I did not know what to do with this impression and mentally compartmentalized it for the duration of the evening so that I could complete my assignment at church.

I next thought about it on the way home, wondering if maybe I had not simply had an aberrant thought. Why would I receive such an impression? We had the "perfect" mix of two boys and two girls, and at age 35, I was relatively confident that my wife was not going to be real keen on the idea of another pregnancy. At that point in time (1988), that was the age where women were being encouraged to close the factory and pregnancies were deemed "higher risk" – how times have changed.

I went home resolved not to say anything about the "vision" or whatever I had experienced, but the curtain that covers the glass panel in my forehead that allows my wife to read my mind must have been open because she wanted to know "what was up." When I said "nothing," she called me on it, and browbeat me long enough for me to share my experience with her.

To say that she was aghast would be a mild understatement and she had me recount the entire experience again. As I expected, she was not of the same mind as I was, but to her credit and own testimony and faith, said that she would think about it. Time passed, until one day she came to me and said that if I were that certain about our need to have another baby, she would agree to it.

Needless to say when we welcomed our youngest daughter to the family and she grew into the two year old I saw sitting in a white dress on a white chair I had an even stronger testimony that the Lord does communicate with us, and we all are entitled to personal revelation if we desire it and keep ourselves worthy of receiving it.

CHAPTER 49

BLACK AND WHITE

"You keep the commandments and you don't look for
excuses, rationalize behavior, or try to find gray areas.
You don't try to push the limits; you simply keep the
commandments because you know it is the better way."
Dieter F. Uchtdorf

Because of my ward and stake callings, I spent fifteen of our first eighteen wedding anniversaries at scout camp because our ward/troop went to the same camp the very same week every year. That was almost reason enough to move to Cincinnati!

In any event, I did enjoy my time with both of my sons, their friends, and all of the young men from our stake during these sojourns to Camp Napowan, Wisconsin, and had many wonderful *learning* experiences either while in attendance or on the drives to and from the camp.

I have a strong recollection of a conversation that I had with my stake president that began in the shower [of all places] and continued for literally a couple of hours around the campfire as we came to the determination that despite protestations to the contrary, the world remains black and white. There is no gray. Gray is nothing more than a shade of black. It is no different than being pregnant – either you are, or you are not. There is no such thing as a "little pregnant."

I thoroughly appreciated hearing this sentiment from someone in authority because even at that time in our history, people were already beginning to cut corners, rationalize behavior, and to make excuses for not living completely in accordance with all the laws of the Gospel.

Between my penchant for perfectionism, the zero defect environment of tactical nuclear weapons, and an utter fear of committing malpractice (the result of not being perfect as an attorney) I had already possessed a pretty strong sense of right and wrong before joining the Church, and genuinely appreciated the "black and white" nature of the church in general, its ordinances, and the standards required to remain a member in good standing.

Even by the time I was in my early 30's, I was already tired of hearing about how the world was becoming a gray place in which to live. As previously noted, I appreciated the comments and testimony of my stake president and the manner in which they dovetailed with what I had learned in the temple in that everything has its opposite: good and evil, light and darkness, pleasure and pain.

I have a testimony that Satan would have us believe that the world is gray and that a little short cut, or submission to small temptations, won't stunt our growth or impede our progress on the path, but I know better. I am not going to drive as close as I can to the edge of the mountain road, but will always choose to err on the side of safety and to avoid even the appearance of straddling the very distinct and discernible line between good and evil.

CHAPTER 50

HERITAGE

"Each of us has a heritage—whether from pioneer
forebears, later converts, or others who helped shape
our lives. This heritage provides a foundation built of
sacrifice and faith. Ours is the privilege and responsibility
to build on such firm and stable footings."
Thomas S. Monson

Over the years I have heard countless stories about people who have
left the church because they were "offended." Fortunately for us while
we were in our infancy as converts to the church, we were surrounded
by many loving people who embraced us, nurtured us, and made us feel
welcome. While it was not all roses and rainbows, nobody went out of
their way to insult us or to belittle our status as converts or did anything
that I can deem *offensive* to us.

Gratefully, early on in my course of study of all our latter day
prophets, I learned that the only one who loses in this scenario would
be me, and vicariously, my family. Brigham Young is credited as saying,
"He who takes offense when no offense is intended is a fool, and he who

takes offense when offense is intended is a greater fool." When I first read that many years ago, I did not quite grasp the subtle nuance that Brother Brigham expressed with this thought. Fortunately, it did not take us long to figure it out.

As most people are aware, the Church of Jesus Christ of Latter Day Saints places a great amount of appreciation and reverence for the settlers who founded the church, suffered the indignities and persecutions of the 19th Century, emigrated across the plains in wagons and handcarts, founded the Great Salt Lake Valley, and formed the basis of *pioneer stock.*

In 1995, our older son was on his mission, and we were sending off our oldest daughter to college at Utah State University in Logan, UT. I was serving in the bishopric as a counselor, and while attending the wedding reception of our bishop's son, found ourselves seated at the table with my fellow bishopric counselor. He and his wife were born and raised in Utah, and still found it hard to live here in Chicago, also known as "the mission field." I did not realize how much of a challenge it was for them until that fateful dinner. Susie was teaching early morning seminary and the other counselor was her point of contact within the bishopric. He had always been very complimentary of her efforts but in hindsight I realize that his praise was somewhat lefthanded because it would follow along the line of "nobody would ever know that you didn't grow up in the Church," as opposed to "nobody would ever know that you are a convert."

Their children were younger than ours, with their oldest, a son, being the same age, as our middle daughter. We were making small talk after dinner, and as BYU graduates themselves, they wanted to know why our daughter was going to school at USU as opposed to a local school here in Chicago. When we replied that "you marry who you date, and we wanted her to date LDS boys," he solemnly nodded his head in agreement, and announced, "that is very good advice." Score one for us dumb converts.

If the conversation had ended there, it would have been a lovely evening. Instead, he then added, "but my father gave me even better advice." When Susie asked what it was, he replied that his father said "while it is important to marry a member of the church, it is even more important to marry a member of the church *with a heritage in the church.*"

Needless to say, you could have heard a pin drop at our table, and even though I was squeezing my wife's leg under the table as a signal to let it go, Susie calmly threw gasoline on the fire when she asked, "so what I hear you saying is that if your son David liked my daughter Katie, and they fell in love, you would discourage them from getting married because Don and I are converts and don't have a *heritage* in the Church?"

Without blinking an eye, or even a moment's hesitation or thought, he quickly replied, "Yeah, I guess that is right."

We managed to avoid any bloodshed while in the Church, but once we closed the car doors, Mount Susie erupted, and it was at that point that Brigham Young's counsel popped into my head and I was able to provide some comfort to my [offended] wife.

While I know that the mindset that you are only a *pioneer* or have a heritage in the church if you walked across the plains, I have come to embrace the belief that Susie and I are the pioneers in our family. We now have three generations of active Latter Day Saints in our family. My grandparents as they came through Ellis Island were most assuredly pioneers too. The fact that the first time I went to Utah was by airplane does not make me any less a member of the Church entitled to all the rights and privileges afforded us by a loving Heavenly Father.

I know for certain that any number of people would have been offended by the remarks we heard that night, and some would even have used them as an excuse to turn their back on the Church. But that is how I know that the Church is true: because it survives in spite of all of its members.

CHAPTER 51

HEY MEATBALL

"The first principle of the gospel is faith in the Lord Jesus
Christ. Faith means trust – trust in God's will, trust
in His way of doing things, and trust in His timetable.
We should not try to impose our timetable on His. . . .
Indeed, we cannot have true faith in the Lord without also
having complete trust in His will and in His timing. . . ."
Dallin H. Oaks

It happened nearly twenty five years ago. I was still practicing law in
Chicago, and Rick was newly released from active duty with the Army
and working at Motorola.

Well, it was the day after Labor Day, and on the way to our respective
offices, Rick and I had breakfast at Richard Walker's Pancake House,
and he looked as lousy as he purportedly felt. We were celebrating the
fact that the promotions list for lieutenant colonel had come out, and
that I was on it. Rick was also informing me that when I exchanged
my gold oak leaves for silver ones and officially outranked him that if I
was waiting for him to salute me that I was in for a long wait. This was

funny because up until then he had always been promoted about nine months ahead of me, meaning that he had date of rank and technically outranked me. He had been promoted to First Lieutenant, Captain, and Major all before me, and each time had absolutely reveled in the fact that he outranked me. While it was all good natured fun, truth be told, I was looking forward to him having to snap off a salute in my direction if we were ever in uniform outside our Reserve Center and other folks were around. Sadly, it never happened, but I am getting ahead of myself.

We made it a quick breakfast that day because Rick felt like he had the flu. I encouraged him to go get checked out, but like me, he was stubborn about the need of going to doctors. As a result, when we were done eating, Rick left for work, and I went on to the courthouse for a prove-up and some other trial matter and did not give it another thought until Friday morning. It was then that Sally called Susie to tell us that Rick was being admitted to the hospital. Apparently, he had stopped at the Emergency Room on the way to work and after they did some initial blood workups, they determined that he had AML Type III Leukemia, and he was being admitted in reverse isolation.

To this day we do not know how he contracted it, and, that he did not have it three weeks prior when he went to his doctor for his annual physical because we went back and checked the results. P.S. we had the same doctor!

We went and visited with him on Friday night, and we were the ones who had to put on caps, gowns, gloves, and masks on to protect *him* from anything that we might be bringing into the room with us. At this point we were not worried because if you are going to contract the disease as an adult, AML Type III is the one you want, because you have a 50-50 chance of going into remission, and an 80% of staying in remission. So, the odds are in your favor if it is treated right.

Ironically, Rick's boss at Motorola had suffered the same diagnosis only the previous year, and she determined that Rick needed to be moved from the, and I quote, 'po-dunk community hospital' down to Rush-Presbyterian in the City, and beat the disease in the same manner that she had done the year before. They moved him by ambulance on Sunday afternoon and when we went to visit him, he was feeling better; more energy, good attitude, and things were looking up.

That evening we were visiting him and having fun, when he complained of a headache, and so they did an MRI and discovered an ever so slight bleeding in his head. Purely as a *preventative* measure, the doctors then moved him to the ICU. Of course, once he got there, he was still entertaining the staff, watching television, telling jokes, and actually feeling better with each passing day, just as we had hoped he would as he responded to the treatment.

Well, it was getting late, and so we said a prayer together, and then Rick's son Bob and I gave him a blessing. I remember that Bob anointed him with oil that had been consecrated for the healing of the sick and that it was then my responsibility to seal this anointing and to be the voice of the blessing. Needless to say, I was more than just a little nervous, just as I often am when faced with life and death situations. This was certainly not a father's blessing, or a blessing given at the start of the school year. However, during the blessing, I remember that Rick "would teach the gospel again." We all interpreted this to mean that Rick was going to be okay and resume teaching the early morning Seminary class that he taught to kids at church every morning on their way to high school. In fact, the exact impression I received on behalf of Rick was 'you will continue to teach the Gospel.' We all took that as a very favorable sign that he was going to get well soon and be part of that lucky group that goes into remission and stays there. I was going to get that salute yet. We went home on that high note, and genuinely felt that Rick was going to be okay.

Monday came and went, and Rick was doing better. Tuesday, we visited, and the ICU staff was telling us how much fun they were having with him because as patients went, he was pretty low maintenance for them, and entertaining to boot. We had every confidence that our prayers, as well as those of many people across the country, were going to be answered. After all, 45 is too young to leave this world, especially with a wife and seven kids dependent upon him.

Wednesday came, and I was downtown for an Army assignment, and met Susie and Sally at the hospital for a late afternoon visit. Rick was entertaining us, and since our kids were at home, needing help with homework, we opted to leave just as his dinner arrived.

At this point, Rick got a very quizzical look on his face and started asking us questions about his dinner, and then the words started coming out in a jumbled order, and then with the syllables mixed up, sort of like an eight track tape being skipped between the tracks, and it became evident to us that he was having a stroke right before our eyes. While we knew that part of the treatment for the leukemia and the slow blood leak made this a possibility, after several days of care and steady progress we assumed that the worst was behind us.

Rick then lost consciousness, while staring directly at me, after which they started doing bi-hourly CAT scans and MRIs and with each passing one, we could see the bleed overtaking the healthy part of his brain. We were going back and forth between his room and the chapel where we were all fervently praying, though in my heart I already knew that he was not going to make it. I was angry, I was disappointed, I was confused. We had prayed, I had given him blessings, and we had all heard that he would teach the gospel again. How could this be happening?

When people ask me why I had that impression, all I can do is shrug and convey to them that even as a layperson, I know enough about the brain to know what parts of the brain control what bodily functions, and I knew that he was at the very least in some deep trouble even if he survived. He was not going to be the Rick we knew unless a miracle were to occur. This realization shook me, as did the look in his eyes as he lost consciousness. It was at first confusion and then settled into one of understanding and acceptance. Also fueling this feeling of dread inside me were the doctors encouraging us to assemble the kids from around the country and asking whether he had a Living Will and Medical Directives. I told them that he did, and when they asked me how I knew, I simply told them that I had drafted them on his behalf in my capacity as his attorney. These documents later turned into a blessing for his wife when I was able to comfort her and inform her that Rick had relieved her of the burden of deciding for him what to do in terms of prolonging his life; he had made that decision of his own volition under better circumstances. This also promoted a peaceful feeling for all of us.

We stayed the night and I remember the staff providing us blankets and pillows for the ICU waiting room, how cold I was all night long, and that I spent a good bit of the night up and about walking the halls because it was the only way I could stay warm. We obviously made arrangements for our kids, but I cannot tell you what they were, much as I wrack my brain to this day.

It got to be around 0200, the bleed was severe and the shunt that they had put into his head was drawing blood off, but it was a losing battle. I knew at that point that he was gone; that the machines and the additional blood transfusions would keep him alive until all the college kids got home, but that he was no longer a part of this world. When I looked at him, I could almost feel his absence if that makes any sense at all – sort of like attempting to prove a negative.

Sally asked me to administer to him again, and I somewhat nervously complied. It was just Sally and I in the room, and because I typically do not remember the actual words I say after I have voiced the blessing, and ordinarily would have had to rely on her memory, the fact that she audibly gasped enough to startle me when I voiced that he would continue teaching the Gospel with the additional verbiage "but not in this Life," I too could remember it. This was heartbreaking for both of us, and everyone with whom we later shared it.

At this point I realized that my friend was in transition and was going to be teaching those on the other side of the veil. I so wanted to know what he was experiencing, but to look at him there was no outward change to his countenance or evidence of what was happening to him.

The kids all got in from Utah, and about 3:00 that afternoon the medical staff started disconnecting him from the ventilator and other machines that were keeping him alive. He surprised all of us by not dying. He kept breathing on his own for about twenty five more agonizing minutes. It was anguishing to watch everyone in the room gathered around him, crying, and aching to see him struggling to stay with us. Even the doctors and nurses in attendance were crying which I found to be incredibly shocking, because they deal with life and death situations every day, but *this* was not an everyday occurrence for any of us. Most ICU patients are comatose or in bad shape when they are on that ward. Rick was the life of the party for a good three days before he took a turn for the worse and these professionals were genuinely sharing our grief.

I think about that day every so often, trying to replay it in my mind's eye, and whenever I do, I remember that it was more a *feeling* that I experienced when he left us. I mean one minute he was there, laboring to stay with us, and then it was as if he let go of an imaginary or metaphoric anchor, and he sort of just floated off....spiritually.

So that was Thursday afternoon. We all left the hospital, pretty much in a state of shock and exhaustion, and finally went home for a much needed shower, change of clothes, some real food, and to sleep in a bed. On Friday, Friday the 13th mind you, we made arrangements for Rick's funeral to be conducted on Monday, and on Saturday, it was my birthday. I do not remember if we even celebrated it. I do remember that the following year *Sally* threw me a birthday party to make up for the bust the previous year had been.

On Sunday morning I was at church with Susie and the kids. We were singing an intermediate hymn, and suddenly, I hear "hey meatball" as plain as day. In fact, it was as plain as if Susie had turned to me and said it in her own voice. Ordinarily, that would have been Rick talking to his kids, his troops, and to anyone who did not measure up at the moment. Now, it was my turn.

At this point I did nothing. I dismissed it. And I dismissed it a second time when it happened again a minute later, chalking it up to my own vivid and sometimes overactive imagination, and a decided case of sleep deprivation and some emotional exhaustion.

But he persisted. The third time it was "hey meatball, I'm talking to you. Tell Sally and the girls that I am alright. That I am in a much better place, and I'll be waiting for them."

Some of you may be thinking that this was a wonderful occurrence for me. At that moment I was seriously contemplating whether I was losing my mind! What I later learned is that I was not losing my mind, but rather, being given the opportunity of being Rick's advocate. However, at that moment it was so out of left field that it left me feeling shaken. Susie said that she looked over at me when I had stopped singing and knew something was wrong but could not figure it out. She said my color and countenance changed, and it scared her. She thought maybe I was having a heart attack or something. That would have been easy by comparison.

This is when I realized that most people on earth are mortals hoping to have an occasional spiritual experience to bolster their faith and like it or not I was actually having one of those moments, or, my cheese was not only sliding off the cracker but right from the plate onto the floor.

The first thing I did as soon as the service ended was to share the experience with Susie. Somewhat unexpectedly, she thought it was wonderful, and acted as if it was a normal everyday occurrence for a deceased person to be communicating with me! More than just a little perplexed, I let her know that I did not understand her reaction.

While I was all for dismissing it as a figment of my overactive imagination, she insisted that I share it with Sally. I told her if she wanted to share it that she was free to do so, but as for me, no way, Jose. True to form, I lost that argument, and when I ultimately shared it with Sally, you would have thought I had shared something as simple as I had received a telephone call from him while he was alive. Her only frustration was that he did not communicate directly with her! She said she knew he wouldn't come to her because she would not have heard him.

This turned into a great learning moment for me. As it was later explained to me by my Stake President, this was Sally's faith allowing her to accept the fact that as his closest friend that it was perfectly natural for him to reach out to his family through me, especially after I had promised to look after the family in the event anything happened to him.

I learned that it was not as uncommon as I thought it was and that more than a few of the people who attended the viewing that Sunday night had had similar experiences with friends and family members who had passed on. While I felt a little less crazy, it was still a challenge for the logical part of me to accept that no matter how much faith I have and how much I want to believe that I could be part of something as special and unique as communicating with the other side that it could actually be happening!

On Monday morning we had a lovely funeral service at the church building for Rick and proceeded to the cemetery for his military internment. I was able to perform the services of the Burial Detail Commander. It was left to me to present the flag that had draped Rick's coffin to his widow. I could swear that I felt his hand on my shoulder in gratitude as I performed this act. This was an incredibly challenging moment for me because I did not want to cry while in uniform and as a result of suppressing tears all morning long, I had one monster headache. The twenty one gun salute and mournful rendition of *Taps* would have done me in (as it usually does) but for the fact that just as the burial detail had completed folding the flag into the trifold, Rick's son Bob popped a brass button on his uniform, and it made a perfect *ping* off the top of the casket, for all to see. Given that Rick had battled weight while in the Army, often cursing me when I got on the scale for a weigh-in with my full battle dress uniform on, we thought it was an angel or some force of nature injecting a bit of humor.

My final act that day was to prevent Sally from having to pick between her two priesthood-bearing sons and accepting the assignment to dedicate Rick's gravesite. This dedication is an ordinance of the Gospel and is performed under the auspices of the Melchizedek Priesthood and is intended to provide comfort to the family as well as being a petition for the Divine protection of the grave. I felt his gratitude as I completed the prayer. Years later when we buried my own father, I asked my son Jeff who was preparing to serve a mission to dedicate his grandfather's grave. This act of priesthood service is a sacred duty and touched my heart in such a way to further strengthen my faith and testimony.

There was so much to that stream of experiences that greatly strengthened my conversion and testimony. The prayers, the priesthood blessings that over time provided clarity as to the direction of Rick's path, as well as his honoring me to be his mortal advocate, all promoted growth in me. In hindsight it makes perfect sense that he would, even during his departure from this life, continue to be a mentor and teacher to me, and to help me grow in the Gospel. It may have been an example of paying it forward because Rick was a convert of only a few years when I first met him. Whatever the actual circumstance, I look forward to seeing him again on the other side of the veil.

CHAPTER 52

THE CLOTHES MAKE THE MAN

"Living members recognize the need to
put into action their beliefs."
Howard W. Hunter

The most beautiful aspect of our faith and membership in the Church of Jesus Christ of Latter Day Saints is the Plan of Salvation that affords all of us the ability to remain part of an eternal family. To this end, if children are not born in the covenant they may be sealed to their parents as we were sealed to Katie when she was only fifteen months old. Our older children were not born in the covenant, and because I am not their biological father, it was their choice when they attained the age of twenty-one as to whether they wanted to be part of our eternal family.

Karen turned 21 on a Friday. She flew home to Chicago on Thursday night from Utah for a long weekend so that we could be in the temple on Friday morning. Since attendance in the temple begins at age 12 for vicarious baptism and is reserved to age 18 for everything else, younger children are typically not exposed to what goes on in the temple proper. For Karen's sealing to us, we were able to bring our entire family into

215

the sealing room, and in her inimitable style, 9-year old Eliese took one look at me in my temple robes and let loose with a "What the heck are you wearing?" We gave her an innocuous explanation and proceeded on with the sealing ceremony.

That event was more than twenty years ago, and it was literally the very next month that we watched Karen be sealed to her husband in the Logan temple as they established the next generation of family for our eternal family tree. Presumably, we could have waited to perform our sealing during our visit to Utah, but the urgency attached to this sacred rite prompted us to do it when we did. It meant so much to both Susie and I that it was so important to Karen that she be sealed to us for all eternity, and that she did not want to wait one day longer than necessary as evidenced by the fact that we did it on her 21st birthday.

When Phil returned from his mission to Hartford, CT, it was shortly after the dust had settled on his arrival home that he too elected to be sealed to us for time and eternity.

Our two younger children Jeff and Eliese were born in the covenant and as a result were automatically sealed to us.

There were many occasions in the years before our children were old enough to elect to be sealed to us that people would ask us, "doesn't it worry you that you are not sealed to all of your children? What if something were to happen to you or to them before it happens?"

While no offense was intended, or taken, to me these questions by their very nature indicated either a lack of faith or understanding, because we knew that since it was not something within our control, that if tragedy had struck prior to these ceremonies, that the Lord would have "sorted it out" for us and as a result was never a concern for us. The witness I received during the ceremonies served as an additional brick in the cathedral that is my testimony.

CHAPTER 53

OUR FIRST MISSIONARY

"Knowing that the gospel is true is the essence of
a testimony. Consistently being true to the gospel
is the essence of conversion. We should know
the gospel is true and be true to the gospel."
David A. Bednar

As we progressed through our first ten years in the church, we sat through many missionary farewells and heard an equal number of missionaries report on the two years that they spent immersed in the Gospel and teaching those to whom they were led by the Spirit. We had decided early on that we would encourage our sons to serve missions and to fulfill that expectation, but only if it was their desire to do so. Fortunately for us, whether both boys would serve a mission was never a question.

When Phil determined to go immediately on his mission the fall after graduating from high school we were all in favor of it, and he spent the intervening six months working, studying and reading books as assigned by the bishop, and really preparing himself for what would prove to be a pivotal two years of his life. We were all very excited about his call to the Hartford, Connecticut mission where he would labor in a number of communities, and regale us with wonderful tales of his experiences. We were even more thrilled when he would send us flattened, dried, roadkill as additional mementoes.

We were promised blessings as the family of a missionary, and for as often as I heard that, I really could not comprehend what it would mean to our family until we lived it. Providing financial support for our missionary did not seem like a sacrifice. In hindsight, it was a blessing for us to do, and while the fruits of our sacrifices may not have been immediately evident, I do know that we were blessed for Phil's faithful service.

CHAPTER 54

APOSTLE'S BLESSING

"Almost to a man, the Twelve come from humble
beginnings, as it was when He was here. The living
Twelve are welded together in the ministry of the gospel
of Jesus Christ. When the call came, each has put
down his nets, so to speak, and followed the Lord."
Boyd K. Packer

Having joined the Church in Chicago in what is referred to as the "mission field" (any place outside of Utah), we did not encounter apostles and general authorities with the frequency that our children began to while attending college in Provo and Logan, UT. Many times they would call home to Chicago, Cincinnati, Richmond, or Seattle, and casually mention that they heard Elder So and So speak, or they shook hands with President So and So, or they attended a conference or activity and this general authority was in attendance. While delighted and maybe a bit envious that they had these opportunities, I was also amazed at how complacent they were becoming in their attitude.

One of the blessings of serving in the temple were the annual

Don Levin

Christmas devotionals that were usually presided over by an apostle or other general authority. Listening to these fine brethren speak to us in the intimate confines of the temple chapel was always a highlight of the holiday season for us.

Shortly after joining the Church in 1984, I had the privilege of joining a group of faculty from my law school and venturing around the corner to the DePaul Law School in downtown Chicago. We were going to hear from Dallin H. Oaks, a recent member of the Utah State Supreme Court, president of BYU, a University of Chicago law professor, and now, newly ordained Apostle of the Lord Jesus Christ.

Elder Oaks had received permission from the First Presidency to honor this speaking commitment made prior to his call to the Quorum of Twelve Apostles, and speaking at DePaul University would in fact constitute the final professional speaking engagement of his legal and academic career. He spoke powerfully on the separation of church and state, and I confess that much of his talk sailed completely over my head, as well as those of my compatriots. I took some degree of solace in this fact.

While it was not an ecclesiastical event, when I shook hands with him after being introduced by one of my law school brethren as a new convert to the Church, he took my hand in both of us, looked me square in the eye, and absolutely radiated love and concern for me. While his handshake was firm and not much different than the thousands of other hands that I have shaken in my life, there was a distinct *aura* that enveloped him. Yes, he was a man, but he was also an Apostle of the Lord Jesus Christ, and for me, that was the highlight of my sojourn to the symposium that day.

Fast forward a couple of years, and I am now a temple missionary, serving in the Chicago Temple, having been called as a missionary by the First Presidency, when the Chicago temple became the first temple in the world to begin staffing its shifts with locally called [temple district] workers. This was being done in an effort to replace the full-time missionaries drawn from the senior missionary ranks. I vividly remember the Thursday night that we were informed of this fact by Elder Neal A. Maxwell who was in town to conduct many items of

220

business in the greater Chicagoland area. I had just assumed that my call to the temple was a "local" calling and that it did not have anything to do with the missionary department in Salt Lake City. I was sitting with several of my fellow shift workers and this news shook us to the marrow in our bones. I simply could not imagine that my name had been approved by the missionary department and the First Presidency. To say that it made an impression that blew us all away would be a gross understatement.

Later that weekend, we gathered with our spouses in the Temple chapel, and Elder Maxwell spoke very sweetly and kindly to us, thanking us for our service in the temple, and extolled the virtues of working in the temple. As he spoke, I heard, I saw, and I felt, the great love that he had for the work, for the Lord, and for each of us. When he then pronounced an apostolic blessing upon all of us, I felt it was as if the windows of Heaven had been opened above us, and again, I felt something incredible, and I was so grateful that I had been deemed worthy to serve in the temple.

Again, because this was something those of us living far from Utah rarely experienced, the experience was all the sweeter. When I later researched the significance of the blessing, and how they had their origins in the Old Testament, I felt my heart and my testimony swell even larger. I was all the more grateful for having been in attendance and in a position to experience this greatest form of love that the Lord can shower upon us. I felt that I had sincerely been blessed, enriched, strengthened, and afforded a level of protection against the adversary as well as the coldness of the world. Like a small sapling, I felt that I had been nurtured, and given added strength to persevere.

Over the years, and usually through the medium of satellite broadcasts we have been afforded the opportunity to be the recipients of other apostolic blessings usually in the context of our semi-annual General Conferences. Even through the airwaves I can still feel the full impact of these blessings and love the men who have used their authority to bestow these blessings upon us. The Spirit touches my heart, and whispers in my ear the truthfulness and fullness of the Gospel, and for this I am filled with gratitude.

CHAPTER 55

INDESTRUCTIBILITY

"One's life . . . cannot be both faith-filled and stress-free. . . . Therefore, how can you and I really expect to glide naively through life, as if to say, 'Lord, give me experience, but not grief, not sorrow, not pain, not opposition, not betrayal, and certainly not to be forsaken. Keep from me, Lord, all those experiences which made Thee what Thou art! Then let me come and dwell with Thee and fully share Thy joy!' . . .Real faith . . . is required to endure this necessary but painful developmental process."
Neal A. Maxwell

Before we joined the church and immediately after for a few more years, whenever we experienced something like the dimes in my boot or impressions that would either drive us to do something or to avoid a situation, we would quite often refer to it as "spooky stuff." Clearly, Rick speaking to me after he transitioned through the veil fell into that category, but it no longer "spooked" us, or maybe not as much as it used to in the past. We *understood* these manifestations of the Spirit and came to embrace them as evidence that we were worthy, and in good favor with our Heavenly Father. However, all the preceding notwithstanding, if I had not personally viewed and experienced the following events, I would have been hard pressed to believe, much less comprehend, their significance.

As was the custom of the time, my younger son and I were assigned as Home Teaching companions to several families in our ward. As home teachers we were stewards to these families, the eyes and ears of the bishop, and visited them no less than monthly to check on their temporal and spiritual needs, and to share a message with them.

One family was led by a single mom, Greta, with the younger five of her nine children still at home. School had recently ended for the summer, and we were going to be engaged from Thursday to Saturday in a Stake Youth Conference with approximately 150 youth between the ages of 14-18.

Early on Thursday morning we had broken into "families" of 10-12 youth, and spent the day engaged in a variety of activities in and around the church building. We were a host family that year and had literally just bedded twelve teenagers down on two different floors of our home and retired to our bedroom, grateful for the refuge.

It was going on midnight and I was literally just climbing into bed when our phone rang. It was Greta. "Don my house is on fire." She had called me even before she had called 9-1-1 and summoned the fire department! I told her to make that call and that we would be right over. The good news is that all of the kids had been gone, participating in the youth conference, and were dispersed at various houses. Because of the late hour, we elected not to tell them individually but rather to gather them at the church the next morning when we had an idea of what was going on.

We were there in less than ten minutes, and I can't remember if I called him or someone else had, but we were soon joined by the bishop and the four of us stood there and watched Great's rental home burn for the next three hours as the fire department went through their protocol for turning off utilities and determining appropriate ingress and egress points before actually engaging the fire. What a horribly helpless feeling that served to intensify my own fear of ever losing our own home to fire.

By 4:00 a.m. there was nothing else for us to do, so we went back to our house where Susie shared some of her clothes and we situated Greta in one of the kids' rooms.

Over breakfast we learned that she had no renter's insurance, and the landlord's policy would not cover any of her losses, but the kindness of the ward essentially furnished a townhouse for her and met her needs. This act of generosity is yet another aspect of our life as latter day saints that never ceases to amaze me.

On Friday morning before the commencement of that day's activities we met with all of Greta's kids in the Stake President's office, and they took the loss of their home and worldly possessions in stride because "they were all safe, and they had their scriptures." What teenager would think about their scriptures and not mourn the loss of their stereo and cassette tapes? We were completely overwhelmed by their mature attitude. I am still amazed by it to this day. Wow!

We finished Youth Conference on Saturday night, and at that point, all retired to our house where we would house most of them for the following six weeks. That is where this story begins.

Sunday was Father's Day and after church ended at noon, it was agreed that I would accompany Greta to the house to see if there was anything to be salvaged. Because of the inherent danger of the site, and warnings from the fire department, we were the only ones who were going to go to the house.

The fire had burned "very hot" according to the fire inspector. Hot enough that chandeliers and kitchen cabinets had literally melted into surrealistic shapes. Nearly everything in the kitchen, to include appliances, had simply melted in place. The stoneware dishes in the cabinets that had not collapsed were salvageable and provided many evenings of therapeutic scrubbing and discussion on our patio.

Because of the number of very athletic kids in the family, the basement had walls filled with shelves and shelves of trophies – all destroyed by the intense heat of the fire. There was literally no trace of anything ever having been there. The devastation was absolutely frightening.

At one point Greta left to retrieve some trash bags from either a neighbor or our house, leaving me alone inside the burned shell of the house. Talk about an eerie experience. As I explored, I started to discover things that were causing the hair on the back of my neck to stand straight up.

When Greta returned, I very carefully started my guided tour of the things that I had discovered. The furniture, fixtures, and chandelier in the dining room were completely destroyed. The framed pictures and pieces hanging on the walls were destroyed either by fire, smoke, or water. While most were simply gone, there were a few still in place with frames that had melted into very grotesque shapes, all but the completely unscathed portrait of the Savior in the center of the dining room wall. I checked the wall around it, and I could discern where other pictures had been incinerated, or the frames had melted so that the contents of the frame had dropped out the bottom of the frame, leaving picture wire dangling from the nail with which it had been hung on the wall.

From there we wandered very gingerly into daughter Joannie's room. This room was in complete shambles. The fire department's hoses had blown the curtains out through the high-on-the-wall broken windows. At the foot of Joannie's bed was a little table with a 12" television sitting on it. Several months earlier my wife had presented all the young women in her class a 3x5 picture of the Savior in a bi-fold cardboard frame. Joannie had previously told us that she had placed the picture on the top of the television so that it was the first thing that she saw every morning. Despite the horrific condition of the room, Jesus was still sitting on top of the television in pristine condition. As noted, the curtains were blown out through the window, there was, soot all over everything in the room *to include the television* except for the picture itself, and the v-shaped slit on the soot covered surface of the television. I could not imagine how that flimsy piece of cardboard had withstood the fire, the water, the wind only to be standing there in as pristine condition as when Joannie had set it down on the television for the first time. It was at this point we nearly jumped into one another's arms. Okay, so I am starting to discern a trend here.

We then went into Johnny's bedroom, and looked around, and under the bed, which was waterlogged and sagging to the ground, we discovered Johnny's personal journal and collection of drawings in an ordinary cardboard box, obviously protected from the inferno.

We then went into Greta's room and found her scriptures on the bedside table, damp, scented by the smoke, but otherwise unscathed. We started pushing things around so that we could navigate the room and discovered her chest of drawers laying on its back. The outside was wet, covered in soot, and even singed in places. Many of the drawers and their contents were ruined by smoke and water, and in some cases actual fire. However, in the drawers that contained her temple clothing and religious garments, these items were unscathed. Family photo albums that she had been viewing prior to going to sleep that night were also salvageable after we spread tarps out on the floor of our garage and we carefully took the albums apart to dry.

In earlier chapters we have talked about coincidence, luck, timing., miracles, science, and tender mercies. This experience certainly stretches the limits of these various concepts. Having viewed it with my own eyes, I have no doubt that there was divine intervention here. While all of the things that did survive could have been replaced with relative ease, they were still protected against damage and survived despite incredible odds to the contrary. I know that those items that were spared brought the family comfort in the following weeks and remain a testimony of their faithfulness.

CHAPTER 56

INTO THE CRUCIBLE AGAIN

"There is no obstacle too great, no challenge too
difficult, that we cannot meet with faith."
Gordon B. Hinckley

Much to my surprise, after only two [extraordinarily successful] years in Cincinnati as a Regional Sales Manager, I was encouraged to apply for the role of Division Vice President. Ultimately, when the dust settled after a brutal battery of both panel and one-on-one interviews, I came out of the grinder ranked number 1 out of 24 candidates for the eight [newly re-organized] positions. I had approached the process with some trepidation because all I wanted to do was to be a long term care insurance guy, and the new DVP role required me to be familiar and licensed in the fields of both long term care insurance *and* financial services which really did not hold a lot of interest for me. Nonetheless, I went through the drill, and after turning down a couple of DVP roles, ultimately accepted the Northeast Division, which turned out to be the number one division.

My Dad was pleased with this new role, and to show the degree of *nachas* that he was feeling, and that I had been forgiven for retiring "early" from the Army, he presented me with general's stars and a general's leather dress belt. I know, a little bizarre, but meant from the heart.

The fanfare around the new re-organization, the fact that I would be a salaried W-2 employee with a very nice base salary and an equally large bonus opportunity, and an expense account made it exciting. The idea of moving to Richmond, VA and of being based "at the flagpole" would provide even more fuel to my meteoric rise in the company. All of this far surpassed any hopes and dreams I may have harbored. I also found it to be very humbling.

I was feeling great…until I became aware of one exceptionally large and glaring term of employment for the new position: namely the requirement for several FINRA licenses, to include the Series 7, 24, and 66 licenses. Our Chief Sales Officer, the four new Senior Vice Presidents (SVP) and the DVPs who did not already possess these licenses would all have to study for them, and successfully negotiate some brutal exams.

After my experience with the Bar Exam, I really did not want to go down this path, but they gave me five months from my start date to complete the exams. P.S. Nobody met this end of May deadline, and it was nearly ten months later (October) before I took the last and easiest exam (the 66) only to have the company trash our three year plan after only a brief nine months and revert back to separate LTCI and financial service channels. The entire painful process of earning these three licenses was ultimately for naught. I could have screamed.

For me, the fear of failure reared its ugly head again. It became worse when the CSO failed the Series 7 exam the first time he took it, and when my immediate boss failed both the 7 and the 24, I was starting to sweat. However, I did have enough self-confidence to believe that I could study and negotiate these tests easier than they could with their respective experiences in the financial services world. I thought they had enjoyed a leg up on me, but apparently I was wrong on that score.

I began in the new role concurrent to our annual leadership meeting, conducted at the stately Jefferson Hotel in downtown Richmond, and it was magical. I was extremely comfortable in the new role, and felt like I could make a real contribution to the company while leading my division and also assuming "championship" (leadership) roles with various staff sections within the home office. We sold our home in Cincinnati quick enough to qualify for a nice bonus that the company offered, found a house we would build in Richmond, and life looked great. Unfortunately, I was already knee-deep in the self-doubt process because my fear of these exams was palpable. All I could think about was the potential *humiliation* AND loss of my job – there was no going back to Cincinnati because that position was filled. It was clearly nightmare time all over again.

What is ironic about this situation is that the most important strategy for me has always been setting and achieving goals. Because I believe that the brain is truly a goal-seeking mechanism that deals in absolutes, not distinguishing between positive and negative, I always have my long term and short term goal lists, and my daily to-do list with which to attain the former. I am equally convinced that the best goals truly are characterized by the acronym SMART (Specific, Measurable, Attainable, Realistic, and Timebound), and this is what I attempt to always convey to my followers.

One of the terms of my employment is that I would spend 70% of my time [that first year] on the road in the Northeast where I had twelve regional managers reporting to me. I would fly from Cincinnati to either New York or Boston each Monday and return home on Thursday. While traveling I was also juggling studying for the Series 7, removing chapters from the ridiculously large four inch binder to study on the plane, in the hotel room at night, and to take practice exams while at home. To say that I detested the practice exams would be a gross understatement. There was many a time that the only thing that kept me going was a positive mental picture of the celebrating Susie and I would do when these nasty exams were behind us.

I spent a week in Richmond at a hotel next to the campus taking a five day review course. At the end of each class day I would walk over to the campus and check in at headquarters. One day I remember being tutored by the CSO on market activity, and realized I was being mentored by a guy who had failed the very exam that I was preparing to take in less than a week. Not exactly a confidence builder. At the time, the first-time pass rate for this exam was under 50%. The good news is that I was willing to accept help from every quarter, and ultimately scored a 76 on the exam. Since passing was 70, everyone good naturedly accused me of "over studying." Phew. Hallelujah! One down.

I started the arduous task of preparing for the Series 24 following the same study process. I was still traveling every week, we re-located from Cincinnati to Richmond during this time, and life was hectic. Now that I was based in Richmond, I was in the office on Mondays and Fridays, and this made it far easier for me to engage in my championship roles of Leadership and Training. I considered myself fortunate to have been able to grab both roles that fueled my passion for the business.

I always utilized my ride into the office to rehearse my day and to organize myself, and I continued this practice with prep for the 24. There were two possible scenarios: the first, in which I failed the exam (like many of my peers had already done) and had to take it again, no biggie, no shame (except in my own mind) or the second, where I passed the exam, and then attended our national agent conference down in Orlando, FL, and was literally toasted each night at dinner as news of my successful completion of the exam spread throughout the organization. The desire to achieve this positive outcome was enough to motivate me to continue to plod on through all the practice examinations and review sessions while continuing to travel extensively and to simultaneously build a new house and relocate my family.

The two-day review course for the 24 took place in Manhattan, and I flew up there on Monday night, was delayed, and instead of arriving at 5:30 anticipating a nice dinner and a good night's sleep, I arrived at nearly midnight. I found myself in a rather interesting neighborhood where at 3:00 a.m. all the local fish suppliers and their buyers were right outside my window! It was so ridiculous and because I was awake, I went and worked out, came back to my room, and took a shower. I then realized that I still had a real case of *shpilkas* (butterflies floating around in my stomach) that I decided to say a prayer.

I didn't pray that I would pass the exam or anything like that, but only that my mind would be receptive to the techniques and intricate details being reviewed, and that ultimately when I sat for the exam in that sterile testing center, that my best would be good enough. I no sooner finished that prayer that I had a very calm and peaceful feeling come over me, and I felt like I was back on top of my game. I was ready to be the Boy Wonder again, even if I was a few years older and a step or two slower.

Arriving at the review center down on the Battery end of the island, I soon determined that I was one of only two people in a class of fifty five who were there for the *first* time. For about half the class this was their *third* visit to wonderland. While this might ordinarily have freaked me out, I remember smiling to myself, and thinking, "watch me. One and done baby."

As it was, the only day that I could even get an appointment to sit the for exam was on a Saturday in Glen Allen, VA. It also happened to be the day of my assistant's wedding, so my absence was even more conspicuous, and the pressure to pass the exam a little greater. With well wishes from my wife and kids, I drove to the testing center, and scored another 76. Two down!

My SVP and I were on the 0600 flight from Richmond bound for Orlando, but I think I could have flown there without the plane. I was on cloud nine. We were checked in at the resort and at the pool shortly after 1000. The day at the pool, enjoying the sun, some good food and drink, was exactly what the doctor ordered, and by the time our first official event (dinner) came along that night, I was on top of the world.

The actual celebration of my accomplishment exceeded my expectations, as each successive night more and more people arrived and were met with a dinner that we hosted. There were toasts in my honor each night, which served to reinforce for me the power and importance of positive self-talk.

By the time I got around to taking my last exam, the 66 (which is a combination of the 63 and 65 exams rolled into one) it was the end of October. As previously noted, I had no sooner finished this exam, also with a score of 76, than the company trashed our three year plan after only nine months and reverted back to separate LTCI and financial service channels. The entire painful process of earning these three licenses was ultimately for naught. But my testimony of prayer, positive self-talk, and preparation – the 3 P's, -- was reaffirmed.

When we finished the first year of the new plan, the positions of 4 SVPs and 8 DVPs were consolidated into 6 DVPs. I was one of the survivors, and in addition to my 12 regional managers, now had my own team of 8 staff members to support the efforts in the field. I was in hog heaven, as I finally had the autonomy I had expected but did not realize in the first year.

I mentioned that in addition to my salary and bonus, that I enjoyed a very liberal expense account. In fact, it was a large pot of money allocated for travel expenses, training, marketing, etc. I learned that some people simply cannot handle a corporate credit card, and that telling them to spend it as if it was their own money does not make a difference if they are frivolous with their own money as well. I actually had to take a credit card or two away from people who abused it and make them use their own personal card subject to review and reimbursement.

Being a member of the Church and not drinking alcohol pretty much provided me with the liberty of eating some nice meals on a regular basis and to still maintain the most efficient T&L cost center. By the same token, because people *knew* I was a member of the Church, they also *watched* me like a hawk, and for that reason my drink of choice was always Sprite with lime, so as to avoid any appearance of impropriety.

Further accentuating my distinct style of doing things, I spent between $4000-5000 a year on books for my various book clubs with managers, staff members, and district managers on occasion. Gift books to my peers became an expectation for our quarterly leadership meetings.

Perhaps the best thing about this time in my career is that I was free to practice my faith openly and without apology. The fact that I did not drink was never an issue. When someone noted in one of our leadership meetings that I was the only person they knew who ever passed all three exams on the first try, another person in the room attributed it to my "clean living." I would like to think that this may have had something to do with it, but that the 3P's – prayer, positive self-talk, and preparation had been the real difference for me.

While I still battle my fear of failure on a regular basis, my attitude is quite different. I have nothing to prove to anyone; I don't have to seek anyone's approval, and if it interests me enough to try to do it myself, what is the worst thing that can happen – I mess it up and have to call a real expert in to finish the job. Often if it is a project around the house that I decide to do myself, I can usually grind it out.

CHAPTER 57

THE KIRTLAND TEMPLE

"We must have all things prepared and call our solemn
assembly as the Lord has commanded us, that we may
be able to accomplish his great work: and it must be
done in God's own way; the house of the Lord must be
prepared, and the solemn assembly called and organized
in it according to the order of the house of God."
Joseph Smith

After leaving New York and settling in Eastern Ohio, in December
1832, God commanded Joseph Smith to build a temple in Kirtland,
Ohio. We have a lovely watercolor painting of that temple which I
commissioned from a friend of mine as a Christmas present for Susie
while we still lived in Chicago. We had a youth conference that took
us there one year, and we had both been enamored with the building.

The Prophet and several others saw the Kirtland Temple in a
vision, which provided its design. Construction began in June 1833, at
a time of great poverty in the Church. Work slowed in 1834 because
many brethren were absent with Zion's Camp. When they returned,

Joseph Smith labored with others in the sandstone quarry, and vigorous efforts to build the temple resumed. Church members made enormous sacrifices to complete this "House of the Lord."

On March 27, 1836, the Prophet Joseph dedicated the Kirtland Temple, repeating the ceremony several days later. Beginning in January and continuing past the dedication, many Church members witnessed heavenly manifestations culminating in Jesus Christ's appearance to Joseph Smith and Oliver Cowdery to accept the temple. Moses, Elias, and Elijah also appeared to Joseph and Oliver to restore priesthood keys for the salvation of all mankind.

Most of the Saints moved away from Kirtland in 1838. The temple fell into disrepair, and its ownership was challenged. The Reorganized Church of Jesus Christ of Latter Day Saints, now known as the Community of Christ, gained title to the building in 1880. They restored and beautified this sacred place and maintain it today as a historic site with guided tours. They will also allow groups to rent it by the hour for the purpose of having their own meetings.

In 2005, I was the Stake Young Men President for our recently created stake in Virginia, and though we were the "new" stake, the other half of our old stake was committed to tagging along with us for our planned Youth Conference to Kirtland. Personally, I was extremely excited at the prospect of seeing Kirtland because I had always felt a connection to Nauvoo and other Church historic sites in the Eastern United States.

Our plan was to rent the Kirtland temple and conduct a testimony meeting, complete with the administration of the sacrament for our youth. It troubled me that in addition to the hourly rental fee, I also had to pay on behalf of the stake a $2 per person "head charge" to secure the building. To me, it seemed that the Community Church was nearly desecrating the temple with their "strictly business" approach to the edifice.

Despite the way we finally found ourselves in the temple, we had an absolutely wonderful meeting. The spirit was strong, and I cannot imagine that anyone present was not overcome to some degree. The highpoint for me is that we had arranged for the six members of the two stake presidencies and several of the bishops to actually pass the sacrament, after the two stake young men presidents had blessed it. As I blessed the bread, I knew that it would be a an experience that I would never forget. Because of all the history in that edifice, and because it is still largely the original temple in all its splendor, I was grateful to be there, and worthy enough to participate in that sacred ordinance.

It is my hope and prayer that at some point that the Church of Jesus Christ of Latter Day Saints will resume ownership of the temple so that it can be again considered something more than a national historic landmark.

CHAPTER 58

THE HAND LEAVES THE GLOVE AGAIN

"When the challenges of mortality come, and they come
for all of us, it may seem hard to have faith and hard
to believe. At these times only faith in the Lord Jesus
Christ and His Atonement can bring us peace, hope, and
understanding. Only faith that He suffered for our sakes
will give us the strength to endure to the end. When we
gain this faith, we experience a mighty change of heart,
and like Enos, we become stronger and begin to feel a
desire for the welfare of our brothers and sisters. We pray
for them, that they too will be lifted and strengthened
through faith of the Atonement of our Savior Jesus Christ."
Robert D. Hales

It was September 2005, and I was in my third year as divisional vice
president, and attending a leadership meeting in of all places, downtown
Chicago. We were staying at the Marriott Hotel on Michigan Avenue,
the same hotel where my commencement ceremony from law school

had occurred. On Wednesday, one of our free evenings, one of the guys suggested that we do something "Chicago-ish" and I recommended that we attend a night game at Wrigley Field and see the Cubs do battle. Since it was also my birthday, I could not think of a better place to spend it if I had to be away from home and family. The idea was quickly ratified, and my California counterpart suggested that we take a limousine to the park. I nixed that idea and suggested that we take the El so as to stay consistent with our theme of "doing Chicago," and that we eat some genuine Vienna beef hot dogs, and deep dish pizza at the ball park for dinner. He was nervous, and for whatever reason this amused me. It had been years since I had ridden the El, but hey, when in Rome….

This would have been a great trip for me but for the fact that I was worried about my Dad and his health out in Arizona where he was still residing. We had spoken on Sunday night, and while he was looking forward to my brother's visit from Chicago, he was not feeling quite himself. I asked him if I needed to change my tickets and he said no.

I was scheduled to go out and visit my dad the following Monday, and we were both looking forward to doing some shooting in the desert, and simply hanging out. While we were speaking by phone no less than weekly, I had hopes that we could spend some quality time together and have a deep discussion involving our relationship, life, and ultimately death, because several of our recent conversations had touched on that topic.

I flew to Chicago for my meetings first thing Monday morning, and after checking in at my hotel, something prompted me to call my dad. He was at the Tucson airport picking up my brother, and thought he was feeling better. That made me feel better, and we confirmed that in a week's time he would be picking me up at the airport. My afternoon meeting was followed by a business dinner, and I went to bed that night still feeling uneasy though I could not place my finger on why.

Having not slept well, as I often do the first night in a new hotel, I was up early, and after getting in a workout in the fitness center and meeting a couple of my peers for breakfast, we kicked off our meeting.

On the first break of the morning, I had a strong impression to call my dad, which I naturally followed up on. He was still not feeling that well, and after talking to one of his doctors, my brother was going to drive him to the VA hospital in Tucson from Sierra Vista, about a 90 minute drive for some routine blood work. My dad promised that either he or my brother would call with an update. I asked him, "do I need to come out?" to which he replied no. He wanted me to come out the following week as planned.

When I did hear from them later that day, it was to learn that the doctors had decided to keep him over night due to "abnormalities" in his blood results. My next question was of course "Do I need to come out?" And again, the answer was no.

On Wednesday, the blood work was of great concern, resulting in more tests. Do I need to come? No. You have a ticket to come visit next Monday, and it will be nice to have company two weeks in a row. I remember checking in from the ballpark, and my Dad telling me to eat a hot dog for him. He always loved a good Chicago hot dog.

Thursday. To this day I am not certain what happened, but my father passed into a coma, and ultimately died. Two of my brothers were there. Apparently, the radiation that one doctor was using to treat a skin condition, was more than should have been utilized, and had actually forced my father's body to develop leukemia. It took them until Thursday morning to diagnose that condition.

For a long time I felt that the circumstances of his death denied me some degree of closure because the manner in which I had been raised, and how even up until his death, there was always so much more expected of me. Over the ensuing months I experienced some anger and frustration at not being there at the time of his death but then realized that it was very likely that circumstances being what they were, the words that needed to be said would probably have not been uttered.

I flew back home on Friday to Virginia, to prepare for immediate departure to Sierra Vista. We were all in a bit of shock to say the least.

On Monday we all gathered in Sierra Vista, staying at a hotel in town. My father's widow was in the house, and it did not seem appropriate to crash there. Since she spoke only broken English, it fell to us to organize his funeral service at the mortuary as well as to organize the details of his military funeral at the local veteran's cemetery located on Fort Huachuca. The funeral director was LDS, and very accommodating. In terms of the military side of things, it did not hurt that I was Colonel Levin, burying Colonel Levin.

We spent a lot of time at the hotel reminiscing, and it was nice to have most of the family, kids and grandkids, present to say goodbye.

My three brothers were quite distraught. My most vivid memory of that extended time together is of the three of them standing on either side of the casket, stroking my Dad's face, his hair, or his arm. They could not understand why I did not want to participate in it. I attempted to share the Plan of Salvation with them in bite-sized pieces. I shared that Dad as we knew him, was already gone from the shell of his body. Like the proverbial hand leaving the glove, there was nothing of his essence remaining in his body. I know that they could not comprehend what I was saying, but they were comforted by the thought that he was not really gone, and that we all had the chance of seeing him again in the next life, predicated on our faith and the life we choose to live on this Earth.

Having been a member of the Church for twenty years at this point in time, I found added meaning to the Plan of Salvation, and spoke of it during my remarks that day. I know that these remarks were of comfort to a large number of the family. Nonetheless, there was enough of the Jewish drama and finality for some of them that this was viewed as a tragedy because my dad had only turned 69 the previous month.

Out of respect for my father, and because it was a military funeral per his request, I was in uniform that day as well, and was able to convince the burial detail NCO that it would be more than appropriate if he were to direct the honor guard to surrender the expended brass casings from the twenty-one gun salute to me for further distribution to grandchildren and other family members. I recently found out that my wielding my influence as a colonel was one of the more vivid memories of the day for two of my brothers.

As for me, it was the reality that I was the oldest member of the family now, and as the de facto patriarch, it was my responsibility to connect the family, generations past and generations future, into one continuous chain. As the center link of the immediate five generations spanning my grandparents to my grandchildren, it would be my responsibility to ensure that this work was completed.

My other vivid memory of that day was watching my soon-to-be missionary son dedicate his grandfather's grave, and the way this sacred rite softened the hearts of several family members who had earlier expressed hurt feelings. I have no doubt that it was the Spirit that touched their hearts and made them receptive to the simple but elegant prayer offered by an extremely nervous young and newly-ordained Elder.

It was all these little things that have continued to strengthen my testimony and conversion.

CHAPTER 59

SAYONARA

"In this work there must be commitment. There
must be devotion. We are engaged in a great eternal
struggle that concerns the very souls of the sons and
daughters of God. We are not losing. We are winning.
We will continue to win if we will be faithful and
true. We can do it. We must do it. We will do it.
There is nothing the Lord has asked of us
that in faith we cannot accomplish."
Gordon B. Hinckley

"Forget yourself and go to work."
Bryant S. Hinckley

We sent our second missionary off in 2006 all the way to Tokyo.
While Jeff was growing up, a finicky eater and pretty much an introvert
we used to tease him that the Lord would send him somewhere remote
where he would get to eat delicacies like dog. Well, we were close. In
Tokyo (later Nagoya) he taught a great many Filipino investigators, to

whom *Balut,* fertilized duck embryos were a delicacy and rare treat. He was able to indulge on no less than two separate occasions.

Even though he had a year of college under his belt, we did worry about sending him so far away for fear that he would be home sick or not be able to adapt to the work or the language. We were at the temple one night when I slipped into the Celestial Room and said a prayer and received the assurance that not only would he be fine, but that he would greatly prosper while on his mission.

As expected, Jeff had a great mission, was rarely homesick, and came home with a brighter testimony and even more prepared for college and life. We too were greatly blessed while he was gone. I had always heard that the family of the missionary is also blessed for the sacrifice of sending off a missionary, and I always thought that this was another trite thing to be shared with mothers anxious about sending off their babies. I will say that we were blessed with health, *nachas,* and a great appreciation for the work as we read his incredibly detailed letters each week.

Never having had the opportunity to immerse myself in the work and the scriptures in the same manner as both of my sons, I allowed myself to live vicariously through them and experienced my own *nachas!*

CHAPTER 60

BROKEN CODE

"The trouble with us today, there are too many of us
who put question marks instead of periods after what
the Lord says. I want you to think about that. We
shouldn't be concerned about why He said something,
or whether or not it can be made so. Just trust the Lord.
We don't try to find the answers or explanations. We
shouldn't try to spend time explaining what the Lord
didn't see fit to explain. We spend useless time."
Harold B. Lee

    I am a closet author. I love to write. From the very first Officer
Efficiency Report (OER) that I received as a second lieutenant in the
Army up until the final one received upon retirement, I have always
been acknowledged for my written and oral communications skills.
I have spent the better part of the last twenty years writing a weekly
newsletter or leadership column and have now progressed to writing
articles relating to my profession for industry journals. When I am able
to carve out the time, I allow my creative juices to flow in the form of
books in any number of genres.

I would like to think that my writing has become part of my legacy, not just because there are tangible books on the shelf with a bona fide ISBN and Library of Congress registration, but because each book captures a part of my essence. Welcoming each final bound version of the newest book is analogous to welcoming a new member to the family. Even after thirteen books, it does not get old.

While living in Virginia, I became a member of the James River Writers Guild, and it was interesting to visit with budding authors, and to take advantage of conferences where I could meet professional writers like David Baldacci, or to speak with literary agents and reviewers and to pick up tips. One of these tips was to write about things you know and that you enjoy. Having written about the military legal system in my first novel, and blending historical fiction with the modern day in the next, it only seemed natural to draw on my experience as an attorney and a member of the church to craft another story.

Somewhat autobiographical, and with a dash of literary license, that is how *Broken Code* came to life while I was on my sabbatical from Genworth Financial and the long term care business, working on building my own consulting business, and secretly feeding my dream of becoming a full-time author.

Because so much of the story was being drawn from my actual legal career, and some unfortunate experiences with members of the church who did not feel that it was *appropriate* for me to represent people who inadvertently found themselves on the wrong side of the law, going so far as to threaten to leave me or to actually do so, there is a great deal of my raw emotions in the novel.

Writing dialogue drawn from family members, children, and other attorneys made it easy to write as well. What I did not count on, and to this day cannot explain, is the sheer amount of Church doctrine, scriptural references, and modern day revelation that is present in the body of the work. As previously noted, I am NOT a great scripture scholar, and yet, I would either be working on a section of the outline or writing the actual manuscript, and scriptural references, anecdotes, or quotes from church leaders would seemingly magically appear in my head. The internet was still largely in its infancy, and the Church was still very much a printed matter organization, meaning that the internet and the church website were not available to the degree that they are today. I have had friends tell me that the depth of both the legal and religious knowledge makes it a unique book to read. To me it is absolutely amazing, and I do not think for a minute that I wrote it all by myself.

I will say that when I have read it over the years, I am still amazed at how it all flows together as a story, but more significantly how inspired I was in terms of the depth and breadth of doctrine and scriptures weaved into the tapestry of the story. I have no recollection of where it all came from, and now thirteen years later recognize the assistance I received from the Spirit.

Couple this with pieces of the law that would pop into my head – I actually used some of the things that I either dreamed about or woke up thinking about while writing the story to win a few of my cases. The famous loophole in the law happened, but only after I had a dream and subsequently wrote about it in the story. True fact.

I just pulled a copy of it off of the bookshelf and fanned the book open to the beginning and found a wonderful quote attributed to our hero of the story, Douglas John Long, Attorney and Counselor at Law. "Life is a fragile set of scales that require constant balancing…" It was true when I wrote the book, even more so today in this even faster, more furious, and disposable world.

The epilogue put a nice bow on the story and contained a wonderful quote from President Harold B. Lee: "A Testimony is fragile. It is as hard to hold as a moonbeam. It is something that you have to recapture every day of your life." Amen.

CHAPTER 61

THE GAZEBO

"You don't know me; you never knew my heart. No man
knows my history. I cannot tell it: I shall never undertake
it. I don't blame any one for not believing my history.
If I had not experienced what I have, I would not have
believed it myself. I never did harm any man since I
was born in the world. My voice is always for peace."
Joseph Smith

Telling a story such as Alex's is by far the most unique project that
I have worked on in the course of my life. It gave me an appreciation
for the authors I respect such as David McCullough and Doris Kearns
Goodwin, and the painstaking work they do to share history as if it were
merely a story. In this case, it was more than just a story, or tapestry
of pictures and images. Over the next six months I would often have
to stop and remind myself that this was not merely an anonymous
historical account but rather the record of his life!

I was working hard at establishing my consulting business, working
with some pretty powerful business leaders who wanted to join me,

and it was exciting. We were in a meeting at yet another Panera located somewhere in Richmond, VA when my wife Susie called me, and began talking at 120 miles per hour. From what I could gather she was pretty excited and had a lot to share with me. Since it was already after 5:00 in the afternoon, I promised to wrap up my meeting as quickly as possible so that we could talk about her experience as soon I arrived home.

That afternoon Susie had ventured down to the Virginia Holocaust Museum for a tour in conjunction with her book club from Relief Society. Alex Lebenstein, a Holocaust survivor who served as a *docent* at the museum had served as her group's tour guide. What I later learned to be the norm for Alex, a regular 90 minute tour took over three hours as he would inject many of his own experiences throughout the tour.

When I arrived home, Susie was extremely animated, and informed me that I needed to write this man's story and that I should call him immediately. As I was scheduled to fly to Phoenix the very next day and had several things to still prepare, I told her that I would call him when I returned at the end of the week. That was not the right answer, and she quickly dialed Alex's number and handed me the phone. We determined that we would meet in two weeks, on a Saturday, in his apartment, which ironically was about a mile from my office on the Genworth campus. Coincidence? Not likely.

Our meeting was set for 2:00 in the afternoon. My thought process involved a couple hour discussion, after which Susie and I would go for dinner at one my favorite Vietnamese restaurants North of the river. As it was, we talked for seven hours, during which Alex asked me point blank why I wanted to write his story. When I shared that my grandmother's sister had died in Auschwitz, he nodded, and simply said, "okay, you can write my story." It was at 9:00 that Alex then suggested a late dinner at the very restaurant that I had wanted to go where we continued our discussion until midnight. I watched him devour an entire fish, head to tail, picking it clean, which later inspired several anecdotal accounts in the book.

As one might expect on a project of this scale, the memories of a man his age might not be as sharp and focused as desired. However, often, as we peeled the onion and went through taping sessions, reading sessions, and editing sessions, details of memories long since forgotten, repressed, or safely hidden away, would come roaring back providing us greater insights. Sometimes a phone call to contemporaries on one continent or another would clarify or amplify points of contention.

Over the years since the end of the war there have been many of these historical accounts captured by other survivors and historians. Often time these records conflict with one another. I attempted to be as accurate as possible, and to use only the most reliable of sources besides Alex's own memories. If, however, there are any mistakes, misconceptions, or inaccuracies, they were unintentional.

As we captured Alex's life for all posterity, we did not want to over generalize the events, but attempted to provide the reader with an historical context so as to better understand the events as they happened and impacted the life of a young boy. We also tried to tell it from one man's viewpoint rather than that of a country or certain group of people.

For whatever reason, Alex always thought it was noteworthy for everyone to whom he presented the book to know that Chapter 5 was the first chapter written at the beginning of the project. It was a natural place for me to start, especially after having heard the *Kristallnacht* story nearly a dozen times during presentations at local schools and at the Virginia Holocaust Museum. Being proud of the chapter, I subsequently presented it to Alex as a sample of how I saw the book being put together. While the reading went well, and Alex was pleased with the result, as the project progressed, and my wife Susie and I tagged along with Alex to many of his presentations at various schools in the area, I still ended up re-writing this chapter more than a few times. With each passing revision, it became apparent to all of us just how emotionally charged the words contained in this narrative were to all of us engaged in this project. What had once been merely a story or historical account became nearly as real and painful for us as it was for Alex almost seventy years ago. We attribute this to the fact that our love for Alex continued to grow during this same period. We felt his pain, his absolute terror, and the level of despair being experienced by the three Lebensteins as they hid first in the gazebo and then in the cemetery enclave, and attempted to place ourselves there alongside of them, projecting what each of them must have been feeling most notably during that cold desolate period in the cemetery when death was mere inches away. No doubt, for Natan Lebenstein, Alex's father, it was the taking of the final vestiges of any dignity he might have once mustered and retained. For Lotte it was clearly pure terror and pain. For young Alex, it was the beginning of an incredibly cruel odyssey that few young people his age would survive, and it was also the end of his childhood, and the loss of innocence. When we later viewed still pictures of the enclave, and video of Alex sprawled on the ground in front of the enclave we felt the terror all the more.

As parents we all feel a desire, or even a duty, to shield our children from the vulgarity and ugliness that the world has to offer. Today, one of our largest challenges is to protect our children from the evils of images that come into our home via television and the Internet. We attempt to shield our children from these images that can first desensitize and then to forever stain their souls. Gratefully, none of us must physically shield our children from the ravages of an existence where continued life, or the finality of death, can be decided and assigned by the mere pointing of a finger or the nod of a head.

I spent my teenaged years chasing girls, driving cars, and typically worrying about what the impact of a minor case of acne might have on my life. A voracious reader and devoted aficionado of History, I spent a great deal of time learning vicariously, through words that described the tiny sparks of good and the horror of the bad, associated with what historians now describe as the Holocaust, the Final Solution, or more vaguely, World War Two. I heard tales and saw faded photos of distant relatives from the *Old Country* who had perished in the camps, bringing some modicum of reality to the madness.

Alex Lebenstein, spent the same formative period of his life living, breathing, seeing, hearing, and feeling, the horror that was Kristallnacht, the *Ghetto*, and finally, *the Camps*, and up until the day he died at age 82, carried the physical, mental, and emotional scars of what must assuredly be described as the most heinous chapter in the history of Man.

Amazingly, to this day, there are still those who persist in attempting to convince the world that none of this ever happened; that it was a giant hoax perpetuated by politicians. Fortunately, wise leaders like General Dwight Eisenhower insisted on there being a record compiled of what liberating forces found in the camps that littered the European countryside. It was my intent that this book would also dissuade anyone who ever had even a glimmer of doubt.

As I previously mentioned, I remember as a child, encountering these survivors on the streets of downtown Skokie, Illinois. Skokie is located outside of Chicago and represented one of the largest concentrations of Holocaust survivors in the 1960s. I remember walking with my grandparents and viewing the odd tattoos that defaced the forearms of these people. I was told never to point or to stare, but rather allow these people to attempt to resume some form of normalcy in their lives. Alex needed only flash to the recesses of his own memories to recall the satanic blood and horror that was his own childhood; the ruthless dedication of those who operated the trains, gas chambers, firing squads, and crematoria with the efficiency of a large scale corporation that ultimately led to the death of millions of people in the span of eight years as the world went temporarily mad.

I have had the opportunity to walk some of the hallowed ground in Germany where the blood of countless millions of innocents was spilled, land where neither vegetation nor insect, nor wild animals for that matter, can survive due to the still contaminated ground, poisoned by the insecticides used to kill countless people deemed "inferior" by those who viewed themselves as the master race. It is eerie to stand there and to listen to the whispers that still call from the faded and crumbling buildings; more than whispers at times, as the wind howls, filling the air with cries of mothers and children, as well as voices of those powerless to protect them or stop the killing. One can only <u>imagine</u> what it was like to be separated from his family, to suffer the agony of not knowing the fate of these loved ones. If one was fortunate enough to *know* the fate of loved ones, then one could only inwardly mourn their passing and attempt to accompany their spirit out of this mortal life by keeping them in our thoughts, and thereafter remain focused on the sole goal of one's own survival. Alex knew the fate of his father but had to cling to the hope that his mother would survive so that they could be reunited at war's end.

It was my honor to assist Alex, who actually lived it, and who was never able to forget the faces, the sounds, or the smells, as they remained forever emblazoned in his memories; who now desires to tell his story before his own life ends, so that the children will know. It is a story important enough for all of us to learn and to remember, and to share with the children of future generations. There have been many books written on this subject, and like other aspects of our history, this one too is gathering dust. The very essence of the Truth, as well as the eyewitness stories fraught with the emotion and passion of these times, is being lost to future generations with each passing day as more and more of those who lived this horror leave this life.

The tragedy is that the natural man is an enemy of God, and if he does not know of his history, he will be destined to repeat it. For this reason, this unique story must be recorded, and added alongside the accounts of others, that the children will know, and that the memories of millions who perished will be honored, and future generations will be spared the blood and horror of a time when the world truly went mad.

This was one man's story of survival and subsequent re-birth. It was intended as both a testimony and a legacy; an accounting of the triumph of good over evil, and how the will to survive can burn brightly even in a world filled with darkness. It is also a story of how faith can be restored, and the manner by which the power and influence of children, present and future, can bring about change for the better in our world. It is a story of the beauty and innocence of children and the influence that they can be and why it is still possible to have hope for the future.

More than anything else, this is the amazing life story of the sole survivor of the entire Jewish community of the town of Haltern am See, Germany. It is the legacy that he now shares with thousands of children in both the United States and in the Federal Republic of Germany, and through them, with generations to come.

Having visited with Alex on the porch of his apartment in the late fall and hearing the rustling of dried leaves on the sidewalk and watching his visible reaction to the sound that they make, leaves me no doubt that he still could recount the bone-chilling horror of that fateful night as easily as you and I might recall what we had for lunch yesterday. This is the lesson that must be taught to all that will listen to his message.

My life is forever changed for having known this man. I have learned much about life, the desire to do good for others, and about simple gratitude from this man. He has helped me bring a greater perspective to my own existence and honed my skills to really prioritize what does and does not matter in this blink of an eye that we call Life. I suspect that he has done the same for the countless *thousands* of young people for whom he took the time to address and to impart his wisdom, even if they are not aware of it at this point in their life.

Part of my legacy will always stem from the time we spent working with, learning from, and serving Alex Lebenstein. Make no mistake, he was incredibly difficult to work with at times, as he remained an 11 year old boy emotionally in the physical body of an 80 year old man. If he felt that you were attempting to manipulate, dominate, much less control him, his anger would expose itself with great volatility. I also have no doubt that he was another one of those milestone markers along my path.

What started out as a *Mitzvah* – good deed – turned into a great adventure that touched my heart, allowed me to exercise what I believe are gifts that I have received from God, and ultimately strengthened my own testimony of God, the role he plays in our lives, and why this life is a mere speck of sand in an ocean that is the eternal universe.

CHAPTER 62

MIRACLE OF FORGIVENESS

"It is by Obedience that we gather Light into our souls."
Dieter F. Uchtdorf

I always look forward to General Conference, and the Priesthood Session on Saturday evening. That was usually the time that I spent with one or the other of my sons, and we would cap off the night by going for ice cream or donuts.

April 2008 was another one of the few times that I attended conference without one of them, as they were both physically far away. I can remember exactly where I was seated in the chapel when I received another of what I had started to refer to as "Chippenham flashes."

For several weeks I had been receiving spiritual promptings that were leading me to believe that I was going to be called as bishop of the Young Single Adult Ward that served the three greater Richmond area stakes, or literally about a quarter of the state of Virginia.

This particular "flash" directed me to read *The Miracle of Forgiveness* tomorrow morning. To this point I had read it three times in 24 years of church membership, and I will candidly confess that it is not one of my favorite books because I had long felt that Pres. Kimball took a very hard stance on a number of issues related to morality.

The first time I received it, I remember thinking, "I am not going to read that book again. I have read it three times, I don't like it, and the last time I read it was only about five years ago."

About five minutes later I received the same impression, though candidly it was a little firmer in the tone and the depth of the *feeling* I experienced. Again, my mind ran to enjoying sleeping in a little bit, enjoying breakfast, watching a session of general conference at noon, followed by a siesta, and then the concluding session later in the afternoon.

It was probably about ten minutes after those somewhat rebellious thoughts that I received a very distinctive impression that not only communicated with my brain, but also took hold of my heart and the rest of my body and I was directed very pointedly that I *would* read the *Miracle of Forgiveness* in its entirety tomorrow.

Aside from the time that Rick had communicated with me during Sacrament meeting, I had never been subject to such a direct and powerful communication from Heaven. My bravado at not reading the book quickly dissolved and I began to mentally plan how I would complete my reading assignment with the proper mindset. I went to bed that night without telling Susie of my intentions for the next day.

The music for the priesthood session that night was provided by a joint Institute Choir from Logan and Orem. That meant that had Jeff been in school, and not in Nagoya, Japan, he would have been singing in Priesthood! I had already reserved three tickets for October Priesthood so that I could attend it with both Phil and Jeff, but other events conspired against us from going to Utah that fall. I cannot recall a time when we have been able to do that as a trio. Now that we all live in the West, I remain hopeful of doing that very soon.

The next morning, I was up early with the dogs, and started my reading at around 0600. Susie slept in until after 0900, and with all that had been going on in terms of suspected callings, things going on professionally, as well as simply keeping up with life, she was really wondering in her words, how I was "functioning at all, given the total lack of sleep that you are working under." I did not know why I was not sleeping, though I did not feel particularly tired. After breakfast, I shared my experience of the previous evening, and continued my reading, and read until the fourth session of Conference began at noon. In between sessions I continued reading and finished *The Miracle of Forgiveness* as directed.

I found that my reading of the book this time had a totally different impact upon me, and that I felt certain organic changes taking place within me. I viewed and internalized President Kimball's words from what seemed like a totally different perspective.

As we all know, hindsight is perfect 20/20, and as it was later explained to me by a few men for whom I have tremendous respect, this was the mantle of bishop ever so slowly settling down onto my shoulders, and that my reading of the book served several purposes, but most significantly, as an exercise in obedience. It also served to provide necessary instruction so that I could 'hit the ground running,' as well as to allow me to experience a true change in my own heart.

This experience alone, aside from the calling that came 48 hours later, is something that I will remember for the rest of my life, and is another integral part of my testimony on how the Spirit operates and why we must always keep ourselves in a state of readiness so that we do not turn a deaf ear to these spiritual whisperings.

CHAPTER 63

CHIPPENHAM

"You are more kind and compassionate in dealing
with others. You don't judge or criticize or gossip. You
are more aware of others' feelings, and it becomes
natural to look for ways to serve and help."
Dieter F. Uchtdorf

I am so glad that as members of the Church of Latter Day Saints
that we are in fact a recordkeeping people. As I pondered what I wanted
to write about this chapter, I was drawn to the entries in my personal
journal for this time period. I can honestly say that I have not looked at
them in the twelve years since I wrote them, but will say with a feeling
of humility that I am so grateful for having had the discipline and desire
to be obedient in keeping a journal. More than a walk down memory
lane, it served to stir the embers of my testimony and the wonderful
time this was in my life.

I was surprised at how much I had forgotten about the days leading
up to my call as bishop, the feelings that I experienced, and how many
wonderful people were part of my life at that time.

Ironically, I also thought that this would be an "easy" chapter to write, and I was astounded that it took me a great deal of time. Needless to say, I was writing this chapter simultaneous to the previous chapter and experiencing a great deal of emotions as I recounted this milestone event in my life.

Had I elected to recount the many journal entries that I read for the two weeks leading up to, and immediately after, the calling being extended by a loving and devoted Stake President, this chapter would have been in excess of twenty five pages long and far exceeded the message that I want to share.

As noted, the six weeks that led up to the calling were filled with what I referred to as "Chippenham Flashes" or thoughts that would randomly pop into my mind, even while I was engaged in other activities. I was teaching a class at the Jefferson Hotel when the completely unrelated and extraneous thought popped into my head, "you should call an Assistant Executive Secretary to oversee home teaching." In addition to losing my train of thought, I must have looked puzzled, because several people were prompted to ask me if I was okay.

The first few thoughts puzzled me, but I soon started capturing them on my computer as a word document, and by the time of the call, I had nearly two full pages of these random bullet-point thoughts. When I was finally able to properly categorize these thoughts as additional private tutelage by the Spirit, it was a great testimony builder.

When the call was extended to us in our living room, I *knew* that this call had come from God. It was humbling, and yet, I knew that I was prepared and would be buoyed up when required because I had a firm witness that the Lord qualifies those He calls.

After the president had left us, I then shared my entire list of flashes with Susie, and I think she was genuinely impressed when she said that she expected nothing less from me. I them pointed out to her that this was not Don thinking of this stuff, but rather inspiration that I had been receiving.

By the time Sunday rolled around, I was ready for all the secrecy to end. I remember at one point having had the thought "Hard to believe that 45 minutes from now we will be sitting in Sacrament, and I will be sustained as the bishop. How crazy is that?!?"

At that point we were still meeting in the stake center, and because I was still the stake clerk, we were hanging out in the Stake suite until it was time to go in and greet people. Several of the kids wanted to know if I knew who the new bishop was, and I just said, wait 20 minutes and you will find out.

At exactly 1320, I was sitting next to Susie, and I was asked to stand. It was very cool to be sustained, and to be called to take my place up on the stand by the president. He then had Susie bear her testimony, after which I did as well. I cannot remember when I was as calm and comfortable as I was doing it that day.

After the meeting ended, we went into the Stake President's office where I was ordained a bishop and then set apart as a bishop "with all the priesthood keys, as president of the Aaronic Priesthood in the ward, the presiding High Priest, as well as a common judge in Israel." The President explained to all those gathered that it is quite technical, and that the first couple of times that he did it, he had a post it note on his hand to remember it all. The blessing took nearly five minutes, and even then, he forgot to mention that it was the Chippenham Ward that I was to lead over, so he did that part again by himself!

I will share anecdotally that after being set apart and the cat being out of the bag, and we were home for the night, we called each of our children, and the best reaction came from our daughter Katie who showered me with no less than three "shut up's" and two "oh my goshes" clearly astounded that her dear old dad would be called as bishop.

While it was an incredibly challenging calling, it was also the most spiritually rewarding calling in which I have ever served. For as much as I thought I knew about repentance, faith, and charity, I did not know squat, and learned a great deal myself.

Whenever people would ask us how we were enjoying life as empty nesters we would simply reply, "what empty nester? We have 180 kids again," and that is how we viewed our time in the Chippenham Ward. These kids became our life for the four years leading up to our rather abrupt move across the country to Seattle, Washington.

Don Levin

I consider this time to be one of the greatest gifts that the Lord has shared with me, and remain grateful to this day for all of the wonderful moments, most of which I will never be able to share with another soul, I experienced within the four walls of my office in the Monument Avenue chapel.

The spirt that prevailed in our Fast and Testimony meetings is the greatest that I have ever experienced in any of the nine wards in which we have lived and served and had absolutely nothing to do with me.

It was awesome to be known as the "Marrying Bishop" as opposed to the "Burying Bishop" as one of my peers had the onerous distinction of being, and we literally shared in the joy of over fifty weddings during our time in the ward. Today we (Susie) keep tabs on all of our kids and are delighted when we hear about the birth of another baby or another milestone achievement.

I remain eternally grateful for the privilege of having served in this calling and having my testimony strengthened countless times as I witnessed miracles, broken hearts and contrite spirits, and countless miracles of forgiveness.

CHAPTER 64

SOMETIMES THE ANSWER IS NO

"Petitioning in prayer has taught me, again and again, that the vault of heaven with all its blessings is to be opened only by a combination lock. One tumbler falls when there is faith, a second when there is personal righteousness; the third and final tumbler falls only when what is sought is, in God's judgment – not ours – right for us. Sometimes we pound on the vault door for something we want very much and wonder why the door does not open. We would be very spoiled children if that vault door opened any more easily than it does. I can tell, looking back, that God truly loves me by inventorying the petitions He has refused to grant me. Our rejected petitions tell us much about ourselves but also much about our flawless Father. By inventorying our insights, from time to time, it will surprise us what the Lord has done in teaching us. What we have learned in the past can help us to persist in the present. By tallying the truths and keeping such before us, we can also avoid lapsed literacy in spiritual things. If we will let Him, the Holy Ghost will bring all the important insights to our remembrance."

Neal A. Maxwell

I loved every aspect of my life… my wife, my kids and grandkids, my calling as bishop, all those whom I was serving, occasionally getting the chance to do some writing, a little bit of travel, all of it… except my professional life. In the name of re-inventing myself, something that we all had to do from time to time at our company, I had taken a huge step backwards, and because I was in my prime earning years, I genuinely felt stymied.

Durwood Atkins was still the CSO, and after having cleaned house a couple years ago and driving all the DVPs out, to include me, he was loading the ranks of DVPs and General Agents with all of his old cronies, or at least outsiders to the organization. He had completely reversed the process of hiring only from within which had fueled tremendous growth over the years as successful people were rewarded by being allowed to climb the corporate leadership ladder.

As a result, I was out of the corporate side of things and back in the field as the Virginia Agency marketing leader, a district leader, as well as Associate General Agent.

I spent a week up in Falls Church, VA attending GAMA International's Essentials of Leadership and Management where I was the only long term care guy. The vast majority of the class was comprised of financial advisors from First Command, an organization of largely retired military officers in their second career as advisors catering to the active military community. I fit right in, and it was great to spend time with them, and during lunch I talked to them about selling long term care insurance while they imparted practical wisdom to me that would enhance my marketing efforts to financial advisors and other professionals in the greater Richmond area.

I came back from the class fired up, and I was really chomping at the bit. I had a whole new agenda that I wanted to implement but had an exceedingly small patch of the garden in which to plant my new seeds.

Ironically, the DVP that oversaw our agency was someone that I had worked with while a DVP myself, and he encouraged me to apply for the recently vacated (death) Mid-Atlantic Agency. When I asked about Durwood's prohibition about hiring from within, he indicated that he had a green light to hire someone experienced, and quickly, because it was the #1 agency in terms of lead potential. In any event, he thought we could do an end run if necessary. This agency covered Pennsylvania, Maryland, and Delaware, some of my old Division's stomping grounds. I was excited at the prospect of getting to spread my wings again, to run my own agency again, and to build up a new book of renewals that would pay me into the future.

When I shared this opportunity with Susie, she was enthusiastic as well, and having gone to college in Pennsylvania was willing to re-locate when necessary. I drafted one of my business plans, and when finished, thought it was a winner. I submitted the plan and it was greeted with enthusiasm by the DVP.

Part of my modus operandi to making large decisions is to prepare one of my "Ben Franklin's" in which I attempt to objectively weigh all the pros and cons associated with the decision. After I had done that, I then discuss the document with Susie, and ideally make what is an obvious decision one way or the other. Subsequent to that taking place, I then prayed about it. Given the opportunity I prefer to do this praying in the temple because I think the "bandwidth" is a little stronger there.

Following that course of action, I drafted the Ben Franklin, and the Pros won in a landslide. We saw truly little in downside and a whole lot of potential associated with the opportunity. My single largest regret was that I was only in my second year of my ministry as a bishop, and I genuinely felt as if I was making a difference and loved my calling. Nonetheless, because I was in my prime earning years, had two children in college, and I needed to be making money so as to facilitate retirement in a timely manner, I prayed about the decision and did not get a clear feeling either way. That was unusual for me. So, I prayed again, with the same non-result.

Our ward had occasion to travel up to the Washington DC Temple for our monthly temple day and I resolved to find some quiet time on my own during that trip to pray in earnest about the decision. I even went to the Temple fasting that day.

I no sooner was situated in a chair in the corner of the Celestial Room and had started my prayer by expressing thanks for the potential opportunity when I heard a very distinct. "No."

Always fearful that an overactive imagination could be at work, I repeated my prayer, and this time managed to articulate all of the positive reasons that this move would be good for me professionally, for our family financially, and why I wanted to follow through with the opportunity. This time, the NO was softer, and followed by "not at this time."

Feeling a little more than desperate, I repeated the prayer, accentuating all of the positives and why it was only *fair* that I get this opportunity given all of the professional frustrations that I had experienced over the past three years. Again, "no, not at this time."

I was dumbfounded. How could this be happening? I had been praying for an opportunity to get "out from under" and to get back to my sales leadership roots, and I have the top agency all but offered to me with a nod and a wink. How could I walk away from that opportunity?

As I confessed in a previous chapter, I am not a great expert when it comes to the Scriptures, but this time I had one pop into my mind, or have it *placed* in my mind. Proverbs 16:9. "In their hearts humans plan their course, but the Lord establishes their steps." As soon as I heard that, and pondered it for a moment, I knew that the answer had to regrettably be NO. I was destined to stay where I was for another season, and to continue to serve as bishop of my ward. This thought filled me with some consolation.

As soon as I had that thought, a warm feeling filled me, and I felt peace replace the frustration that I had been experiencing, Then John 16:33, "I have told you these things, so that in me you may have peace. In this world you will have trouble. But take heart! I have overcome the world." When that thought popped into my head, I knew my destiny, at least for the short term.

Because we had carpooled up to the temple, it was not until after we arrived back in Richmond that I was able to share with Susie what had transpired in the temple. She was shocked. Shocked at the answer, and even more so that I was willing to accept the answer, for I basically have always had the reputation of "damn the torpedoes, full speed ahead." This time was different.

Obviously when I had to convey my decision to the DVP I could not go into the detail of my temple experience, so I simply told him that circumstances had changed, and that while I would ordinarily have jumped at the chance, that I would have to wait for the next one. I remember how I approached that conversation with a great deal of trepidation because I feared that he would think I was an absolute idiot for turning it down, but he was very gracious, and thanked me for my efforts in terms of the business plan.

I will admit that whenever things became frustrating at the office and I remembered that I willingly turned down my own parole from my current situation, I would take comfort in my calling and the successes that I was enjoying in helping people.

Ultimately, this was a wonderful faith promoting experience, and I know that my testimony grew as a result of it. I have every confidence that what appeared to be a total sacrifice on my part was as much a lesson on the law of consecration and why obedience is so important.

CHAPTER 65

STAY THE COURSE

"Well was it said of old, 'Where there is no
vision, the people perish' Proverbs 29:18. There
is no place in this work for those who believe
only in the gospel of doom and gloom.
The gospel is good news. It is a message of triumph.
It is a cause to be embraced with enthusiasm."
Gordon B. Hinckley

We did not leave Virginia, electing to stay the course as directed. Unfortunately, with each passing week and month, the frustration was mounting. On a subsequent trip to the temple accompanied by prayer, my answer came in the form of "stay the course." I found that this was a lot easier said than done. I was also impressed to find a favorite talk from General Conference that Elder Jeffrey R. Holland had delivered back in 1999: "Some blessings come soon, some come late, and some don't come until heaven; but for those who embrace the gospel of Jesus Christ, they come. To any who may be struggling to see that light and find that hope, I say: Hold on. Keep trying. God loves you. Things will improve. Christ comes to you in His 'more excellent ministry' with a future of 'better promises.' He is your 'high priest of good things to come.'"

Was it all a test of faith? It did not matter. I tried to stay out of the agency office as much as possible, working out of the offices of some of my financial advisor "partners" while scheduling a great number of events and meetings that kept me in the field either marketing, or working with and training my new agents. This was old hat for me, and I was building something for myself even if it meant more money in my boss' pocket.

As it was, not departing for the Mid-Atlantic meant another two plus years of professional frustration, but a number of things that I worked on and developed came to fruition and we did enjoy a modicum of success that included platinum status as the number 2 district in the entire company, qualification for the platinum incentive weekend to New York City which was another milestone moment, and ultimately the incentive trip to Paris, France with the bonus day to the Loire Valley. It also allowed me the time to really hone several projects on which I was working that ultimately enabled me to hit the ground running when the *right* opportunity came along two years later.

I kept up the positive self-talk, and encouraged myself to control what I could control, and to let everything else roll off my back. Unfortunately, my work was being stolen from me. The first long term care insurance producer One Card System ever to exist was the one that I developed after my time with the First Command guys up in Falls Church. I used it successfully in my district, and yet somehow it became my boss' work. I will never forget the time we were sitting in a General Agents meeting (with the few Associate General Agents also in attendance) when as they went around the room, the boss started talking about *his* One Card System. Not *Don's* One Card, or even the *Virginia One Card* which would have been okay, or even OUR One Card, but when I heard *MY* one card come out of his mouth – my gosh, I was sitting right next to him – that was when I knew I had to get out.

At this point in time I loved the weekends, particularly Sunday, even if they stretched to 10 or 12 hour days because I was energized the entire time I was at church until I got home and loosened the tie, at which time I was toast. But come Monday morning, and it was back to the grind, I was chafing and maybe even slowly dying professionally. But with Durwood still at the helm calling the shots and blocking any advancement, all I could do was put my shoulder to the proverbial wheel and control that which was in my control. As noted, I recruited, trained, and launched a bunch of new agents, developed my own lead platform, and tried to be as autonomous as possible. Being the #2 District in country also certainly fueled Virginia's rise to Platinum status, but again it was all about the boss, but I suspect more than a few people knew the score and we were being noticed.

The Texas Agency opened up, and while I applied for it, ironically, the DVP that was running the East and who would have helped me get into the Mid-Atlantic, saw the handwriting on the wall, and he bailed out and *he* took over Texas. That was a blow, because with all the military presence in the state, I had a definitive plan on how to work that market. I felt like I was slowly sinking to the bottom, to never see the light of day again.

The new DVP was a nice guy but from another channel within the company. Not really a long term care guy, I struck up a friendship with him, and even offered to help him get acclimated since half of the East was my old division in the Northeast. Interestingly enough, we had the same birthday – we were literally only about four hours apart in age. He was both receptive to, and grateful for, my coaching, and when I suggested that the best way for him to learn what we do in the field would be for me to come visit he and his wife in their home and conduct a bona fide home interview, they were so enthralled that they became clients that very day when I sold them a long term care insurance policy.

He knew that I was getting worked over by my boss, who was doing everything possible to ingratiate himself with him, and he became a confidant. Very quickly he figured out that I was only biding my time and tried to be helpful by being respectful and supportive. All the while I was dying a little bit more with each passing day. I was not sure whether I wanted to stay the course and started praying for some way out. I even contemplated going to work for another general agent and taking over one of his states for him out West, figuring that getting closer to the kids and grandkids that were starting to show up in abundance was worth the move. Those talks started getting real, and I once again began constructing a new Ben Franklin, but other things would happen that would keep these plans from coming to fruition.

CHAPTER 66

TRANSITIONS

"You ae caging the tiger that has controlled your life. It
will shake the bars, growl, threaten and cause you some
disturbance. I promise you that this period will pass...
As you stand firm, it will pass."
Richard G. Scott

As the business contracted, so did the leadership hierarchy. We were
now down to two DVPs – East and West. Ironically, I had helped to hire
the West guy years ago, even though it was a foregone conclusion that
he was going to join us because he was an old pal of Durwood. Even he
was telling me that I needed to get out of Virginia.

On one of his trips to Richmond (he lived in Minnesota), I invited
him to breakfast. Recognizing that the 23 agencies of the company were
split 11 in the East and 12 in the West, I knew I had to get this guy
on board. Imagine my surprise when during breakfast at the hotel he
announces that he does not like me. Excuse me? How do you respond to
something like that? I tried to peel that onion to determine if I had done
or said anything to offend him during the time we worked together,

and he said no. Though after a few more questions he conceded that he had not liked me when we were DVP peers because I "always had the answers, and made the job look easy." Yikes. This was going to be one long uphill putt.

To this day, I do not know what prompted me to respond as I did, but I asked him to be my mentor. He was equally shocked by the proposal, but to his credit and our mutual benefit, he agreed. My first assignment that day was to read Herman Hesse's *Journey to the East* and to call him with my thoughts. When I told him that I had read it, and nearly everything that Hesse ever wrote in a college course years ago, he smiled, and I like to think this was the genesis of what developed into a great relationship. Ultimately, he became my biggest fan, and we would talk regularly. Later down the road, once we had moved to Seattle, he was always there to encourage the next big step to include things like, "you should double the size of your agency next year..." The turn-around in our relationship was nearly unbelievable to those who knew from where we had started.

At this same time, an Executive Headhunter contacted me and said that another company was interested in me. This company was looking for a Senior Vice President for the State of Virginia with three offices in Roanoke, Richmond, and Virginia Beach. I would be reporting directly to the Executive Vice President. It was intriguing enough that I interviewed for the role and was almost immediately offered the position. When I pointed out to them that I was not a life insurance or annuity guy but rather a long term care guy, their response was "no, you are a senior sales leader with a proven record of success. The product knowledge is easy to acquire, the leadership is not." This was in June 2011. When I told them that I was not available until the first of the year, they said, "we'll wait. You are worth the wait." I was on cloud nine. For as much as I hated the idea of leaving the long term care industry, I finally had an escape raft.

Things really started to accelerate when almost simultaneously to the offer from the other company, the New York agency suddenly came open. The incumbent was heading home to Texas to semi-retire and to work under the new GA down there. Hmm. Interesting. Needless to say, my creative juices clashed with my competitive juices (New York was absolutely crushing it in terms of premium at this point) and I wanted to interview for it. My first point of contact was unfortunately an interview with my nemesis Durwood. He discouraged my applying for the role but would not give me a concrete reason as to why I should not pursue it.

Within a week or two as the process dragged on, the reason for me not to apply for it became clear: Durwood was being removed from the Chief Sales Officer role (ding dong the witch is dead) effective June 30, and effective July 1 *he* was taking over The Empire State. Oliver Stone could have a field day with the speculation of how all of this had shaken out. In any event, Darth Vader was heading home to the Empire State with an incredibly soft landing after significantly trashing our business for too many years.

Adding insult to injury, Durwood attempted to recruit *me* to run Upstate New York as a separate sub-agency. While I should have laughed in his face, I was desperate enough that I actually considered his vision for a few days, until he made the "opportunity" into a complete start up for me by excluding the existing agent force in the area. This move would only benefit him. I also remember that the entire time I was talking to him it was reminiscent of the moment in *It's a Wonderful Life* when George Bailey is shaking Mr. Potter's hand. With that image flashing in my mind, I went home and quietly put the Ben Franklin for Upstate New York into the shredder. The good news is with the other company's offer now in hand, I now had an ace up my sleeve.

I had met Pete, Genworth's new president at a conference a few months earlier, and after being seated at his dinner table on the first night, he had sought me out several times during the conference "just to talk." One morning I was sitting in the lobby reading the newspaper when someone walked up and kicked my shoe. When I looked over the top of my paper, it was Pete, and with a nod of his head, he muttered, "coffee. Walk with me. We need to talk." There were also several occasions when I would receive phone calls from him just to confirm certain company policies or to provide input on proposed changes to product or procedure. It was a remarkably interesting time for me. Was I a former Somebody, or just a voice from the street that he could trust?

So, as a courtesy, the next time I saw him on campus, I let him know about the offer from the other company, and I was a little shocked by his reaction when he looked me square in the eye and said, "You aren't going anywhere. *Laurel* is coming on board in about a month, you will be one of her first orders of business." Laurel? Well, that confirmed the rumor that the next CSO was a woman. But that I would be one of her first orders of business, yeah right.

Shame on me, but I was seated in my office in the Virginia agency when Hurricane Laurel came whirling through the office. When she saw the nameplate on my desk, she pointed at me, and said, "You and I are supposed to have lunch asap. Expect a phone call from my assistant." Knock me over with a feather.

It was only the next week when I went to that first lunch across the street at the Westin Hotel with an agenda of what I wanted to say and an internal agenda of what I did not want to discuss. Well, we hit it off that very first lunch, and in a matter of minutes she had me spilling my guts about everything from my do-not-talk list. I shared with her many times thereafter that it was probably a good thing that we were not married to one another. We had another two lunches over the next three weeks and established a good relationship. Over time, Laurel became a good friend and enthusiastic fan. When she would later come to Seattle to visit us, she fell in love with our grandbabies, and we would often have to search her carry-on luggage to ensure that she had not absconded with them.

It was during our Platinum Trip to NYC in October that Laurel and I would begin *serious* discussions about where I wanted to go as a General Agent. With New York, Texas, the Carolinas, and Virginia unavailable, my prayers had left me with an impression that I should seek "new birth and go forth." I did not understand it until I was perusing the New Testament and found 1 Peter. I was then impressed to review the agency rankings and almost immediately was drawn to PNW Agency. The Pacific Northwest. Washington, Oregon, and Alaska mired in last place. Another potential resurrection job like Cincinnati had been ten years earlier.

When Laurel asked me where I wanted to go, I quietly said "PNW."
The answer surprised her, and her next question was "have you lived
there before, are you trying to get back there?"

I smiled, and said, "No. I spent six weeks there while in the Army,
but otherwise, no ties to the area. Being in Seattle or Portland would
make seeing the kids in Idaho and Utah a lot easier, but it is a dying
agency. It needs new life, and being in last place, there is no place to go
but up." She smiled sweetly – a smile I later learned how to read – and
clearly loved that answer. Interestingly enough as soon as the words were
out of my mouth, I *knew* that it was the right answer, and I had found
my destiny. There would be new birth in PNW.

Two weeks later, Human Resources posted a vacancy for a General
Agency position in...the Pacific Northwest. Both DVPs were excited to
sponsor my candidacy. I dusted off my, by this time, well-worn business
plan, only this time feeling a surge of faith and confidence that not
only was it going to happen, but that we were going to absolutely rock
in this new role.

The interview process was fun! The six-person panel discussion, the
individual interviews with the two DVPs, and of course with Laurel, all
took place on Monday, in mid-November. On Monday night I received
a call from my newfound benefactor in the West inviting me to join
the three of them in Laurel's office the next day. It was a mysterious
invitation that even my client the East DVP could not shed light on.
He too had been invited to attend and that was all he knew. Since my
previous job offers had taken no less than eight weeks to materialize,
I knew something was up, but I could not put my finger on what it
might be in this case.

I prayed that night and had a solid feeling that I was going to get
an offer for the job, but that something was different. I could almost
smell the change in the air, which around Genworth was not hard to
do since we seemingly endured *annual* re-organizations. While I enjoy
change enough to embrace it and initiate it, my Spidey senses were
definitely tingling.

As often happens when I go to bed praying and thinking about
things, my subconscious kicks into gear and we go to extra innings.

When I woke up the next morning, I had two seemingly disconnected thoughts from two vastly different sources. Maya Angelou wrote, "If you don't like something, change it. If you cannot change it, change your attitude." I pondered that for a while and realized that new birth was only going to occur if we changed the attitude of the agent force in the PNW. And I felt okay about that, because I am convinced that attitude can be a great change agent and can also be a great force multiplier.

Another semester long course in college had centered on the writings of Kurt Vonnegut. "We are what we pretend to be, so we must be careful about what we pretend to be." With that resonating in my ears, I knew that I needed to go to this meeting in Laurel's office with an open mind and humility in my heart.

Laurel was all smiles, and the guys were strangely quiet, when I walked into her office at precisely 1:30 as directed. The two guys were seated in front of her desk, and when she sat down behind her desk, that left the chair to the side of her desk for me to sit in as she announced, "you blew everybody away yesterday – even those who knew you – and you ARE our leading candidate for the Pacific Northwest, and we wanted you to be as read in on what is going to change in 2012, as well as to get your insights on our proposals."

She then launched into a near hour-long dissertation of the changes that were coming to the General Agent contract, the financial aspects of the role, as well as changes for the agents in terms of compensation, the production of company generated leads, and what they perceived as the needs of the PNW agency. I sat there and listened, making comments when appropriate, feeling wonderfully comfortable while making them.

When she finished her overview, I was afforded nearly an equal amount of time to ask questions, share my perceptions, and to add my two cents to the process. For all that time, it was only Laurel and I talking. "I thought it was only fair that you knew about all of these changes that will be enacted on January 1, because these changes are pretty significant, and we wanted you to have all of the facts before you decide to literally move across the country."

At this point I seized this initiative, and very casually said, "okay, so roll back the tape an hour or so, and am I correct in assuming that as the leading candidate, if I like these proposed changes, that we are done?"

Laurel then swiveled in her chair to face the two guys and asked, "did you hear anything from Don that would change the decision we made last night?"

A couple of "nopes" and head shakes, and she then swiveled back to me, and said, "Don, I want to formally offer you the role of General Agent of the PNW, and welcome you to our leadership team. This will be effective December 1, but with the expectation that you will start immediately in terms of planning and talking to people out there. This is the first major leadership decision that we have made as a leadership team, and I am thrilled with it. We are going to put the spotlight on you because you are going to be the prototype of the new GA in this company of elite LTC planning specialists. You have done it before, and you are going to do it with a new crop of agents now. It will be about new growth."

When I immediately accepted the role, she was surprised, and asked if I wanted some time to think about it or to discuss it with Susie. Recognizing that the changes would get us closer to family, make what we were going to do in Seattle even more financially advantageous to us, and that Susie wouldn't care about the nuts and bolts of the changes, I quietly reaffirmed my acceptance of the role.

My buddy in the West label my performance the "best 'assumptive close' he had ever seen," and added that I had come in and sat down like I was part of the leadership team and that we were all partners." Laurel then added with that same winning smile, "as of today he *is* a partner in our leadership team."

After a big hug from Laurel, and firm handshakes from the guys, I walked out with my friend from the East who then told me, "you absolutely nailed it yesterday and today. You demonstrated that you *are* coachable, and that you are humble – a combination that cannot be beat. Congratulations, and I am proud of you."

When I went back to the hotel with my new boss for the West, I asked him pointblank, "how do you really feel about our working together?" Without any hesitation, he looked straight back at me and said, "I am thrilled. You earned this opportunity in every way imaginable." It was a great moment.

It was hush hush until the following week, but after that the news spread fast, and there was a lot of excitement. A Ben Franklin quickly determined that we would be better served in Seattle rather than Portland, and we started preparing to move across the country. It was a great Thanksgiving!

I called the other company, and they were more than gracious, and completely understood my decision and did not feel like I had jerked them around, leaving the door open if I ever changed my mind down the road. I was going to be back in the game.

When I prayed for confirmation of what already felt like a wonderful decision and accompanying opportunity, the words of Matthew 25:23 came to mind. "His Lord said unto him, 'Well done, good and faithful servant; thou hast been faithful over a few things; I will make thee ruler over many things; enter thou into the joy of the Lord." This time the answer was YES. We were going to Seattle.

CHAPTER 67

ISLE OF TEARS

"When our hearts turn to our ancestors, something changes inside us. We feel part of something greater than ourselves. Our inborn yearnings for family connections are fulfilled when we are linked to our ancestors through sacred ordinances of the temple. Because of the importance of this work, the Church has built temples closer to the people, and family history research is being facilitated as never before. Methods to find and prepare names for temple ordinances are also improving."
Russell M. Nelson

We were in New York City for a "platinum incentive" weekend that I had earned by virtue of having had the #2 sales district in the country. This was the very same trip on which Laurel and I began our discussions in earnest about what it was going to take to keep me with the company and taking a pass on the other company's looming offer.

This extended visit to NYC featured a three-night stay at the Pierre Hotel on the edge of Central Park, right across from the Plaza Hotel, a couple of Broadway shows, extravagant dinners, and some free time to sightsee or in our case, to travel to Ellis Island, also known as the Isle of Tears.

The first time I heard the song *Isle of Tears* performed by the Irish Tenors, it was an incredibly emotional experience for me because it immediately conjured up an image of my beloved Grandma Mary coming through Ellis Island in 1913 as a mere ten year old "greenhorn" not speaking English, only knowing that a brother waited for her in America.

> *On the first day on January,*
> *Eighteen ninety-two,*
> *They opened Ellis Island and they let*
> *The people through.*
> *And the first to cross the threshold*
> *Of that isle of hope and tears,*
> *Was Annie Moore from Ireland*
> *Who was all of fifteen years.*

Source: <u>LyricFind</u>
Songwriters: David Downes
The New Ground / Isle of Hope, Isle of Tears lyrics © Liffey Publishing Ltd.

For many years both my cousin and I had attempted to find the ship on which she had come over from the Old Country. We had the rough date of August 1, 1913, but no idea of the actual ship and more importantly the exact name (or variation) under which she had traveled. The process of sifting through hundreds of ships' manifests over the years had not been fruitful, but as my wife and I made our plans for our Saturday morning sojourn via the subway to the ferry dock and out to the Island itself, I had a high degree of confidence that we would be successful in our search.

I awoke very early that morning, left our very tiny [and extremely overpriced] room for a quick workout in the fitness center, and then to take some time by myself in a quiet corner of the lobby where I said a prayer that we would be successful in our efforts to further unite our family – generations past and future – on our trip to Ellis Island.

Almost immediately I was overwhelmed with a feeling of warmth, joy, anticipation, and felt the presence of my grandmother. I should note that during the time I was bishop that my experiences with prayer had become greatly heightened, but what I was feeling at that moment far exceeded those standards. I went upstairs and rousted my wife so that we could wolf down our breakfast and get on the Subway to the Battery.

I felt my grandmother's presence the entire time we were traveling down to the Battery ferry terminal, and even remarked how wonderful this experience already was for me. My wife continued to caution me to temper my emotions, and to keep my expectations reasonably in check, but I *knew* we were going to be successful because of that prayer. I could literally hear my grandmother calling "Hi Handsome" to me.

We stayed on the ferry when it docked at Liberty Island, and I was chomping at the bit as the gang plank was lowered on to Ellis Island. I literally pulled my wife by the hand once the ferry was docked on the island and we ran into the main terminal where we were met by a Ranger. He informed us that we should start on the third level and work our way down if we were interested in seeing everything in one visit. When I told him that I wanted to go into the archives, he looked at his watch and advised that even though it was early, we could have as much as a three hour wait inside.

When we walked into the archives, there was absolutely nobody ahead of us, and after paying for a swipe card and finding a computer terminal began our search. A very helpful young lady (graduate student) assisted us, and in a matter of only ten minutes we had refined and manipulated our search several times when all at once we had found my grandmother and one of her other brothers on the manifest of the SS Rotterdam, which arrived at Ellis Island on August 4, 1913. The manifest clearly identified her as MASHE LISCHE, accompanied by her brother Itzek, en route to her brother Max Liss in Chicago, at an address that I clearly recognized. Susie had goose bumps, and I was doing all that I could to not burst into tears in front of this young lady.

Even now, some nine years after the fact, I am amazed at how guided we were that day. The fact that there was nobody ahead of us in line at the archives (which had already been open for a few hours by the time we arrived), there was an available terminal for me to utilize, and the fact that even after twenty five years of sporadic review of these records, we were literally directed to the proper ship and manifest with the assistance of a young lady who will probably not remember how she was an angel to me that day.

To say that finding this manifest and picture of this ship was the high point of the trip for me would again be a gross understatement. While it would be another six years before I was settled enough to really begin my family history work in earnest, the memory of that day, and the manner in which we were guided by the Spirit, was another milestone for me along my Path. The veil was very thin that day, and I am grateful that I had the opportunity to feel my grandmother's spirit once again in close proximity to me.

CHAPTER 68

THE EMERALD CITY

"Men make history and not the other way around. In
periods where there is no leadership, society stands still.
Progress occurs when courageous, skillful leaders seize
the opportunity to change things for the better."
Harry S. Truman

We had completed the Ben Franklin, reviewed it, and concluded
that Seattle was the place for us to be rather than Portland, so we
started plans to go West. I would make a couple trips in the month of
December, then enjoy the holidays in Virginia, and then Susie would
come out in January to start house hunting.

I tried a succession of extended stays and "cheap" motels, and
finally settled on one literally around the corner from our eventual
office location. Susie did not like it when she came out, but it worked
for me and met my needs or in other words, it was convenient and
relatively cheap.

I was excited for the opportunity and up for the challenge of having
my own agency again. Between the other agencies that I had "fixed"

and the Army units that I had turned around, I was confident – not cocky – that with an eye towards attention to detail, a focus on people, and the basics of blocking and tackling, we could restore PNW to the top ranks. The new structure that Laurel had outlined for me filled me with even more enthusiasm because the opportunity to maximize my earnings was there as well. I felt that I had some time to make up for, especially if we wanted the freedom down the road to serve a mission or to help our kids establish themselves.

My three year plan originally called for us to finish in the top ten the first year, but then realized that if we were going for top ten, that we may as well go for top seven and make a statement. Cracking the top 7 [of 23] would also reward Susie and I with whatever incentive trip was being offered that year. If we accomplished this milestone, the next year we would shoot for the top four and platinum status, and after that, well, we would see where we stood at that point.

While I felt confident that I could bring to the agents the "love and attention" that had been missing in their lives, I was also convinced that this gig was going to be all about servant leadership and that while I could go in and re-shape the agency in my image by force, all would be better served if as a transformational leader I modeled the way.

I should also make it clear that the vacancy in PNW was not created solely for my benefit. My predecessor Ted had clearly earned being fired after literally flying this once high-flying agency into Mount Rainier. He had retired as a young man, and when the new GA model was launched, he came back. Unfortunately, he ignored the agency, and was out of state pursuing a girlfriend every other week. Absentee leadership does not work. I discovered that some of the agents clearly resented the lack of attention, while others could have cared less so long as their precious leads kept flowing. Some interesting dynamics.

I was the new guy. From the East no less. I had never encountered this type of bigotry before but was well aware that the differences between the agencies in the West and East were actually palpable. I had seen them over the years, but never paid attention up until now, when I most decidedly had a dog in the fight.

I was trying to balance humility and my own coachability with providing leadership. It was remarkably similar to the experience in Cincinnati, and in dealing with parts of the Northeast. I conducted one on one interviews with all the agents, in which I did a lot of listening. I treated them all as fact finding conversations. I limited my communication to painting a bright picture wherein the PNW was back on top and where each of them fit into the picture. I wanted to spark some excitement and enthusiasm leading up to our first all hands agency meeting.

Because I wanted an identity for the agency around which the agents could rally, I solicited about a dozen different ideas that ranged from The Orcas (indigenous to Washington, Oregon, and Alaska) and Trailblazers, to the Pathfinders and Mariners. I surreptitiously slipped in my proposed Wolf Pack, and by the end of the meeting that we held at the University of Phoenix, we were the PNW Wolf Pack, because as Rudyard Kipling so eloquently said it, "For the strength of the Pack is the Wolf, and the strength of the Wolf is the Pack." The best part is everyone thought it was a group decision.

I was also looking for an office location, more central to the region, and the highway network and ultimately moved it an hour south to the Tukwila area.

At the same time Susie was working with a realtor to find us a house. It clearly was a seller's market, and the pickings were slim. We ultimately found a "short sale" by a bank, down in Bonney Lake. I was not thrilled with the distance and drive from the office, but we were getting a little desperate. Sadly, I was not really all that thrilled with the house, but we bought it anyway. It must not have been meant to be, because we waited over two months for the bank to reject the offer.

I was flying back to Seattle from Orlando on Wednesday evening, when during a stopover in Chicago, I cleared voicemails and learned that we did not have a house because of the decision by the bank. When I reported this to Susie back in Virginia, who was contemplating the arrival of our movers the following week, things became a little animated. My mission: find us a house in Seattle.

I landed in Seattle at midnight and took a taxi back to my office where I had left my car. It was always my practice to check out of the hotel or extended stay if I was physically out of town and to stash my stuff in the office. Since it was going on 0100 and I was going to be in the gym at 0530 anyway, I slept on the floor in my office, saving myself a night's lodging. That is called frugality. Susie says it is my being cheap. Whatever.

I woke up at 0500 and took stock of our situation. Our movers were coming the following Thursday because the closing on the house was the next day. We would be homeless in eight days. I said a prayer that I would be able to find a house that met our needs and that would make Susie happy. For whatever reason, Bonney Lake kept popping into my mind. I would [selfishly] reject it, but it kept coming back. While it was a nice enough small town, it was at best a 40 minute drive for me, and usually longer, to the office. Nonetheless, that was the venue that kept coming back to me, even though we had looked in at least a dozen other towns and cities.

I went to the gym, showered, and by this time it was a civil enough hour for me to call our realtor. When I asked her what she was doing that day, she said that she had to show another couple around the area. I told her that I was *buying* a house that day, and she was welcome to accompany me, or I would do it on my own. She agreed to *meet me,* rather than chauffer me, and I was off to Bonney Lake, not quite sure where I was going to look.

I went to look at one house that I had a vague recollection of, and when I arrived there I noticed a house down the street that had been previously reported as sold when we went through the neighborhood was apparently back on the market. When I made an inquiry at the sales office, I was informed that the buyer's financing had fallen through just the day before and the builder was quite anxious to sell it. My ears perked up on that note, and I was even more anxious to see it.

When my realtor arrived, we walked through the property, and I liked it… a lot. Because Deb had been with Susie in dozens of houses, and knew what Susie was looking for, I asked her somewhat tongue in cheek whether she thought Susie would like it. Her answer was that if Susie did not like it, she would move in with me. I felt confident that I had the female vote. I called Susie, and she recalled having been in a similar house on the next block, and with the aid of some cellphone technology, I was able to share enough of the home's features to determine that we would buy it.

The negotiations were pretty much a non-event. The salesperson had tipped her hand that the builder was anxious to sell, and I had the money with which to buy. We bought the house at a good price, and peace reigned on earth. We had a house. Coincidence? I think not.

We had our office, we had our home, and things were coming together on all fronts. We closed very quickly and had keys to the house when the movers arrived with our household goods. Unfortunately I was not in town, and that left Susie alone to receive all of our household goods. Fortunately I arrived home shortly thereafter and we were able to quickly get settled in. It was quickly time for our next adventure: Walter.

CHAPTER 69

MILLION DOLLAR BABY

"My testimony to you is that miracles do happen! They are
happening on the earth today, and they will continue to
happen, particularly to those who believe and have great
faith. Miracles occur frequently in the lives of humble,
fine Latter-day Saints who have the faith to make them
possible. My feeling is that the greatest of all miracles is
the one that happens in the life of a person who really
learns how to pray, who exercises faith to repent, and
who lives the gospel in a simple and obedient way."
Glen L. Rudd

We were in the midst of the 2011 holiday season, and life was
good! After some trials that had really tested us, we believed that we
had turned the corner and that better days were definitely ahead of
us. I had just started my new position as the General Agent for the
Pacific Northwest on the first of the month, but was still in Richmond,
Virginia, essentially home for the holidays.

We were hosting our daughter Eliese and her husband Landon who
were visiting from Utah. Since this was Landon's first time on the East

Coast, we were touring Washington D.C., and having a lovely day; even the traffic up I-95 between Richmond and D.C. had cooperated. We were three days from Christmas and I was really looking forward to having a great Christmas especially because our future looked so bright with our upcoming move to Seattle to take place later in the Spring. The move would bring us much closer geographically to all of our children and grandchildren, and we were entering another phase of our life.

Our son Jeff (Donald Jr.) and his wife Marie were expecting their first baby, and we were pretty excited about it. At this point Baby Donny as he had been dubbed, was eighteen weeks along, and we had no reason to suspect any problems before his April arrival.

Susie and the kids were inside a museum or something because I was actually sitting in the car by myself finishing up a business call when Jeff and Marie called to break the news to us that there was something wrong with the baby, and that they would probably lose Baby Donny within the next two weeks unless they took the doctor up on his offer of "dealing with it now." I was shocked. First, because this was like a lightning bolt out of nowhere, and second because the doctors would spring the option of termination on young kids in the same breath that they alert them to a problem. I still cannot reconcile whether this was callousness or the impersonal aspect that medical practicality sometimes requires. In any event, because they had had a little time to process the news, they were in a better position to comfort me than I was able to comfort them. But even at that moment, something told me that the doctors were wrong, and that we were still going to have this baby.

Even though I was not supposed to tell anyone but Susie because it was their intention not to tell anyone but the grandparents for fear of putting a damper on the holidays, it was impossible to hide it from Eliese and Landon. Because we were so close to the Washington DC temple, I swung in there and added the three of them to the Temple's prayer roll, hoping for the power of prayer to influence the science of the situation.

Apparently the diagnosis for Walter (they subsequently changed his name from Donald Jeffrey III to Walter Jeffrey working from the premise that after he was gone that he would be in the company of his maternal grandfather, Walter, who had previously died) was that he was suffering from Hydrops and a probable Diaphragmatic Hernia with undetermined consequences at this point. I did not know enough to even hazard a guess as to what was going to become of the baby, *but* I still had that *feeling* that he was going to be okay. I have been accused of wishful thinking in the past, but I genuinely felt at peace with saying all that I did with my out loud voice.

Well, we talked the next day, and my son was even more pragmatic about the outcome, and when I protested, all he did was refer me to the web to check out what the two medical conditions were all about. When I went online to research both, I was stunned. The babies with Hydrops often suffer from malformation which contributes to their high (99%) mortality rate. Things were not looking good for the home team. To this day, my heart aches when I think about it all. My heart was in my throat, and I prayed like never before. I cried on and off for three days, until early on Christmas morning when I received a strong impression that he would be okay. When I shared this impression with Susie, and later with the kids, they all looked at me with a degree of sympathy and attributed my beliefs to a certain degree of denial on my part.

Even though the doctors pretty much had written the baby off and had told my kids that with the 99% mortality rate, that they should consider *all of their options,* I was still feeling strongly that we were going to have this baby. In hindsight I believe that this experience strengthened my testimony more than I can even comprehend.

To this day when I relate this story and people ask me *why* I felt as strongly and confident as I did, I can only say that I had experienced a witness that we were going to be allowed to host this very special spirit. It was beyond mere faith, but I firmly believed then, as I do now, that when we *choose* to view the world around us without demanding to know the whys, the when's, and the how's, that we can then reap the rewards of our faith. It is what enduring to the end is all about. Real obedience means accepting Heaven's Plan for us unconditionally, without complaining, and realizing that we are always subject to His will. It also means *listening* for His will, so that we are receptive to the soft whisperings of the Spirit. Again, I must wonder in perfect hindsight how many times I *missed* hearing these soft whisperings because I thought I knew better.

Despite these assurances from me, the kids pushed back, and then I just told them that *somebody* must be in that one percent [survival rate], and it might as well be our own little Tiny Guy. When Jeff was younger, he always called me Big Guy, which made him Little Guy. It seemed only natural that his son would be Tiny Guy.

Ironically, rather than being comforted by my assurance, my son said, "Dad, I know you are the eternal optimist, and I love you for it. But we have accepted the fact that we will probably have a stillborn baby in the next week or two, and you need to accept it too." Because I know that you don't win arguments by attempting to change people's perceptions (because this perception is usually their reality), I elected to be supportive and a better listener if they wanted to talk and to scale back the fervor of my own feelings when called upon to share them.

The more they, and others, pushed back on my impression, the stronger my convictions became. A subsequent trip to the Temple and private prayer in the Celestial Room confirmed for me that we were going to have this baby, and while there might be challenges, that he was going to come to our family and have a profound effect on all of us. To this end, I have shared with many people that the greatest gift that I personally received while serving as bishop was the gift of discernment, and the enhanced capability of listening to the Spirit. I was reassured by my Stake President that if I continued to nurture this connection, that I could maintain it even after my release from the *calling* of bishop; or as he testified to me, "once a bishop always a bishop" because we are *ordained* to that office.

The doctors commonly referred to Walter's condition as CDH, but to the rest of us it stood for the more ominous *congenital diaphragmatic hernia* and in plain English is a birth defect that impacts the diaphragm. The most common type of CDH is a Bochadalek hernia, and is essentially a defect in the diaphragm – usually a hole, or a shredding, which allows the abdominal organs to push into the chest cavity, essentially hindering proper lung formation. Walter had a *huge* hole in his diaphragm which messed up his insides to no end. His heart was actually on the right side of his chest, and his stomach, liver and spleen, and a good bit of his intestines were on the left side. We had no idea whether he even had a second lung until after he was born, but I am getting ahead of myself.

With mixed feelings for the internet, I learned that CDH can be a life-threatening pathology in infants and a major cause of death due to complications associated with respiratory distress but can be dealt with effectively if diagnosed early as with Walter. The fatality rate for CDH hovers in the 65% range, so we were not out of the woods even if we defeated the Hydrops problem, because individual rates vary greatly dependent upon multiple factors; size of the hernia, organs involved, additional birth defects or genetic problems, amount of lung growth, age and size at birth, type of treatments, timing of treatments, as well as complications such as infections and lack of lung function.

Hydrops fetalis includes the retention fluid throughout the body — around the brain, the liver, a severe abdominal swelling, and carries with it a 99% mortality rate, so I knew that Walter was going to have to be a fighter if he were to survive at all.

The good news about CDH now is that unlike when I was being born, or even when our children were being born, this condition can often be diagnosed before birth, and surgery could be done before he was even born if deemed medically necessary by the doctors. We have a friend who had a grandbaby with CDH, and the surgery was done while in utero and was a complete success. At this point, it would be up to the doctors and largely depend on the severity of the condition.

My biggest fear centered around the fact that infants born with diaphragmatic hernias experience respiratory failure due to both pulmonary hypertension and pulmonary hypoplasia. The first condition is a restriction of blood flow through the lungs thought to be caused by defects in the lung. Pulmonary hypoplasia or decreased lung volume is causally related to the abdominal organs' presence in the chest cavity which causes the lungs to be severely undersized, especially on the side of the hernia. My grandson's left lung was the size of my pinky when he was born and just grew and grew and grew once all the other organs were removed from around it, greatly resembling an unfolding and expanding air mattress.

301

With two very scary health issues, we knew that logically, and maybe medically, the odds were stacked against us. The survival rates for infants with CDH vary but have generally been increasing through advances in neonatal medicine. In case you have not seen the advertising, Primary Children's Hospital in Salt Lake City is a great place to have a baby with any form of health issue. Nonetheless, the scientific data does not address the power of prayer and how miracles DO happen, even if not easily discernible.

The holidays came and went. The dreaded two weeks in which we expected Walter to die passed. Then another two weeks. We kept praying in ever increasing numbers. Pretty soon we were approaching thirty weeks and with even more prayers from a lot of people across the country, another milestone doctor's appointment revealed no presence of Hydrops. I will never forget the relief this news brought me as I was shuttling back and forth between Richmond and Seattle, looking for and establishing a new brick and mortar office, buying a house, recruiting, and making plans for a big year. *God had heard our prayers!*

Before I knew it, April was on the horizon, and after physically moving our household goods from coast to coast, we were now scheduled to depart for an incentive trip that I had earned to Machu Picchu in Peru. Billed as a once-in-a-lifetime trip, we were genuinely excited about it. But the trip was not to be for us, because when my daughter-in-law called me at the office and asked if instead we would consider being at the hospital when Walter was born, scheduled to occur the day we were to depart, we said yes. We did not regret taking a pass on the trip, but certainly did not realize that we were actually beginning an incredibly memorable experience that would far eclipse anything that the trip promised to offer us.

Walter was born at 39 weeks, weighed seven pounds plus, and we thought he was gorgeous. In reality, not so much. When I look at pictures from that time of his life, I am physically disturbed by his appearance, and the twenty six machines to which he was attached, half of which were pumping him with medications and/or oxygenating his blood.

On the night he was born, Jeff and I accompanied him on his "air flight" to Primary Children's Hospital via the glass pedestrian bridge that connected it to the hospital next door. Jeff and I were then invited into the Neonatal Intensive Care Unit (NICU) where we administered to his son for the first of many times in the coming months. He was so fragile, and while it clearly looked like the odds were against him, the blessings that we pronounced on him always promised that he would grow strong and survive to enjoy life.

The first step in management after birth is a gastric tube placement and securing the airway (intubation). The baby will usually be immediately placed on a ventilator. Extracorporeal membrane oxygenation (ECMO), is also used as part of the treatment strategy at some hospitals as the baby's condition warrants. ECMO acts as a baby heart-lung bypass and goes in through the side of the neck with a venous cannula being inserted into the jugular vein or the common femoral vein, allowing the blood to exit the body and begin its trek through the ECMO circuit, where it is then scrubbed, oxygenated, and passes through a filter before being returned to the body via a second cannula into the baby's own circulatory system where it makes its rounds before returning to the ECMO circuit to be oxygenated again. In essence, the ECMO circuit acts as the baby's lungs. Had we known then what we know now, i.e. how dangerous it was to him, maybe we would have been even more concerned. Ignorance truly was bliss in this instance.

Dangerous or not, the use of these machines keep the babies alive and buys the doctors time to stabilize the baby, perform any necessary surgery, and to help them survive recovery while gaining strength The thing is that babies require extra blood volume and hefty doses of blood thinners in order to keep the circuit running without clot formation, which could be potentially fatal. Even though the baby is not using his lungs, an oscillating ventilator may still be used to keep some air in the lungs so that they do not fully collapse while not being used. During ECMO the pulmonary artery has a chance to rest, as it were, thus hopefully reducing the presence of pulmonary hypertension, one of the biggest complications of CDH cases. While the CDH repair can be done while the baby is on ECMO, they usually wait because the blood thinners increase the risk of bleeding complications. After eight days of ECMO, Walter was weaned off the machine. We then waited an additional day or two for our grandson to be free of ECMO before he had his surgery. Once the baby is taken off ECMO the carotid artery is sealed and can no longer be used. When repairing the hernia an incision is made in the abdomen. The hernia can sometimes be simply stitched closed but in more complicated cases a patch may be required. A synthetic patch can be used but will usually require replacement later as the child grows. A more natural patch can be created by slicing and folding over a section of abdominal muscle and securing it to the existing piece of diaphragm. In Walter's case they used some of the existing muscle, but the hole was so big that they used a piece of Gortex. Every time I put on my Gortex rain jacket to go outside, I think of the lad. I do not smile because it reminds me of the sheer terror that we experienced until we knew the outcome of his surgery.

While they fix the diaphragm, they usually get everything rearranged the way God intended. In my grandson's case that meant pulling his stomach, liver and spleen and a bunch of intestines back down into the abdominal cavity. Well, they start with an incision through the abdomen and they pull all these organs *out* of the body, and then replace as much of them as they can into the abdominal cavity based on available capacity. In some cases, these "spare parts" are left outside the body for future placement! In Walter's case, they all fit back inside, and as soon as they were out of the way, we discovered his second lung, and we all took a deep sigh of relief, no pun intended.

As expected, the heart and lungs moved back into position on their own, once all the other organs were out of their way. They then closed the incision, and we waited for him to heal. When he was born, we were so grateful that he was here, and alive, that we didn't really notice how swollen and grotesque he was from the ECMO and meds, but you couldn't miss the fact that the skin of his stomach was laying on his spine because the space behind it was completely empty. He had a big barrel chest, and looked like a bruiser, but his insides were all mixed up. To this day, we are not absolutely certain that everything is where it is supposed to be and are reminded by the doctors to be mindful if he ever expresses discomfort or reports pain in his abdomen.

Prior to the surgery I also administered to my son, and it was one of the most powerful blessings that I have ever been a part of. When all was said and done everyone was in tears. I never felt more like a patriarch or worthy priesthood holder than at that moment. It is another one of those moments that will always stand still for me and is another foundational block in my testimony.

The surgery took only a little over an hour and went exceptionally well. I remember when the doctor came out to tell us the good news, we were all in tears, so grateful for a loving Heavenly Father, and for the surgeon's hands that were able to perform this miracle.

While we were receiving our good news, in an adjacent family waiting room another family was receiving the horrifying news that their baby had died. The wails of anguish that emanated from the mother and grandmother were absolutely horrifying, the mere thought of them still capable of making me cry. I do not think I will ever forget the sheer agony that I heard in the wailing and tears. It naturally served to make us even more grateful for our favorable outcome.

As it was, Walter was in the NICU for four and one-half months after he was born, on twelve medications at one point, to include morphine, and had they wanted to move him, it would have required the presence of 26 medical personnel to handle all of the tubes, buttons, and machines that he was hooked up to at that point. For this reason, they sterilized his bay in the NICU and performed the surgery there rather than attempting to move him to a regular operating theatre.

Shortly after Labor Day, Walter was discharged from the hospital and along with his mommy and daddy, lived with us for seven and one-half months, in Washington, because it nearly took a village to take care of him. He had a feeding tube – his "g-tube" – and we fed him with a regulating pump 23 hours a day through it.

As he got older, we adjusted the feedings to more or less correspond to our feeding times, but the kid never experienced hunger, and because of all the tubes that he had had shoved down his throat, he had developed an oral aversion, and so never took a pacifier, or ate or drank anything, or even sucked. Because he was also an active kid, I can remember many occasions watching him do headstands in the pack 'n play in the family room all the while praying that he would not inadvertently pull out his feeding tube. This did happen once, but fortunately *Grandma* was on duty and quickly replaced it in his abdomen, inflated it, and life resumed. While I am certain that I could have, and would have, risen to the occasion, I know that we were all blessed to have Grandma "Dr. Mom" Susie on duty.

When he was just about three years old, we took him to the hospital in Seattle and after a weekend of basically starving him we taught him how to eat – yogurt and other stuff – and then weaned him off the feeding tube. This involved several months of commuting to the hospital largely handled by Mom and Grandma, with occasional cameo appearances by Dad and Grandpa. It was nearly miraculous to watch this transition.

After that, we had to teach him how to drink. So, from March until July we would give him fluids through his g-tube, until we knew that he was consuming enough fluids to avoid dehydration.

The tube came out for good just after he turned four, and we were on our way. By the time he was four, he was wolfing down three slices of Little Caesar's as quickly as you and I would.

Today, Walter is a healthy 8 year old, who loves to ride his bicycle, play basketball, and to build things. He has a wonderful imagination and a sweet spirit about him. I would like to think that in his case miracles and medical science went hand in hand. When I view the sheer number of scars on his neck, chest, and stomach, I cannot help myself from grimacing, but they do not bother him. For this I am extremely grateful.

Many children who go through this experience often die when they are three, four, five, or six years old or the diaphragm re-herniates prompting more surgery. That fact was never far from my mind, but I always chose to believe that Walter was sent here for a purpose. Prior to starting school he was diagnosed with mild to moderate autism, and that is a battle we are all waging now, but in the big scheme of things, it simply does not matter to me for I find myself completely captured by his innocence, wonder, and sweet spirit. While I love all my grandchildren equally, I cannot help but believe that Walter was sent to our family for a special purpose.

How has this extended odyssey impacted my testimony? I have never felt like my priesthood mattered more than during the time that Jeff and I were administering to Walter daily, calling upon the powers of Heaven to heal him and to make him strong. I do not know too many Vegas gamblers who would have given us any odds on his survival, much less development, but with Faith, odds are of no importance.

I still remember the faces of many of the NICU nurses, and give thanks for the strength of their personal constitutions, because quite a few of them felt that they were there as if fulfilling a calling, usually after having suffered the loss of their own child. When I observed the love and compassion with which the NICU nurses would tend to these tiny little babies for months and months and months, sometimes to lose them in the end, I knew that I was in the presence of mortal angels.

CHAPTER 70

PLATINUM

"A story is told of a woman who was upset that her
son was eating too much candy. No matter how
much she told him to stop, he continued to satisfy
his sweet tooth. Totally frustrated, she decided to
take her son to see a wise man whom he respected.
She approached him and said, 'Sir, my son eats too much
candy. Would you please tell him to stop eating it?'
He listened carefully then said to her son, 'Go
home and come back in two weeks.'
She took her son and went home, perplexed why he
had not asked the boy to stop eating so much candy.
Two weeks later they returned. The wise man looked
directly at the boy and said, 'Boy, you should stop
eating so much candy. It is not good for your health.'
The boy nodded and promised he would. The boy's mother
asked, 'Why didn't you tell him that two weeks ago?'
The wise man smiled. 'Two weeks ago I was
still eating too much candy myself.'
This man lived with such integrity that he knew his advice
would carry power only if he was following his own counsel."
Jorge M. Alvarado

After several weeks in Salt Lake and the all the related drama, trauma, and emotions attached to Walter's birth, surgery, and miraculous existence, it was time to get back to Seattle and to get to work full time. Working remotely from SLC had been a challenge, but I knew it was the right thing to do. We may have lost a step or two, but nothing that the team could not pick up in the second half of the year.

The plan for this first year was to focus on attention to detail in all that we did, to include Marketing. Rainmaking, Recruiting, Teaching, Training, and to really pull the lever on Placement Rate. This would be accomplished by doing a lot of listening and learning myself. Rather than paying some "professional coach" $10,000 for 2 hours a month of time, my buddy Todd and I decided to coach one another...for free. Those Thursday morning sessions were invaluable to both of us, and we genuinely helped one another as both of our agencies started an ascent in the rankings. I was not selling but was spending time in the field with new agents and even veteran agents. I kept the spotlight on them. I prepared a weekly newsletter, keeping things fresh. I was all for spotlighting success both in the newsletter and on the weekly training calls. I conducted monthly All Hands in-person luncheon meetings in both Seattle and Portland.

By mid-year things had really started to take root. The Wolf Pack was starting to work and hunt as a team. Susie and I were welcomed with a lovely housewarming party that was hosted ironically at *our* new house. We were deluged with a large basket stuffed with local delicacies and goodies. The team was bonding and growing at the same time. I was taking nothing for granted and tried to make prayer an unofficial part of my business plan. I had learned from several influential business/church leaders that while it was not appropriate to bring business practices into church leadership roles, it was more than appropriate to bring church principles into the business world. I have every belief that this was an integral part of our success this first year.

Like an ancient submarine with battered ballast tanks, we ever so slowly lifted off the bottom and started our ascent in the weekly office rankings. By the summer were in the middle of the pack, and still rising. By the fall, we were in the top ten and still rising. We sailed through number ten in the rankings, and it looked like nothing could stop us from finishing in the top seven. We threw a couple more logs on the fire and kept the locomotive engine stoked. Our new agents were coming on strong as well.

We had hung in there in the dog days of summer and soon found ourselves in the top seven for a few weeks. The guys ahead of us saw this image in their rearview mirror getting ever larger. It was the wolf pack chasing them.

We went into the fourth quarter looking like we could go all the way to platinum and finish in the top four. This was heady stuff if not darn right surreal. Carl the West DVP was cheering us on, and Laurel was calling from Richmond with support as well. We had a lot of fans cheering for us. We threw everything we had at it, and when we went into the last month of the year when the reports stop coming in (the traditional blackout period that is supposed to add an element of suspense to the year's end), we were forced to extrapolate and project our numbers against those of the other agencies. I secretly had any number of home office people helping in this pursuit, and I was beginning to think that we were going to be there when the dust settled. Because it was an Olympics year, and I knew that fourth place does not get anyone a medal, I set my sights on number three. My counterpart in Northern New England had the same goal. While there was no difference whatsoever, neither one of us wanted to finish number four.

In early December I flew to Richmond and presented my business plan for 2013. I wanted it to stand out against the other 22 agencies, and since Seattle is known as the Emerald City, I elected to build my business plan with a Wizard of Oz theme.

Despite the levity, and clever presentation with the Oz theme, front and center was still an attitude of humility. I was grateful that we had achieved all that we had done in 2012, and wherever we finished, it was definitely the comeback story of the year.

In January we were in Dallas for our annual National Career Agent Conference, and the results were still unknown. When the big Saturday night party finally happened, it was New York, Texas, PNW, NNE

Don Levin

in that order. We were platinum and had taken home the unofficial Bronze Medal.

That was a great night, and our team really came together. While the other agencies had arrived at the National Career Agents Conference with agency t-shirts or polo shirts, I had purchased each of them a nice fleece jacket and that night handed out a Platinum Agency patch that they could attach to the breast of the jacket. I loved it when some of the top producers in the country admired the jackets and complimented the team. We would be a contender for next year even though New York and Texas were heavyweights and had to be considered favorites.

By this time, I had spent six months as an assistant Ward Mission Leader with responsibility for the YSAs – 120 of them. Nobody knew where they were, and my mission was to 'clean up' the rolls and get them to either the YSA branch or active in our home ward. After completing what I thought was largely a made-up assignment, I was then called as the First Assistant to Curt, the High Priest Group Leader. Having served as the HPGL in Cincinnati, I was able to really step up and assist my HPGL especially when he was gone traveling twice a month to Alaska!

It was shortly after getting back from Dallas that I started to receive the now familiar "flashes" that had accompanied my calling as bishop in Virginia. I was surprised, but not shocked this time around. By mid-February they were coming fast and furiously nearly every day.

Mark, our bishop, with whom I had been having a series of discussion about his coming onboard to the Wolf Pack was due to complete his five years as bishop in August. The plan was to potentially make something happen in terms of a new career for him in the Fall.

We had a stake conference in March, and surprise, Mark was called as our new stake president, necessitating his immediate release as bishop. The HPGL was called as the new bishop and I was called as the new HPGL. I was somewhat surprised by this considering the "flashes" that I had been receiving but did not say anything. However, when I had a discussion with Mark about it a couple of months later, he asked me when I started receiving the flashes. When I told him the exact date in February, he shared that he himself had been in the Seattle Temple on that very day and it had been revealed to him that he was to be the next Stake President and that either Curt or I would be the bishop, with the other as the HPGL who is sometimes thought of as the second bishop of the ward.

To this end, when I was called as the HPGL in Cincinnati by the Stake President, he said "Brother Levin, I have good news and bad news for you. The good news is that you are the second bishop to the ward; the bad news is that you get the adults," reflecting the emphasis that the bishop is supposed to place on ministering to the youth.

Mark made it very clear that it made perfect sense that I would have been receiving those flashes at that time because it was not until several weeks later that he ultimately received an answer as to what calling each of us would occupy. In his mind it finally came down to the fact that Curt knew the people better, had never been a bishop, and I had been. He also emphasized that he had every belief that the Lord knew that I was rebuilding the agency and that it was critical for me to be able to focus my energies there at this time. Of course, with 300 of the 365 households in the ward under the High Priests, I was still a busy boy, with a personal home teaching route of eight families!

I was somewhat disappointed, but at the same time extremely grateful that the Lord still knew me and that moving across the country had not moved me off his radar screen. Curt delegated as much as he could to me, the Elders Quorum President, and Relief Society President. We had a strong core of faithful members, and home teaching went up dramatically as we shared a powerful vision with our 37 high priests.

Susie and I hosted a Platinum Dinner in April, and Laurel flew in for the event. We indulged 90 agents and spouses with a wonderful cocktail party, surf and turf for dinner, and Laurel graciously picked up the bar tab. As it was, that was an $8,000 dinner tab for yours truly, but was worth every penny. It was a festive night and by this time we were well into what would be an even more memorable 2013 campaign.

Susie had gone home with the kids from the restaurant so that I could drive Laurel back to her hotel by our office, and we could have a casual debrief and some quiet time. Imagine my shock when as we pulled into her hotel and went in for a night cap, she looked me in the eye and said, "So how is your recruiting going?" I laughed out loud! "Seriously? At midnight on a Friday night, you want to talk about recruiting?" We had led the company in recruiting in 2012, and were already leading in 2013, and the new agent production and new agents themselves were continuing to fuel our meteoric rise.

"So....," she asked again.

"Do you want me to say that we are going to be number one in 2013?" I asked.

"YES!" she nearly shouted.

"Okay then. We will be number one," I said, and as soon as the words were out my mouth, I had a witness that it was going to come to pass. It was not arrogance or ego – it was more like a prompting or affirmation.

"There are a lot of people in the home office who would *love* to see that happen," she said with a big smile. As it was, we were already in the number one position, and had been there since the start of the year. We led the race from the opening until the checkered flag was waved. We never let up, and unlike last year where it was a dogfight between NY and Texas, we absolutely crushed it. There was a whole lot of "daylight" between us and the rest of the field. The biggest challenge was that the rankings largely pitted us against ourselves because all the metrics were about year over year growth. After a strong year like the one we had, the odds were against us, but we kept the pedal to the metal, and owned it.

Atlanta in January 2014 was nearly surreal. We were number one, and we knew it going in, even if it was not official. Our position atop the rankings on the first of December was virtually unassailable. The team wanted to wear the same fleece jacket as last year, and this time we already had the second platinum patch that declared us the number one agency on the jacket. They did the strutting, and it was wonderful to watch. It validated all our efforts. I was just grateful that we had been successful.

Part of the pomp and circumstance of being #1 is the personalized lyrics of the song which is commissioned by our trip coordinator and sung by the group ensemble known as The Watercoolers. I recently found a CD with a recording of this event and it brought a smile to my face as I was able to enjoy it again. It really was a magical night as they sang to me about me. Susie was there along with my son Jeff, and it was great to have nearly the entire agency with us when we went up on stage for our team photo.

In March, we were in Atlanta for GAMA International's LAMP meeting with over 3,000 industry leaders in attendance. I was in a tuxedo that night, because as the company's number one agency leader I would be recognized as First in Class. It is an extremely prestigious award, and one that I had no clue as to its significance until several years later when I was part of the brokerage world and other General Agents would acknowledge it since it was part of my vitae and was on our website. Laurel was my escort that night, and that night really cemented our friendship as I accepted the insurance industry's version of the Oscar award. I know that Laurel was another one of those faces on the milestone markers. From the first lunch together, we had clicked, and because of my past roles with the company, we had enjoyed an incredibly special give-and-take relationship. I am grateful that our paths crossed, and that I had a leader that I could turn to for support, candid advice, and true leadership.

In the late spring, we were off to Barcelona Spain to catch the Norwegian Epic for a three country cruise in the Mediterranean. It was an incredible experience as we were tucked away up in the very exclusive Haven area of the ship. The platinum qualifiers were up there, and I cannot remember when I felt more content. I remember sitting out on the [private] sundeck one evening, looking up at the stars, and saying a silent prayer of thanks for the opportunity that we had enjoyed the last two and one-half years. The stars twinkled back at me, and I knew that it would probably never get as good as this again, and that we needed to be mindful of our actions and to always retain an attitude of gratitude as we lived in the moment.

CHAPTER 71

END OF THE ROAD AND A NEW BEGINNING

"It is a curious thing, Harry, but perhaps those who are
best suited to power are those who have never sought
it. Those who, like you, have leadership thrust upon
them, and take up the mantle because they must, and
find to their own surprise that they wear it well."
J.K. Rowling

Despite the success we were enjoying in the Pacific Northwest, the death spiral of the company's career sales force was reflective of the continued decline of the entire traditional stand-alone long term care insurance industry.

The Spring of 2014 was the end of the magic even though we did not know it at the time. After the First in Class experience, another blow out Platinum Dinner to celebrate our number one status this time, and what turned out to be the final incentive trip, this time to the emerald Isle of Ireland, I knew we were just about at the end of the road. The industry was continuing to contract, a good bit of my peers seemed to be content with "playing out the string," and there was even a lethargy settling on the agent force.

Poor Laurel. We spoke regularly, and I was attempting to be a support to her at this time, and to help out for the greater good, but I knew we were taking on water. I also knew that people would view her like Captain Smith of Titanic fame, and it was unfair.

In a move that really was nothing more than a zero sum gain, the 23 agencies were consolidated into 13. Since we were all independent, self-sufficient entities, there was no savings associated with a reduced full time employee headcount, brick and mortar offices closed, etc. The thought process was that the thirteen of us would be more profitable, but all it served to do was to reduce the leadership influence by nearly half. The problem is that a good number of the General Agents had been brought in from the outside, did not know the business, and lacked the commitment to the product, the company, and by extension, the industry. Because of my relationship with Laurel, I made it clear that in a lot of cases, they kept the wrong people in place, which in hindsight sealed our collective fate.

We picked up seven more states taking us all the way across the Great Plains to Minnesota. Lots of territory, but not so much in population. In fact, it became a running gag that I now had 42% of the United States land mass in my agency, but only 9% of the population. Unless I could sell long term care insurance to cows, the only real benefit to the territory I picked up was Minnesota. We hit it hard, and I was recruiting in Minneapolis every other month, and trying to make it a threepeat for ourselves, but more importantly to have Laurel's back for a change. Because of our stellar back to back years, and because I picked up a greater "denominator" based on the added territory, we could not maintain the pace, and finished in 7th.

The December 2014 leadership meeting in Chicago was like visiting a sick friend in the hospital as we had an ultimatum placed in front of us regarding alternatives if we did not pick up the pace as a sales channel. While I really wanted us to be successful, when I looked around the room, I did not see the team that would make it happen. Over the last three years, Jeff and I had accounted for about 70% of the new recruiting in the company, and when you stop bringing in new blood, you are done. Nobody in that room was interested in growth; they were merely thinking in terms of survival.

If December was like visiting sick friend, the spring was the bedside vigil. In March we were in Orlando for the LAMP meeting, and our private company meeting. It pretty much degenerated into chaos and since Plan A thus far was a failure, the conversation turned to what Plan B looked like if the company shut us all down. This was a horrible time, and I was told by more than few people that they were looking to me as the "voice of reason" and because of my influence with Laurel. Laurel was still hopeful that we could save the company (as was I) but a few of my peers told me point blank that they *wanted* their independence and that the handwriting was on the wall anyway. I remember at this time having an extraordinarily strong impression that reinforced, nay confirmed, my beliefs that we had more than one Judas in our midst.

Ironically, I was being heavily recruited for what appeared to be a solid gig with another carrier right in Seattle. Unfortunately it would require me to reacquire the very FINRA securities licenses that I had allowed to lapse back in 2013 when I was assured by Laurel and the rest of the leadership team that I would never require them again.

It was the first week of May in 2015 when we were informed that the game was over and that call was tantamount to attending the wake, and the next day we broke the news to the agents. In addition to my agency of ten states, they attached a leaderless agency of five additional states to me for the balance of our existence. The end of June would be the time for the funeral. The career shop that had pioneered the industry would soon be no more. I began mourning because the likely alternative was for all of us was to be absorbed by any number of other career shops or field marketing organizations. They wanted our agents and could have cared less for us general agents. I was bothered by it because this was the world that I had known for the last sixteen years and did not know what life was going to bring for us. This was extremely distressing to me, and I seriously wondered what I was going to do for the remaining years of my work life. We had had a good run the last several years, but we were not across the finish line yet.

One of my former DVP peers had landed the role of national sales leader with a competing brokerage a couple of years before, and he was actively recruiting me to join their team as one of four regional directors and his heir apparent. He and his wife flew up to Seattle to wine and dine Susie and I, and I went to their office in Seattle for two days of meetings. I was "wanted for my strategic and tactical leadership, the ability to craft a vision, my attention to detail and ability to get it done." It was all very flattering, but it did not *feel* right, and when I prayed about it, I had only a cold feeling permeate my body. Despite how attractive it looked, it was the same George Bailey-Mr. Potter dynamic all over again. Nonetheless I kept the lines of communications open.

We were also doing conference calls with other brokerage firms that Genworth had arranged who were giving us their best pitches on why we should join their teams along with our agents. One of them was so insulting, that the call which was scheduled for an hour in duration was pretty much over for most of us in less than fifteen minutes. The other call, which resulted in over half of the general agents ultimately finding a "soft landing" with that brokerage had promise, but when I prayed about that opportunity I did not get any confirmation that it was the path that I was to follow. I felt a great responsibility for finding the best opportunity not only for myself and my family, but also for my agents and their families. The impression I was receiving in answer to prayer was "wait." Wait for what? Time was fleeting, and the lifeboats were filling up.

Things were happening very quickly and when it came time for my private call with Laurel and Adam (our most recent president), the second week of May, I was still trying to regain my equilibrium. I still felt like I had a good game to play, and a solid team to put on the field. I shared with them that I have been around units and installations that have been deactivated and so it was a little Deja vu for me yesterday, but that I am not ready to furl my colors. I offered to be a national agency or run the remnants of Retail as a single agency and that in the past week I think we had taken some huge steps forward.

Apparently they agreed, because Adam quickly shifted gears and told me what I needed to be an independent agency; the scale on which

I needed to operate; and the role I needed to fill as the CEO as I built an infrastructure. He then informed me that I "had far more options than most of the other GAs because you have done things over the past several years that have generated options and choices that surpass those of your peers." When all was said and done, he invited me to come to Richmond to discuss receiving a brokerage contract. Because he wanted things to happen as quickly as I did, Laurel's assistant called me with a plane ticket the very next day.

Richmond was quite an adventure. My private time with Laurel was great, and her advice was to focus on making this new adventure fun and uplifting for myself. As soon as she said it, I *knew* which path I was to pursue. I respectfully declined the other offers and set about building my own brokerage. There were plenty of new challenges and opportunities to learn humility all over again as we stood at the base of the mountain looking up.

As we transitioned from a regional agency to a national brokerage and started conducting more and more of our agency training and operations virtually, we quickly determined that staying in Seattle was no longer necessary and that we could in fact move closer to our children and grandchildren in Boise, ID. While we had considered this an ideal retirement plan, we also realized that there was nothing preventing us from implementing it now and making family the priority it had always been in the past.

Because of some surgery that had her confined to the house for several weeks, Susie spent countless hours looking at homes online, and found nothing that captured our imagination or really met our needs. The day that she left the house and experienced her first freedom, I saw her iPad on the island in the kitchen, tweaked the search ever so slightly, and up popped what appeared to be the perfect house. In as much as we were going to Boise the following weekend for our granddaughter's baptism, I called the realtor and told him that we were interested in viewing the house. It was the only house we viewed while we were in Boise that weekend. I am now writing this memoir sitting in that house. You just *know* when it is right.

CHAPTER 72

CUBS W1N

"Believe in Miracles
Hope is never lost."
Jeffrey R. Holland

The Boys of Summer. When I think of my childhood and associated happy memories they usually coalesce around my spending summer days at my grandparents' house in Chicago, working in the garden, eating non-stop, and at 1:20 in the afternoon congregating around the television set to watch the Cubs home games being telecast on WGN from the Friendly Confines of Wrigley Field located some thirty blocks to the south.

It was probably the lack of night games and the requirement to play every home game in the heat of the day that would literally cause the team to wilt in the dog days of Summer, always precipitating the cry of "wait until next year."

There were some memorable moments along the way, but true to form, they all ended in disappointment. Being a life-long Cubs fan has taught me to root for the underdog, to be patient, optimistic in the face of adversity, and to live in the moment.

323

The Cubs have completed 148 seasons of baseball, second only to the Atlanta Braves at 149. Within this time the Cubs have won 17 National League pennants, 3 World Series championships, 3 pre-World Series Championships and tied for 2 pre-Word Series championships.

The best part of being a Cubs fan was sharing the experience with my Grandma Mary. A loyal fan, she could always be counted on to rattle off batting averages for the hitters and pertinent stats for the pitchers. Along with longtime suffering announcer Jack Brickhouse, and players like Ernie "Mr. Cub" Banks, Billy Williams, Ron Santo, Randy Hundley, Fergie Jenkins, Kenny Holtzman, and Don Kessinger, they were nearly like family due to all the collective pain and agony we suffered through together.

Whereas there was a period of time during the Great Depression and the 1930s that the Cubs regularly made it to the World Series only to lose to the likes of Babe Ruth and the Yankees, as in 1932 when he "called" his homerun to center field, since that time, winning times have been sparse.

The last World Series title was in 1908 during the presidency of Teddy Roosevelt. The last World Series appearance was in 1945 after Harry Truman had ended World War Two with the dropping of the atomic bombs on Hiroshima and Nagasaki. The collapse of 1969 and the Miracle Mets left a horrible taste in everyone's mouth, where it would remain until a division title in 1984 and the blowing of a 2-0 lead in a best of five series. We did not fare much better in 1989, and who will forget the Bartman debacle in the 2003 NLCS? The very thing of nightmares. We made it to the League Championship series in 2015 by wining the wild card game over the Pirates, taking archrivals the Cardinals 3 games to 1 in the Divisional series, but lost (again) to the Mets.

After the success of 2015, we were hungry, and getting off to a 25-6 start certainly captured my imagination, and I kept track of the standings on a board on my office door. The numbers that the team was putting up were impressive and the 103-58 record did not even come close to capturing how dominating they had been from the first game until the last game. They beat the Giants in the Divisional series, to earn a chance to play the Dodgers for the pennant.

October 15 was the first game between these two storied teams. Because of their regular season record, the Cubs had home field advantage. The Cubs won 8-4 at home and I was ecstatic. That ecstasy ended the next day when the Cubs gave away their home field advantage by losing 1-0 to even the series, and to head to Los Angeles for the next three games.

By dropping game 3 by a score of 6-0 and extending their scoreless inning streak to two full games, the team had many naysayers already beginning to think that we may have begun the swoon. I refused to believe that after the season we had enjoyed that we were going to go out this quietly.

Game 4 was fun to watch, and the boys and their bats were back, and the final score was Cubs 10-2, to knot the series at 2-2.

The pivotal Game 5 was again in Los Angeles, but the Cubs dominated, and but for a couple of meaningless runs in the 9th, they overpowered the Dodgers by a score of 8-4 to take the series lead, heading back to Chicago for two games. The odds were in our favor.

Game 6, back in the Friendly Confines, and the Cubs did not disappoint by notching their third straight win by a score of 5-0. We were going to the Big Show. I was so excited when the announcer started shouting "Cubs Win! Cubs Win!" that I jumped up and down, yelled, and celebrated much in the same fashion as I had done with the six Bulls NBA titles, the three Blackhawks Stanley Cup championships, the Bears Super Bowl victory and the White Sox World Series of 2005. Life was good! Theo Epstein, the Cubs President, had worked his magic and we were four wins away from a world championship!

For the last time, the World Series home team was decided by the victor of the All Star Game, and so the American League had the honors again this year. This worried me because the home team enjoys a great advantage in the World Series, and if, we ended up in a Game 7, it would have been great to have it in the Friendly Confines.

The series started at Progressive Field in Cleveland, and the Indians made us look bad 6-0. Disappointing does not even come close to describing the feelings I was experiencing.

But, because Hope springs eternal, Game 2 had the boys show up, and the Cubs bounced back for a nice 5-1 victory to knot the series, and essentially wrest away home field advantage.

Before a standing room crowd of nearly 43,000 fans at Wrigley, the Cubs dropped a heartbreaker 1-0 to go down again 2-1. I was so frustrated. Argh!

As if the Game 3 heartbreak was not bad enough, Game 4 was another nightmare, and we got thumped 7-2, with the Indians holding a commanding 3-1 lead that teams do not come back from in championship series. I was in denial, but still rooting hard.

Fortunately, in Game 5 the Cubs eked out a 3-2 victory to stave off elimination. A lot of prognosticators were saying that they were only staving off the inevitable.

For Game 6 we were at our daughter's house for a birthday party for our granddaughter. Because this was a big game, we were allowed to have the game on. A 3 spot in the first inning followed by a Grand Slam home run in the 3rd for a commanding 7-0 lead certainly made things look good for us. We ultimately prevailed 9-3 to tie up the series and set up a fateful game 7. Have I mentioned how much I hate Game 7s in any sport because it is winner take all, and on any given night, anything can happen. The fact that this particular Game 7 would be played in Cleveland left me feeling extremely nervous.

Game 7. Ultimately it is remembered as a classic, with some calling it the greatest Game 7 in World Series history, comparing the drama and tension to that associated with 1960, 1991 and 2001. We have a bunch of our kids over, and I am too nervous to sit. I watched the entire game while pacing between the kitchen and family room putting about 9,000 steps on my Fitbit.

The Cubs drew first blood in the top of the first with a leadoff home run by Dexter Fowler, the first leadoff homerun in a game 7 in World Series history. I am thinking maybe the Heavens might be smiling down on us. Cleveland ties it in the third. The Cubs respond with 2 in the fourth and the fifth to take what should be a commanding 5-1 lead, only to give two runs back on some bad defense and errors in the bottom of the 5th to make it 5-3.

In what would be his final major league at bat, Catcher David Ross hits a home run to center in the top of the sixth to make it a 6-3 game, becoming the oldest player (at age 39) to hit a home run in a World Series Game 7.

The Cubs have a 6-3 lead with only four outs to go with our ace on the mound. Disaster strikes, and we are tied at 6-6. The momentum has shifted. The Cubs squander a scoring chance in the top of the ninth but retire the Indians in order in the bottom of the ninth to send the game to extra innings.

A sudden cloudburst results in a rain delay of seventeen minutes. Unknown to those of us at the time, during the delay, Cubs right fielder Jason Heyward called his teammates into a weight room behind the Cubs dugout and told them, "We're the best team in baseball...for a reason... Stick together and we're going to win this game."

Some timely hitting, good baserunning, and the Cubs score two runs to take a lead of 8-6 though they left the bases loaded, which made me nervous because if they can score some runs, so can the Indians. A base hit and a couple of more runs would have made the bottom of the tenth inning a whole lot less tense.

Everyone is still in their places. Nobody is moving. Superstition is rampant, and I am still pacing. The first two batters are retired, and I am literally soaking my shirt, and then we spring a leak. A walk, second base on defensive indifference, and a single to center and we are at 8-7. Fortunately, an infield grounder fielded by Bryant with a strong throw to Rizzo at first, and the game ends 8-7, the Series is over, and the Cubs have broken their 108 year drought. Did I jump up and down? Did I yell? No and no. What did I do instead, I literally sat down on the sofa and started to cry.

Silly as it sounds, it was a spiritual moment for me. I felt my grandmother's approval of the outcome, and while it may sound somewhat sacrilegious, the veil was definitely thin that night, settling the question of whether there is baseball in heaven. There were reports of several life-long Cubs fans who were over the age of 100 who died either the next day or over the next few weeks. It was as if they had waited for this special moment before transitioning to the next life. It was sad that Ernie Banks had died the year before without seeing his beloved Cubs win. I thought of Jack Brickhouse, Harry Caray, Ron Santo all for the same reason.

The Cubs became the first team since 1985 to comeback from a 3-1 deficit, and the first team since 1979 to do so while winning games six and seven and on the road.

At the suggestion of my daughter and son-in-law we have commemorated this event with my car's license plate which reads: CUBSW1N.

CHAPTER 73

FAMILY HISTORY

"While temple and family history work has the
power to bless those beyond the veil, it has an
equal power to bless the living. It has a refining
influence on those who are engaged in it. They
are literally helping to exalt their families."
Russell M. Nelson

From the time we joined the Church in 1984 and made the commitment
to honor all the mandates of true discipleship, I wanted to do the necessary
research and compile our family tree. Aside from the spiritual aspects
associated with completing necessary temple ordinances for the deceased
members of our family, I simply wanted to know the history of our family.
Unfortunately, back in those days, the Family History Centers revolved
around the microfiche and microfilm readers and the necessity to request
these resources from Salt Lake City. One would fill out the request and in
seven to ten days after sending off the request the desired materials would
arrive for viewing and potential copying. It was a slow and tedious process,
assuming that one's family tree was readily identifiable.

I was quickly able to prepare my four generation worksheet, which captured me, my parents, grandparents, and nearly all my great-grandparents. Unfortunately, that was where three of my four lines abruptly ended. No matter what I tried, I could not get past that generation. I even went so far as to retain the services of a quasi-professional genealogist who finally shrugged her shoulders and said that I was going to have a tough time with compiling my lineage.

As the years passed, and we were busy with our temple calling, as well as callings with the youth, bishopric, stake, high priests, and other assignments, the press to continue to pursue this rather frustrating work subsided. In reality, I probably rationalized and procrastinated to a certain degree as well.

It was while we were living in Seattle and became friendly with a senior missionary couple who was assigned to our ward that my interest in family history was re-kindled. As I recently joked with these friends when I called them to say hello, their efforts in family history had been both inspiring and frustrating for me to view. At the time we were in Seattle together, he was back to the fourteenth or fifteenth century, tied to the royal lines in England, and had countless pictures of his ancestors dotting the various generations of his family tree. He had exactly what I wanted and was being denied. I made several more valiant attempts and added a few more family members, but for the most part was still stymied. Obviously, my success at Ellis Island was also further encouragement, but the Levin, Lisch, and Hefter lines were not going anywhere in terms of the Old Country. Records were seemingly non-existent because of World War Two or had not been processed to any great degree. I had some hope and minor success with the Meyer line (my maternal grandmother) because they had been here several generations going back to the early 1800s.

Our move to Boise and all the new demands on my time professionally as we established the new brokerage, as well as my newly found desire to write novels, left me little time to think about resuming the family history work. Coupled with the frustrations that I had experienced over the years, I sincerely felt justified in believing that the season for this work in my life had not yet arrived.

For about eighteen months Susie would disappear on Thursday evening to attend the Family History Center. She would come home very excited and recount how she and her newly found friends from our ward had found this person or that person, and added this line to her tree, or found pictures of these people, and her tree was growing new branches. I was using these evenings mainly to write and work on my own creative projects.

In November 2017, as I seriously began to contemplate possible retirement the following September when I would turn 60 and qualify for my military health benefits, military pension, and GE pension, my mind started drifting back to family history work. I knew from reading church publications, listening to talks at General Conference, as well as stories from other people, that the Church's adoption of the internet and establishment of Family Search and partnering with Ancestry.com had dramatically changed the ability to connect the generations. I opened my heart and my mind for inspiration.

Just like when you own a certain type of car you see it everywhere on the road, seemingly every General Conference was filled with messages that implored us to do our family history work. In fact, it was now *family history and temple work* so the fact that I was redeeming the dead in the temple did not seem like nearly enough effort in this important mission of the church especially since I was not doing it for my own family!

One morning I was reading something from the Church and ran across a quote by Elder Scott in which he said, "As one of the twelve Apostles, I would like to invoke a blessing on you that as you pray you will know how the Lord feels about what you are doing. . . . I would like to also invoke a blessing that as you prayerfully ask for guidance in this sublime and important work, that you will have feelings from the Holy Ghost that will guide you." With those words echoing in my ears, I started praying for the ability to serve my family and to connect the generations. I was already extremely mindful that I was the connecting link in the five generation chain between my grandparents and grandchildren, and that it was incumbent upon me to complete this vital work before it was lost forever.

The following Thursday morning, I asked Susie if she was going to the family history center that night. When she said yes, I told her that I wanted to accompany her to put my toes back in the water and to see if there was any chance at success for me.

That night was a turning point for me and my family on both sides of the veil. Jack and Shirley took me under their wing just as they had done for Susie, and the work seemingly opened before my eyes. Within three months my very modest tree of thirty family members had grown to over 500, and then grew and grew and grew seemingly exponentially as I not only drove my family lines straight back generation after generation, but on occasion started "branching" out and filling the lines in with thousands of cousins.

It was in February 2018 when I had the "breakthrough" on my maternal grandmother's line that has literally exploded my tree and allowed me to enjoy a degree of "success" that I could never have imagined.

I read the words of President Henry B. Eyring in which he said, "Think of the Savior when you meet Him. . . . He has trusted you by letting you hear the gospel in your lifetime, giving you the chance to accept the obligation to offer it to those of your ancestors who did not have your priceless opportunity. Think of the gratitude He has for those who pay the price in work and faith to find the names of their ancestors and who love them and Him enough to offer them eternal life in families, the greatest of all the gifts of God. He offered them an infinite sacrifice. He will love and appreciate those who paid whatever price they could to allow their ancestors to choose His offer of eternal life." With those words, I was hooked. We now work just as hard at home on our respective lines as we do when we go to the family history center, and my heart is a lot lighter as I continue to compile the names and stories of thousands of my ancestors.

Especially poignant for me are the ancestors who have served in the military. I love compiling as much as I can on them and honor them in my tree with special tags that I have created. When I have a picture for any of my ancestors, but particularly my fellow military service members, they become real to me. I have had the honor of visiting the

Punchbowl National Cemetery on Oahu, Hawaii, the final resting place
of my twelfth cousin who died at the age of nineteen on the island of
Iwo Jima during World War II. When I knelt at his grave I realized that
but for the grace of God that this could have been my Uncle Eddie's
fate as he too was at Iwo Jima and buried many friends on that island.

I have discovered that I have several cousins who were nineteen year
old second lieutenants just as I had been, only they gave their lives in the
trenches of France during World War One, or later in battles of World
War Two. One in particular died in September 1918, about eight weeks
before the Armistice ended the war in November. What made it even
more tragic was the birth of his daughter in October of that year. It is a
relief and a blessing to know that while they did not know one another
in this life, that they will be able to know one another in the next life
because of the eternal nature of families.

It was shortly after my birthday in September of 2019 that I hit a
major milestone and with Shirley's assistance managed to forge a link
back to the old country on the Levin line. I am now back in the fifteenth
century and some twenty generations. It was so gratifying to find my
roots, and ironically to discover that these roots are absolutely riddled
with generations and generations of rabbis. Yes rabbis, not rabbits.

I have come to both enjoy and love my time performing this work,
and it has become a passion for which I am eternally grateful. While I
have always had a command of American history, I have since acquired a
greater awareness of and appreciation for European history, particularly
as it relates to all the royal houses that are so inter-related. I find it to
be absolutely fascinating.

Recently, before Covid-19 reared its ugly head to disrupt a lot of
good works, our youngest daughter accompanied us to the family
history center on a Thursday evening and spent the evening under Jack's
tutelage and became infected by the work. She was there ostensibly to
bust my chops for not transferring the thousands of family members
that I have in my Ancestry tree to Family Search where she would have
more ready access to it. I have been reticent to transfer it because of
Shirley's admonition that when it is in Ancestry, it is my tree and if I

make a mistake I can always fix it; Family Search is God's tree – don't screw it up, because it is tough to fix.

As a result, I only move my family members – they are more than just names – when I am absolutely certain of the veracity of the data I have and that I will be doing their temple work for them relatively soon.

President Boyd K. Packer of the Twelve Apostles said, "Family history work in one sense would justify itself even if one were not successful in clearing names for temple work. The process of searching, the means of going after those names, would be worth all the effort you could invest. The reason: You cannot find names without knowing that they represent people. You begin to find out things about people. When we research our own lines, we become interested in more than just names or the number of names going through the temple. Our interest turns our hearts to our fathers—we seek to find them and to know them and to serve them. In doing so we store up treasures in heaven."

I know all of this to be true and know that we have been blessed to have done the work that we have accomplished thus far. I no longer must feel embarrassed or avert my eyes when the subject of family history work is a topic of discussion in priesthood meetings, sacrament, or General Conference. I already know that because the Prophet is responsible for all the work on both sides of the veil that this is what we have been commanded to do, and it will continue to be one of my pursuits for as long as I am able to do the work.

Note: while editing this project, I was released after nearly 4.5 years as the Sunday School President in order to "pivot" to lead the ward's efforts in Temple and Family History work. I am grateful for this opportunity to share with people what they CAN do during the pandemic, i.e. prepare family members (names) to take to the temple, rather than focusing on what they CAN'T do, i.e. physically attend church and the temple. This is truly one of the silver linings of which President Nelson has spoken.

CHAPTER 74

TENDER MERCY

"There are very few big and spectacular miracles in most
of our lives. But it is a quiet multitude of little miracles
that makes life sweet and adds to our testimonies."
Marjorie P. Hinckley

I have long since given up on the concept of coincidence. The world
is simply too large and too random for coincidences to occur, and for
this reason I believe that when necessary the Lord will shower us with
tender mercies.

After the drama and trauma associated with the birth of our grandson
Walter, which according to doctors left parents and grandparents alike
with some degree of post traumatic stress disorder (PTSD), by the time
Walter's youngest brother, and the fourth child in the family, was on
his way to Earth, and his mother's health was threatened by various and
sundry issues, we were fearful for his safe arrival.

It was Week 33 of pregnancy when the doctors determined that for
the safety of both mother and child, that they would have to induce
labor. We were at the hospital for the blessed event, but the manner in

which he arrived in the world – in the Intensive care Unit (ICU) – and was subsequently rushed to the Neonatal Intensive Care Unit (NICU) with daddy and grandpa following behind, was all too reminiscent of the events in Salt Lake City six years earlier. He was so tiny, so fragile. We administered to him and began another sojourn of waiting and praying that he would survive and become a member of our mortal earth family.

The challenge with Josh was his age and lack of size and development, but he was a fighter, quickly responded to care, and continued to thrive. Before we knew it, he had spent four weeks in the NICU and was deemed large enough and strong enough to go home.

Adding to the drama of his time in the NICU was when another sibling was sick with croup and everyone was quarantined to their home, leaving it to Grandma and Grandpa to visit the NICU and provide the daily skin to skin contact and the occasional opportunity to feed him. This was special time for us, and was made even more special when we discovered that one of the nurses that was caring for Josh was a recent transfer from Primary Children's Hospital in Salt Lake City where she had been employed when Walter was a long-term resident of the NICU.

She put the family connection together before we fully recognized her as one of the angels who had showered Walter with the medical attention and love that allowed him to survive and ultimately thrive after his miraculous arrival. I know that it was not a coincidence that she was there when we needed more of Heaven's special attention for another of our grandchildren. It was yet another tender mercy shown to us by a loving Heavenly Father.

CHAPTER 75

A PUNCH IN THE NOSE

"You are never too old to set another
goal or to dream a new dream."
C.S. Lewis

With my PNW agency slowly setting into the sunset, I determined that as soon as my son had found himself employment outside of the agency, I might give serious consideration to shutting the doors and riding off into the sunset myself. I accepted a twelve month call to serve as a Church Service Missionary to teach the two-morning a week Job Search Skills Workshop at Deseret Industries, in addition to taking grandson Walter for therapy on Tuesday morning and Thursday afternoon. Those activities along with writing, family history, reading, and "tending the grounds," along with six weeks of planned holiday travel was filling my time with worthwhile pursuits. We were also talking about the potential of some additional local church service that we could perform together.

In October 2018, we were in Salt Lake City for the annual meeting of the National Long Term Care Network of which I am the Chairman of the Board, having been elected the previous year. It was at this meeting that Louie, my predecessor as chairman, approached me about "doing something together" professionally. He had recently sold his agency to Mack and was interested in "keeping his hand in the business" of long term care. When I asked him *what* we should do, he was not sure, but was certain that it would come to him, because he *knew* that he wanted to do something with me. Since Louie was a veteran of the business and had enjoyed a brilliant and successful career in the field, I was intrigued, as it might even represent a lifeline for me as I contemplated a couple more years of work.

Mack learned of our conversation and asked to be included in any adventure we might embark on together. This was an unforeseen opportunity as well.

Over the next few months there were a couple trips to Southern California for me, as we had some face to face discussions. As I prayed about this potential opportunity, I started to assemble a Ben Franklin as well. The big question in my mind was whether it was something I should be considering since it could prove to be a radical departure from the course that I had been charting for myself and the family over the last year. To this end, the more I thought about it, I realized that I needed to really explore the *Why* before even entertaining the idea. As a result, I assigned Louie and Mack "homework" to prepare prior to our first face to face session, and we then spent the first two of our nineteen hours of discussion over two days on the subject of WHY we should form this new organization and what our charter, purpose, and long term goals would be going forward.

After successfully identifying the why, we had productive meetings, and the Ben Franklin grew in detail, which also meant that it was time to do some serious soul searching and setting of priorities. As talks progressed, I started to set conditions such as: I was not willing to move again, certainly not to CA; I was not willing to stop advocating for Walter; I needed to complete my mission; and since I would be working remotely anyway, I was not willing to disappoint my wife by not taking the trips we had scheduled well in advance. All conditions were met with enthusiasm by my new partners.

Monetary terms were discussed, roles assigned, duties detailed, and we set about creating a Partnership Agreement.

As much as I thought I did not want to do this, I knew that I needed to "re-stock the shelves" that had been depleted over the last couple of years when the agency had not been profitable, and I started to pray in a different way by asking whether this new venture was not just that very opportunity to further prepare ourselves for a financially secure retirement and life of service.

The respect for me, my leadership, and past achievements was evident in everything Louie and Mack said and wrote to me. I reached out to other business associates and friends who I knew would have my best interests at heart and they too encouraged me to pursue the new venture so long as it was on the terms that were seemingly so favorable to me.

I went to the Temple to pray, and the greatest impression I received was to ensure that I maintained a balanced life. As I pondered this and the meaning of it, I realized that I was past the season where I should be working 65 hours per week, and that I needed to achieve the proper balance for the other priorities that I had established for myself over the last year.

Things came together, we signed the partnership agreement, and we were off to the races. I was doing things I had never done before, and Louie was intent on helping me be the President and CEO of the quintessential LTC insurance shop. One day I called him Obi-Wan, and he said, "why the hell do you call me that?" When I explained it was because he was the Master Jedi of the LTC industry, he beamed, and said that he liked it, and I "should have said that in the first place." We had a good three or four months run before we were all surprised by a diagnosis of esophageal cancer that suddenly took him out of our lives a month later.

Louie's death was devastating for a lot of people because he cast an exceptionally large shadow. I especially felt it professionally because Louie was a mentor and helpmeet, willing to do anything necessary to help me achieve our goals and for me to grow into the role that we had identified for me.

I went down to La Canada (near LA) to participate in the Celebration of Life that his family put on about six weeks after his death. I shared the Obi-Wan story to everyone's amusement because it was so Louie. I also told his widow that I was going to punch him in the nose next I saw him, because he had done us both wrong by dying like he did. Further, that this partnership was established largely because I wanted to work with Louie and learn from the master. She appreciated all these sentiments.

I was sitting in the chapel waiting for the start of our Sacrament meeting this morning (June 14, 2020), the first time that we have been allowed to attend church in over three months because of Covid-19, and thinking about writing this chapter, when I realized that Louie was another of those milestone faces, and his purpose may very well have been limited to bringing Mack and I together.

But for Louie's vision of a new shop for all of us to work at helping people with long term care insurance products, I know that PNW would have become a memory, and I would in all likelihood be out of the game. As it is, I am still a contributing member of the industry, receiving favorable e-mails, texts, and voice mails for the articles that have run over the past three years, and recruiting new blood to the team.

Nearly as soon as I had this chain of thoughts pop into my head, I began to receive a feeling of confirmation that Louie had fulfilled his mission. I still reserve the right to punch him in the nose next I see him on the other side of the veil

CHAPTER 76

CONNECTING THE GENERATIONS

"Your personal testimony of light and truth will
not only bless you and your posterity here in
mortality, but will accompany you throughout
all eternity, among worlds without end."
Dieter F. Uchtdorf

Shortly after we moved to Boise, I received a telephone call from my daughter in which she confessed to having gone to school to address my granddaughter's second grade class on the Civil War and discovering that the kids knew more about it than she did, or as she expressed it, "they ate me alive." I told her that I was surprised to hear this because she is a certified schoolteacher. She countered with an invitation, or was it a challenge, for me to try a turn in the barrel. She was enlisting me because of the nature of their questions, and because she knew of my passion for the subject. I accepted the challenge and started gathering my Civil War artifacts such as musket balls from the Gettysburg battlefield, belt buckles, the blue Cavalry uniform that I had worn on a

Youth Conference Handcart Trek, as well as baking some hardtack for them to sample. Everyone should sample this treat.

By the time the day of my presentation arrived, I was not only speaking to my granddaughter's class but rather all *four* second grade classes or nearly one hundred kids! It was a fun 90 minutes, and my granddaughter was not embarrassed by my performance.

As I started to do my Family History in the years following that presentation, I was both shocked and delighted to ascertain that I had family that fought on *both* sides of the Civil War. When I was able to locate some *pictures* of these Civil War veterans who happened to be not-so-distant uncles or cousins, and started sharing them with my grandchildren, they were both intrigued and excited. Who knew?!?

My granddaughter started in the Young Women program at church and was exposed to the concepts of family history and temple work, and became enthralled with the work, giving us even more things to talk about. With a little assistance from all the grandparents, I was able to assist her in preparing her own four generation chart, and she now has six generations complete with 32 great-great-great grandparents.

Because she is the only temple-aged grandchild in the Valley so far, we have also had the opportunity to attend the Temple together and to do baptisms for some of the women in my immediate family. It was wonderful to share this experience with her, and to hear what she *felt* during the ordinances as we shared ice cream afterwards. This was a choice experience that we hope to repeat many times and to include her brother and cousins as they come of age.

On a lighter note, both of my grandkids are stoked by the fact that we are related to the royals of England which means that Meghan Markel is the wife of Harry, my 20th cousin, once removed. We don't socialize or even exchange Christmas cards with them, but I know through my efforts that have identified both Rebels and Royals, that I have started to connect the generations within the family and for this I find myself extremely gratified.

CHAPTER 77

THE PLAN

"Happiness is the object and design of our existence; and
will be the end thereof, if we pursue the path that leads
to it; and this path is virtue, uprightness, faithfulness,
holiness, and keeping all the commandments of God."
Joseph Smith

As I related at the beginning of this rather voluminous tale, the genesis of this project stemmed from a funeral in which I was explaining that even the saddest Latter Day Saint funeral is better than an upbeat Jewish funeral. Mainly because there is no such thing as an upbeat Jewish funeral. Death is so final and such an abrupt ending, that Death is feared and even the mere discussion of it is discouraged.

The Plan of Salvation was ordained by our loving Heavenly Father and serves as a roadmap for us to follow while in our mortal probationary state. It is not a plan devised by man or even Jesus Christ, but by the Lord, so that Christ, his first-born spirit son and all the rest of us could progress through this life to exaltation.

There is decidedly a pre-mortal state in which we are taught, followed by this mortal probationary period during which we have our agency tested, and we are allowed the opportunity to acquire knowledge that will serve us when we transition through the veil to the post-mortal world.

The plan of salvation is the Gospel of Jesus Christ. The steps in the plan are:

1. Faith in the Lord Jesus Christ;
2. Repentance;
3. Baptism by immersion for the remission of sins;
4. The laying on of hands for the gift of the Holy Ghost; and
5. Enduring to the end in righteousness.

Over the years we have lived in a large number of wards and stakes and have attended many funerals. One of the things I do as a means by which to honor the deceased is to watch those who attend the funeral service, particularly the non-members who may not be familiar with our doctrines. I like to watch their body language especially as the Plan of Salvation is explained to watch when their hearts are touched by the message and their grief is replaced by feelings of hope and gratitude. I have met several people who were later baptized into the Church because of the message of hope that they heard contained in the Plan of Salvation.

I am so grateful for the Plan of Salvation and the path home to Father that it presents to all of us. It was through the acquisition of knowledge about this Plan that I finally found the answers to the three questions that I had been seeking.

The Plan of Salvation lessens loss in the present and provides hope for a future filled with Light and Truth. I like to think of the Plan of Salvation as the Plan of Happiness.

CHAPTER 78

WHAT'S IN A NAME?

"The name of the church is not negotiable. When
the Savior clearly states what the name of His
church should be … He is serious. And if we allow
nicknames to be used or adopt or even sponsor
those nicknames ourselves, he is offended."
Russell M. Nelson

While I have long been a proponent that the greatest constant in Life
is change, I found solace and peace when President Russell M. Nelson
announced that we would no longer allow the Church or its members to
be referred to as Mormons. By resuming the use of the proper name of
the Church as found in the scriptures we more readily identify ourselves
as disciples of Jesus Christ. We are in fact The Church of Jesus Christ
of Latter Day Saints. Rather than a change, it is a restoration or return
to what the Lord intended when the Gospel was returned to the Earth.

I am a High Priest in the Melchizedek Priesthood and a Bishop of
the Aaronic Priesthood, grateful for the power and authority of these
priesthoods that allow me to act in God's name here on the Earth.

The principles and doctrines that I have learned over the past forty years are now deeply rooted in my DNA, values, and character.

We are the pioneers within our family and have blazed a trail upon which our posterity can find peace, happiness, and exaltation.

CHAPTER 79

PANDEMIC

"We are living in a remarkable age when we constantly
see the hand of the Lord in the lives of His children,"
Our Heavenly Father and His Son, Jesus Christ,
know us, love us, and are watching over us."
Russell M. Nelson

We were on holiday with good friends the first week of March 2020.
We were staying at the luxurious Four Seasons resort in Scottsdale, AZ,
intending to attend some Major League Baseball spring training games.
We had attended games the previous year while our accommodations
had us over 120 miles to the North in Sedona, AZ which made the stay
in Scottsdale a baseball fan's perfect base of operations. With fifteen
major league teams based in the Cactus League, the baseball world was
our proverbial oyster. We drove past many of the stadiums, and yet
when we did, rather than feeling the allure that I did last year, I felt a
sense of danger. I did not know that the danger was the pandemic that
was slowly creeping across our country and would force nearly all of the
country to eventually come to a virtual standstill. When push came to

shove, and it came time to purchase tickets for the game(s), I found that my desire to attend the games had completely waned. When I voiced this lack of desire to my friend, he readily concurred. Coincidence? Again, no such thing.

The Coronavirus, Covid-19, was just beginning its insidious gripping of the country, and as we would later learn, it was spread by person to person contact usually in the context of large crowd gatherings. I know therefore it was a prompting from the Spirit that discouraged our attending these baseball games.

It was also during this week that I began to have the same heightened feelings of concern that had enveloped me on January 16, 1991, the day before the air war phase of Desert Storm had commenced, prompting us to go to Sam's and fill up four carts of groceries and staples to the tune of $961. I wanted to be back in Boise to complete preparations for what I foresaw to be an experience completely unfamiliar to our country. Without wanting to sound like a Debbie Downer or to put a damper on our holiday, I quietly began compiling on my iPad a list of tasks we would complete after our arrival home.

Fortunately, because we have subscribed to the practices of self-reliance, we had the vast majority of what we already needed in the house. Our friends would later tease us that while they were scampering attempting to purchase toilet paper of any kind, they *knew* that we were probably sitting on a sizeable cache. Nonetheless, we bought more of the basics, and even a little extra, as we insured that we would have sufficient for our needs.

I recently had a conversation with a friend who asked me what *emotion* would best describe how I feel about the virus and the entire pandemic. I was quick to answer with a single word: frustration. Because of the fact that I spent the last eight years of my military career prior to retirement either as a Plans and Operations Officer at a FEMA Regional Headquarters, or as a Department of Defense Emergency Preparedness Liaison Officer to all of the other federal agencies that are signatories to the Federal Response Plan as enacted by the Stafford Act, I *know* how things are supposed to happen in situations like we are experiencing.

For fear of making this into a political statement, suffice to say that there is a plan, and those in positions of authority did not ensure that this plan was executed in a manner that was either timely or effectively managed. The cost of this lack of leadership has been the loss of countless lives, an incredible Depression-like economic cost in terms of jobs and economic strife, and an impact on our Society none of us could have foreseen. Having written plans and exercises, trained responders, and helped prepare our country, my heart has been heavy as I watch our country spiral downward with its democracy imperiled and the Constitution seemingly hanging by a thread. I have spent a great deal of my time praying for wisdom…to be imparted to our leaders.

Once we knew that our temporal needs were going to be met, I took a step back to take stock of our situation. Our church was being led by a prophet who not only was the mouthpiece of the Lord, but was also a world-renowned heart surgeon who would grasp the significance of the inherent dangers of the virus as it grew into a pandemic.

We had been prepared, line upon line, precept upon precept, in the years leading up to the pandemic. *Teaching in the Savior's Way* had been a great foundation upon which to begin a series of changes that would serve us well as we went forward with uncertainty into the dark clouds of the pandemic. We were prepared for the eventual stay at home orders and to continue to learn the Gospel through the *Come Follow Me* program, and to administer the sacrament in our own homes because of the modification to our church services in which we became a more home based, church supported culture. We had previously started attending church only two hours per Sabbath Sunday and devoting the third hour to teaching the gospel in our homes.

As the pandemic kept us in our homes, I cannot remember a time that I was more looking forward to General Conference and to be spiritually fed by a Prophet, twelve Apostles, and other general authorities.

President Russell M. Nelson in his Sunday, April 5, 2020, address entitled "Hear Him" shared the following:

> We live in the day that "our forefathers have awaited
> with anxious expectation." We have front-row seats to *witness*

live what the prophet Nephi saw *only in vision,* that "the power of the Lamb of God" would descend "upon the covenant people of the Lord, who were scattered upon all the face of the earth; and they were armed with righteousness and with the power of God in great glory."

You, my brothers and sisters, are among those men, women, and children whom Nephi saw. Think of that!

Regardless of where you live or what your circumstances are, the Lord Jesus Christ is *your* Savior, and God's prophet Joseph Smith is *your* prophet. He was foreordained before the foundation of the earth to be the prophet of this last dispensation, when "nothing shall be withheld" from the Saints. Revelation continues to flow from the Lord during this ongoing process of restoration.

What does it mean for you that the gospel of Jesus Christ has been restored to the earth?

It means that you and your family can be sealed together forever! It means that because you have been baptized by one who has authority from Jesus Christ and have been confirmed a member of His Church, you can enjoy the constant companionship of the Holy Ghost. He will guide and protect you. It means you will never be left comfortless or without access to the power of God to help you. It means that priesthood power can bless you as you receive essential ordinances and make covenants with God and keep them. What an anchor to our souls are these truths, especially during these times when the tempest is raging."

President Nelson concluded with "And, finally, we *hear Him* as we heed the words of prophets, seers, and revelators. Ordained Apostles of Jesus Christ always testify of Him. They point the way as we make our way through the heart-wrenching maze of our mortal experiences."

These words touched my heart, and I knew that however long we were subjected to the restrictions of the coronavirus, that we would be fine. We also resolved that if there was a conflict between following the advice and counsel of elected national or local leaders or our ordained and sustained church leaders, we would *always* follow the prophet.

Interestingly enough, this period of enforced isolation has been a period of productivity and growth for some, while for others it has been a prison. I had a person tell me last week that the highlight of their day most of the time is when they get to take a nap with the dogs. I resolved to make it a period of time during which I could point to certain achievements. I did not want to simply GO through it, I wanted to GROW through it. In addition to completing some long-ignored household projects of either renovation or organization, I wanted to add to my family tree by completing more Family History, and to share with my posterity the lifelong path that has led me to this point in my life and testimony. I hope that I have achieved this last task with the words contained in these pages.

CHAPTER 80

THIRD ACT

"Enduring to the end, or remaining faithful to the
laws and ordinances of the gospel of Jesus Christ
throughout our life, is a fundamental requirement
for salvation in the kingdom of God...Therefore,
enduring to the end is not just a matter of passively
tolerating life's difficult circumstances or "hanging
in there." Ours is an active religion, helping God's
children along the strait and narrow path to develop
their full potential during this life and return to Him
one day... Enduring to the end is a process filling
every minute of our life, every hour, every day, from
sunrise to sunrise. It is accomplished through personal
discipline following the commandments of God."
Dieter F. Uchtdorf

Many times in my life I have wished that I had been born into a
family "of goodly parents" where the Gospel had been the guiding light
and that I might have been the recipient of guidance on what path I
should have pursued. Fortunately, there has been a path for me to follow

and to pursue and discover this guiding light with the help of others that the Lord has placed along the sides of the road.

Some of the things that I know now, and that I hope will benefit my progeny and advance their own purposes in life includes the following lessons that I have often learned as a graduate of the School of Hard Knocks.

- It is about Choosing the Right. More than a trite phrase that we teach our children while in Primary class, it is about making good choices. It is about discerning the difference between Good, Better, and Best, and always striving for the best from an eternal perspective.
- It is about staying on the Covenant Path. There is safety, security, and ultimately happiness by staying on this path. God will never not hold up his end when we make a covenant with Him.
- I know that I want to be an influence for good in the lives of my children, grandchildren, and great-grandchildren, as well as all those with whom I come into contact professionally, socially, and within my community.
- I have learned countless times that the best sermon is the unspoken one. Being an example and modeling the way is the way the Savior taught his disciples.
- We are going to be tossed and battered by waves that threaten to overwhelm us. We need to hold fast to the Rod and to weather the storms that come our way.
- Satan is subtle. As I used to say to everyone who came into my office for counseling, he is not going to pick up this building and move it across the street. He is going to be subtle, and move in inches, slithering like a snake, tempting us to stray ever closer to the line between good and evil.
- I know that it is all about listening for, heeding, and acting upon all promptings that are sent to us. Be doers of the word, not hearers only.
- Testimony is like a muscle; we only strengthen it when we exercise it. To do otherwise is to let it atrophy and wither.

- Faith without works is dead. It is all about walking the walk and not just talking the talk.

- We are all saddled with challenges and difficulties. This is part of our mortal test. I have always reminded myself that I am not alone in these trials and that I will never be given more than I can handle.

- "Are these perilous times? They are. But there is no need to fear. We can have peace in our hearts and peace in our homes." - Gordon B. Hinckley

- "He created us to have Joy! So, if we trust Him, He will help us to notice the good, bright, hopeful things of life. And sure enough, the world will become brighter." - Dieter F. Uchtdorf

None of us wants to be forgotten; we all want to have exerted a great influence on those around us whom we love and to leave a large void when we do finally pass through the veil. We want to be missed. We want to be appreciated. That is called Legacy. I hope that something written in these pages serves that purpose.

CHAPTER 81

WHY I BELIEVE

"Sometimes we can learn and study and know,
And sometimes we have to
Believe, Trust, and Hope."
M. Russell Ballard

Over the last couple of years, I have adopted the belief that when you explain the *Why* everything else seems to fall into place. This is most applicable in the business realm. I find that if I ask people *what* they do for a living they can readily answer me, e.g. I sell shoes, I build houses. If I ask them *how* it happens or how the process works, they can usually provide me with a near immediate response. But ask them *why* they sell shoes or build houses, and an answer may take longer to be formulated. Just yesterday, a former business associate asked me *why* I am not retired and still working at the daily grind. My reply shocked him when I said, "I still believe in what I do; I want to live a life of significance; I want to make a difference in the lives of the people who still need what we have to offer them." I suspect that he was a little overwhelmed by the passion that accompanied the answer, but I also

Don Levin

believe he respected it. In retrospect, I too was surprised by the depth breadth, and passion of my response.

I can say much the same thing about *why* I am a member of the Church of Jesus Christ of Latter Day Saints, though I cannot be as succinct in my answer. If I simply brain dump *all* of the reasons, I guess it would look something like this, in no uncertain order.

1. From the time I was ten years old, and particularly during my teen years, I needed answers. I needed to know God. I needed to know where I came from, why I am here, and where I am going after I die. After thirty five plus years of membership, I have found that the meaning of life as provided by LDS doctrine to be spiritually, intellectually and emotionally satisfying.
2. I needed to know that I mattered. That I was not just another carbon unit. That God knew me, and that He cared about me. He loves me!
3. Like everyone else, I wanted to be part of something larger than just myself.
4. I know with certainty that God is our Eternal Heavenly Father and that Jesus Christ is His Son, my older brother, and that he is our Lord and Savior. That the Holy Ghost is the third part of the Godhead and is a real palpable part of my life for which I am incredibly grateful. I may be accused of irreverence, but he is the ultimate wingman.
5. The Gospel of Jesus Christ defines my purpose for being on the Earth at this time and place. It provides answers to those tough questions. It does make Life fair.
6. At some point, we all must decide who we are and what we believe to be true in our heart of hearts. We cannot rely strictly on the testimonies of others. As a convert it was almost a blessing that it took me as long as it did to determine what I believed.
7. I have learned by heartfelt sorrow, never to ignore a prompting of the Holy Ghost. I believe that this companionship is the greatest gift of our membership in His Church.

8. I know that ours is not a Church of "don'ts" but rather that my choice to observe disciplined obedience to the precepts and doctrines of the Church is actually quite liberating.

9. Further, that Repentance is a wonderful gift to the world. I learned so much about it while serving as a bishop. It is something we need to practice every day of our life.

10. After growing up in a somewhat dysfunctional family, I love the focus that the Church has placed on the family. I admire our five children and the people that they have grown up to become. Yes, we had a hand in it, but the concept of a home-focused, church supported ministry made a huge difference for us. President Harold B. Lee referred to the Church as the "scaffolding with which we build eternal families." I believe it.

11. I love being a priesthood holder and being able to do God's work upon the earth.

12. Along these priesthood lines, I have been able to observe and to be a part of so many miracles that I can readily bear testimony of and to the real existence of angels and miracles.

13. I have been in the presence of the Prophet and Apostles, and while they are flesh and blood men like myself, I know that they are disciples of Jesus Christ and exude an aura that is clearly discernible and make my heart race.

14. Having served in any number of "lay ministry" roles over the years, I have come to appreciate the joy of serving others, and the accompanying growth these opportunities provided to me.

15. I love the Thirteen Articles of Faith. They very succinctly describe our fundamental beliefs. I have found them to be a great blueprint after which to pattern my life. I wish I had been exposed to them when a young child – it would have made my journey so much easier to traverse.

16. I know in my heart that when I remain obedient that the Lord will never allow me to go astray.

17. I love the times when I can listen to a Conference talk, or even a Sacrament talk, and feel inspired by the speaker's message, as if it were being spoken solely for my personal benefit.

18. I love the concept of personal revelation and have been the recipient of it on many occasions.

19. I am a much different person than I was before I joined the Church. I was a good person, with inherent values focused on integrity and ethics, and my conversion has served to only make me a better person. The Gospel has the power to make life more meaningful, more vibrant, and to make us better.

20. Probably the greatest "individual growth spurt" that I have ever experienced is when I was afforded the opportunity to serve as a bishop and lead a congregation of wonderful people. I learned so much about repentance, the atonement, and charity.

21. I so appreciate the concept of Eternal Life. The fact that I will be able to live with my family – past, present, and future – through the eternities, is a wonderful gift from our Heavenly Father. I will remain faithful and obedient so as to achieve this goal.

22. The willingness with which members of the church are willing to unquestioningly serve one another is an amazing concept. In times of natural disaster and other crises, the Church is there… in the form of its members, all lifting where they stand.

23. Everyone in the Church is a teacher, a missionary, and a student all at the same time. We learn from one another, often through the examples that are shared. Life really is a series of parables.

24. We are celebrating the bicentennial of the First Vision experienced by Joseph Smith and the restoration of the Gospel and the translation of the Book of Mormon. I have no problem embracing the beliefs that these events took place as depicted.

25. When I need direction, it is readily available to me through earnest prayer, even if sometimes I do not like the answer

I have come to believe that our destination in the Journey we know as Life is reflective of nothing more than the series of decisions by which we live our lives and progress along the path. In hindsight, we will learn that some of these decisions were rather significant, while others insignificant in importance+. Ultimately, it is all about Choosing the Right. I first chose to believe and have since been provided with opportunities to ratify this very decision time and time again. In a word: Believe.

Don Levin
June 2020

ABOUT THE AUTHOR

Don Levin is the President & CEO of USA-LTC, a national insurance brokerage, and has been in the long term care insurance industry since 1999. Don is also a former practicing Attorney-at-Law, court-appointed Arbitrator, as well as a retired U.S. Army officer with 23 years of service.

Don earned his Juris Doctor from The John Marshall Law School, his MPA, from the University of Oklahoma, and his BA from the University of Illinois-Chicago. He is also a graduate of the U.S. Army Command & General Staff College and the Defense Strategy Course, U.S. Army War College.

In his spare time, Don has published thirteen other books in a wide range of genre, as well as countless articles on leadership, long term care insurance, and personal development.

Don is very active with his church and within the community, and remains focused on his wife Susie, their five children, nineteen grandchildren, one great-grandchild, and two dogs aptly named Barnes & Noble.

A native of Chicago, Don and the majority of the clan now resides in the Boise, Idaho and Northern Utah area.

Don may be reached at don@donlevin.com.